Cameroun

An African Federation

PRAEGER LIBRARY OF AFRICAN AFFAIRS

The Praeger Library of African Affairs is intended to provide clear, authoritative, and objective information about the historical, political, cultural, and economic background of modern Africa. Individual countries and groupings of countries will be dealt with as will general themes affecting the whole continent and its relations with the rest of the world. The library appears under the general editorship of Colin Legum, with Philippe Decraene as consultant editor.

Already Published

T. A. BEETHAM	Christianity and the New Africa
ALFRED G. GERTEINY	Mauritania
RICHARD GREENFIELD	Ethiopia: *A New Political History*
RICHARD HALL	Zambia
ALEX HEPPLE	South Africa: *A Political and Economic History*
NIGEL HESELTINE	Madagascar
JAMES R. HOOKER	Black Revolutionary: *George Padmore's Path from Communism to Pan-Africanism*
RENÉ LEMARCHAND	Rwanda and Burundi
GUY LE LUSIGNAN	French-Speaking Africa Since Independence
HORACE MINER (ed.)	The City in Modern Africa
JOHN G. PIKE	Malawi: *A Political and Economic History*
WALTER SCHWARZ	Nigeria
RICHARD P. STEVENS	Lesotho, Botswana, and Swaziland: *The Former High Commission Territories in Southern Africa*
CLAUDE WAUTHIER	The Literature and Thought of Modern Africa: *A Survey*
DOUGLAS WHEELER and RENÉ PÉLISSIER	Angola

Cameroun
An African Federation

NEVILLE RUBIN

PRAEGER PUBLISHERS
New York · Washington · London

Published in the United States of America in 1971

Praeger Publishers, Inc.
111 Fourth Avenue, New York, NY 10003, USA
5 Cromwell Place, London, SW7, England

© 1971 by Pall Mall Press Limited, London, England
Library of Congress Catalog Card Number: 78-150705

Printed in Great Britain
320.967
R 896c

Contents

Cameroun

List of Abbreviations

ALCAM	*Assemblée Legislative du Cameroun*
ALNK	*Armée de Libération Nationale Kamérounaise*
ARCAM	*Assemblée Représentative du Cameroun*
ATCAM	*Assemblée Territoriale du Cameroun*
BDC	*Bloc Démocratique Camérounais*
CDC	Cameroons Development Corporation
CFA	*Communauté Financière Africaine*
CFTC	*Confédération des Travailleurs Chrétiens Camérounais*
CGT	*Confédération Générale du Travail*
CNF	Cameroons National Federation
CPNC	Cameroon Peoples National Congress
CWU	Cameroons Welfare Union
CYL	Cameroons Youth League
EEC	European Economic Community
Esocam	*Evolution Sociale Camérounaise*
FAC	*Fonds d'Aide et de Coopération*
FED	*Fonds Européen de Développement*
FPUP	*Front Populaire pour l'Unité et la Paix*
FIDES	*Fonds d'Investissement pour le Développement Economique et Sociale des Territoires d'Outre Mer*
IOM	*Indépendants d'Outre Mer*
JDC	*Jeunesse Démocratique Camérounaise*
Jeucafra	*Jeunesse Camérounasie Française*
KNC	Kamerun National Congress
KNDP	Kamerun National Democratic Party
KPP	Kamerun Peoples Party
KUNC	Kamerun United National Congress
KUP	Kamerun United Party
MANC	*Mouvement d'Action Nationale Camérounaise*
NCNC	National Council for Nigeria and the Cameroons
NKDP	Northern Kamerun Democratic Party
NPC	Northern Peoples Congress
OAU	Organisation of African Unity
OCAM	*Organisation Commune Africaine et Malgache*
OK(P)	One Kamerun Party
PDC	*Parti des Démocrates*
PMC	Permanent Mandates Commission
Racam	*Rassemblement Camérounais*

Cameroun

Preface

This book attempts to do two things: to trace the process which led to the formation of the Federal Republic of Cameroun; and to outline the institutions and policies which have taken shape in the new state during the ten years or so which have passed since it came into being.

Both aspects of the study contain features which should be of special interest to those who are concerned with the development of the modern states of contemporary Africa, and in Cameroun's place among them. Both the background and the foreground of Cameroun differ from those of most other African countries in several important respects. Thus the first five chapters of this book deal with the early history of Cameroun's contact with the Bornu and Fulani empires, as well as with the traders of several European nations; and then go on to consider the growth of Cameroun nationalism against its unique background of German colonisation, followed by French and British rule. In the course of doing so, some attempt is made to examine the significance of the two varieties of international involvement with alien rule, under the mandate and trusteeship systems, for the development of political nationalism in the French and British territories; and to describe, and perhaps explain, the violent rebellion which preceded the achievement of independence by the first. At the same time, attention is devoted to the growth of a movement for unifying the two territories.

In the next four chapters, unified Cameroun is surveyed. Its federal constitutional framework is scrutinised, and the methods by which it has sought to weld together francophone and anglophone elements within a single nation are investigated; its economic achievements and deficiencies are explored; lastly, its relations with other parts of Africa and with other countries, including France and the other nations of Europe, are dealt with.

In writing this book, I have been only too conscious of the summary account that it provides of a complicated story, and of the valuable and detailed studies that have been made of each of its facets by scholars whose contribution to the study of Cameroun and its affairs has been prodigious. I have found myself constantly indebted to the formidable array of information which has been assembled in the past by Dr and Mrs Ardener, Professors Gardinier, Gonidec, Johnson and Le Vine, Dr Hugon, Fr Mveng and the late Professor Rudin, among others. I have also been fortunate in being able to draw on information made available to me by various people in Cameroun, and by Mr Colin Legum and Dr Richard Rathbone in London.

I must also thank the following people, who have been kind enough to read and criticise some of the chapters and whose advice has been most helpful though they should not be considered in any way responsible for any faults which appear in the book: Dr Rathbone and my colleague, Mr James S. Read, of the School of Oriental and African Studies of the University of London; Dr S. Robinson, of the London School of Economics and Political Science; my father, Professor Leslie Rubin, and my wife Muriel whose patience and forbearance while I was engaged in the research for and the writing of the book have been remarkable and invaluable.

London   N.R.

For Muriel, Guy and Clive

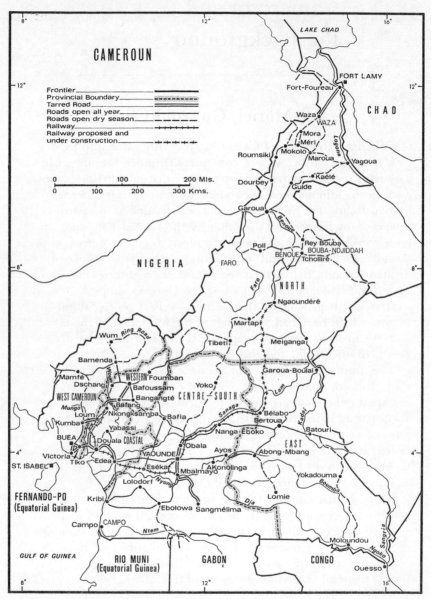

1 Communications in Cameroun

1. Cameroun and its People— the Background

INTRODUCTION

The Federal Republic of Cameroun formally came into existence on October 1, 1961. It was constructed, under the influence of powerful nationalist feeling, from two adjacent territories which had been administered separately as part of an international responsibility. For more than half a century one of these had been governed by France and the other by the United Kingdom—first as a consequence of military conquest, then on behalf of the League of Nations, and finally under the supervision of the United Nations. Before their separation, the territories had undergone single colonial rule as part of the German Empire.

It is worth pausing at this point to reflect on the number of factors which have had a bearing on the formation of the country and its history. Foremost among these are, undoubtedly, the period of alien rule, and the rise of nationalism. The two are, of course, intimately related. But they are hardly unique to Cameroun. Indeed, together with economic underdevelopment, they are among the most prominent features of the experience shared by nearly all independent African countries. In the case of Cameroun, however, it is not simply the fact of alien rule which must be noted; it is the special form—more accurately, the succession of forms—which it took, and which in turn shaped the special characteristics of Cameroun nationalism.

Thus, Cameroun first felt the impact of European colonisation under the Germans through the introduction of western economic, political and administrative institutions. It went on to experience the division of the territory which had been subjected to a single set of European influences for more than a generation. To the purely physical or territorial aspects of this division, there must be added the effects of allocating the individual parts of Cameroun to France and Britain. The two new European powers which now ruled in their respective spheres had distinctive cultures, political

1

traditions and colonial policies, which differed from one another at least as much as each was different from those of Germany. The result was an increasing degree of divergence between the territory under French administration and that under British rule. Even the growth of nationalism, which was directed towards the elimination of foreign rule, involved differences of approach in each of the territories, most notably in the measure of violence that was considered necessary in order to bring about self-rule.

Despite the considerable range of dissimilarities which developed during this period, two other factors already noted had a decisive influence on the ultimate decision to create a single new state by fusing the two territories. One was the territorial unity that had preceded the period of division: paradoxical though it may seem, the existence of a single Cameroun under German rule proved to be an important element in the nationalist programmes of leading political parties in both territories—perhaps the only one they shared in addition to the desire for independence. The other factor was the existence of an international framework within which both France and Britain were obliged to govern their sections of Cameroun. During the period in which they were administered as mandated territories under the aegis of the League of Nations, this was of comparatively little significance, since nationalism was in its infancy, the League machinery was weak, and the mandate system somewhat unclear as to its goals. But the transmutation of the mandate system into the trusteeship system under the supervision of the United Nations made a considerable difference. The fact that the transition took place more or less simultaneously with the emergence of more determined and more articulate nationalist leadership in both the British Cameroons and French Cameroun* may have been coincidental, in the sense that the forces which shaped the United Nations also influenced internal political developments in the territories. But the increasing interest exhibited by the UN in the territories under its supervision as it came to include a greater number of former colonial nations provided nationalists from both parts of Cameroun with a platform

* The spelling is deliberately different for the two territories. Throughout this book, the form used will be determined by the context in which it appears. Thus where the British territory is described, the English form Cameroon or Cameroons appears; and Cameroun is used to describe the French territory. In some cases, the German Kamerun is also employed.

from which they could launch part of their campaign against France and Britain, at first separately and then in concert.

It would be convenient if it were possible to isolate each of the factors mentioned and treat it separately. Unfortunately, this cannot be done. Their effect is cumulative, and results from a subtle process of interaction over a period of eighty years. To a certain extent, the pattern of interaction follows the chronological sequence of events, and it is this sequence which governs the four chapters which follow. Nevertheless, the account of Cameroun's move from colonisation to independence and on to federation can not be complete without reference to some of the other influences which were at work throughout the history of the country's development and had more than a little effect on the political changes it underwent, internally and externally. Among those influences which need to be considered before embarking on an investigation of the history of Cameroun from colony to independence are the geographical situation of the country, the ethnic groups which go to make up its population and their history in the period before Germany established European control over them.

THE PHYSICAL ENVIRONMENT:
GEOGRAPHY, TOPOGRAPHY AND CLIMATE[1]

The external boundaries of Cameroun had to be reconstructed when the country became a federation in 1961, and have not yet been finally settled.[2] During the period before federation, the territorial limits of the French mandated (and later trust) territory were defined, with particular attention being paid to a clear demarcation of the frontiers to the north, south and east where the territory abutted on French and Spanish colonies. The British administering authority had in like manner established a reasonable degree of clarity over the boundaries between its section of the territory and the portions of Nigeria which they adjoined. A similar definition of the border separating the two sections of Cameroun had been agreed between France and Britain from the time that the former German colony was divided between them, and this was enforced with varying degrees of severity in the ensuing years, particularly in the south where the British Southern Cameroons was separated from the French Cameroun.

3

It was the northern portions of the British Cameroons which caused difficulty: at first because the territory placed under British control in the north consisted of two distinct areas, separated by a narrow projection of French territory; and later because neither of these elected to join with the Southern Cameroons and the former French trust in the new federation.[3]

The result is a set of boundaries in the west which are somewhat irregular in shape, and which give Cameroun the form of a slightly distorted triangle. Like most African countries, Cameroun was shaped by a combination of physical occupation by a colonial power—in this case Germany—and the subsequent need to adjust to the requirements of rival claimants to the areas occupied, or the surrounding ones, in order to avoid direct clashes between competing European powers with territorial ambitions. In the process, scant attention was paid to physical phenomena such as forests, rivers or mountains which might in other circumstances have formed the natural boundaries on which man-made frontiers could be based. Similarly, little regard was paid to ethnic considerations, so that frontiers were often straddled by a single tribe. With one exception (the line of volcanic mountains which stretches northwards from Mount Cameroun at the coast and which formed a convenient if imprecise break between the French and British sections in the south) no frontier in Cameroun was determined by natural or ethnic boundaries. One result of this is the wide range of natural features—topographical, climatic and vegetational—in the country; another is the even more strikingly complex and diverse pattern of its ethnic composition.

The wedge shape inherited by Cameroun is symbolic in significance as well. The country finds itself conveniently situated at the junction of two distinct geographical areas in Africa, stretching northwards from the Bight of Biafra to Lake Chad and the fringes of the great desert. It is strategically located so as to occupy the area between the coastal states of West Africa and the western coastline of the equatorial states to its south. The fact that it stretches some 770 miles into the interior has made it an important cross-roads for states with no access of their own to the coast. This, and the possession of several navigable rivers, have been major elements in Cameroun's relations with Chad and the Central African Republic, and there have been economic implications for all three states (as well as the neighbouring Congo (Brazzaville)), through the creation of a customs union which links all these countries.⁴ The fact that the river Benoué is navigable for a considerable portion of its course through Cameroun has also meant that the country has been able to retain its economic ties with the northern parts of Nigeria, to the benefit of both countries.⁵

It is possible to divide Cameroun into four or five distinct regions according to physical or climatic conditions. Looking at the map from south to north, the first of these is the coastal zone. This stretches from near the Nigerian border at Calabar to Campo near the frontier with Rio Muni. In the part of West Cameroun which lies north of Victoria and the slopes of Mount Cameroun, the coastline from Rio del Rey on the Bight of Biafra is jagged, full of creeks and inlets, and possesses no ports. A good deal of the area is inaccessible by any means other than motor launch or the canoes used by the inhabitants of fishing communities. From Victoria southwards, the coastline is dominated by the towering Mount Cameroun (some 13,350 feet high), and is interrupted by the deltas of the Moungo and Wouri rivers. The rocky coast has numerous bays and inlets as well as capes (it includes Ambas Bay and Cape Nachtigal). The two major ports in the country are situated here, Douala and Victoria-Tiko. Between Bimbia, near Cape Nachtigal, and Kribi in the south—another port and a tropical resort area—there is low-lying land marked by swamps, creeks, sand-bars, lagoons and marshes. In this zone, too, the rivers Nyong, Sanaga and Campo join the sea. This is a high rainfall area—Debundscha, near Mount Cameroun, has one of the highest recorded average rainfalls in the world (400 inches a year) while Douala receives some 158 inches annually; but the temperature does not much exceed 80° F (25° C) on average. Buea, the old German capital (and now the capital of West Cameroun), has an annual average of 68° F (20° C): it is situated 3,000 feet up on the slopes of Mount Cameroun, overlooking the bay of Victoria, the lowlands of Tiko and the Wouri estuary, with Douala clearly visible when there is no cloud reaching down from the mountain. The region as a whole stretches some 25 or 30 miles into the interior; it contains fertile volcanic soil (Mount Cameroun is a volcano⁶) and the tropical lowlands have been the base for banana, oil palm and rubber plantations.

Beyond the coastal region, there are low-lying plateau areas, which are situated for the most part in East Cameroun and stretch from the borders with Gabon and Equatorial Guinea in the south-east to Yoko and Garoua in the north. It is through this area that the Nyong and Sanaga rivers flow, along with their tributaries the Dja and Lobo, and the region also reaches to the borders of the Middle Congo basin. The plateaux vary in height from 800 feet to about 3,000 feet and average some 2,100 feet. In one part there are the heavily forested areas which provide the basis of the timber industry at Ebolowa and Sangmelima. In others, there are situated the federal capital, Yaoundé, and the industrial complex surrounding the hydro-electric station at Edea. Also in this area are the granite sectors which cover a large portion of the area from Yoko in the centre to the eastern border with the Central African Republic and consist of undulating land occasionally interrupted by low and isolated peaks. Rainfall is nowhere as heavy as in the coastal areas: Yaoundé, with an annual average of 62 inches receives much the same as Ngaoundéré.

Next, there is a high plateau region, which includes the Adamawa plateau and the mountainous areas of the West Cameroun highlands. Here there are the high, rolling hills with grassland, wooded valleys and relatively small forests. This includes the elevated areas around Bamenda and the Ndop plain of West Cameroun, with ranges of high volcanic mountains which exceed 6,500 feet in places. To the north of Bamenda, stretching towards the centre of the country, there are even higher mountains. These discontinuous ranges are broken by the river Benoué, but the Adamawa plateau has an average altitude of about 3,500 feet. Rainfall is plentiful—ranging between 50 and 100 inches—without being inundatory; the grasslands and savannah have provided the foundation for cattle-keeping by the Fulani and the peoples of the Bamenda area, and the relatively cool climate has left the area free of tsetse fly.

The savannah continues northwards, where it gradually merges with the low-lying plains of the Chad and the Benoué which form the northernmost sector of the country. Although there are the Atlantika and Mandara mountains in the far west, most of the northern region is grassland, with the Benoué plains giving way to steppe as Lake Chad is approached.

6

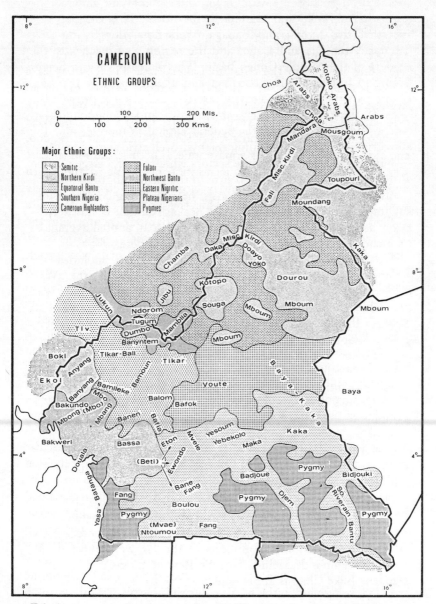

2. Ethnic groups in Cameroun (*after Le Vine, op. cit., pp. 7 and 8*)

7

THE PEOPLE

These geographical regions are contained in a total area of some 183,000 square miles, about 450 miles wide from east to west and 770 miles long from the coast to Lake Chad. The country as a whole is inhabited by approximately 5,200,000 people, giving an average density of a little more than 11 per square mile. The population is, however, very unevenly distributed. In West Cameroun, which has a population of slightly more than 1,000,000, the average is about 60 per square mile. The distribution in East Cameroun reflects a heavy concentration of people in the south and centre of the country, and a large but much more widely dispersed number in the north. Thus the western part of the state —the Western Region[7] inhabited by the Bamiléké people, and the Moungo and Wouri parts of the Coastal Region—contains more than 1,000,000 people and includes the port of Douala which itself has a population of around 200,000. The central portion of the state, which comprises the heavily populated areas around Yaoundé and the neighbouring towns, as well as much of the eastern part of the country up to the forested sectors, has more than 900,000 inhabitants. The north, too, contains a population of well over a million people, with some 700,000 or more concentrated in the portion between Garoua and Maroua.

Demographic factors are of more than passing significance in relation to political and economic developments in Cameroun. Population pressure was one reason for the migration of substantial numbers of Bamiléké people from their traditional areas in the western parts of French Cameroun, and this together with the rapid growth of Douala were among the causes of the rebellion which occurred in the five years before independence and continued afterwards.* While economic development remained focused on the coastal parts of the British Cameroons, it spread in French Cameroun from the coast towards the interior. The extent to which communications as well as economic effort have been concentrated in the central and southern portions of the country are described in Chapter 8. On the other hand, economic under-development in the north contrasts sharply with the growth of its political importance from the time it became established

* See Chapters 3 and 5.

as the power base of the country's largest political grouping, the *Union Camérounaise*, which put Ahmadou Ahidjo in office in 1958.

But neither economic nor demographic influences can be seen in isolation from the ethnographic context in which they have operated. Cameroun presents an ethnic pattern of almost unrivalled complexity, a good deal of which is still shrouded in uncertainty. Attempts to classify the different ethnic or tribal groups have rested on linguistic or cultural characteristics, but have produced major disagreements among ethnographers.[8] Estimates suggest that there may be as many as 136 different ethnic units in East Cameroun, and something like 70 in West Cameroun. Because of its geographical position, Cameroun embraces several of the cultural groups according to which African peoples have been classed. Thus the peoples at the coast include units variously termed those of the Guinea Coastal, Western Atlantic or Nigritic groups; as well as peoples more closely allied to those of the Congo, or with Bantu or Bantoid languages. In the north, ethnic groups are said to relate to Chadic, Western Sudan, or Hamitic blocs. In the centre of the country there are Bantu, Bantoid, or semi-Bantu groups as well as pygmy peoples.

None of these classifications has immediate relevance for the present study. Even without the uncertainty which surrounds the basis of classification, the categories are too large and too closely identified with linguistic or broad cultural features to be meaningful for an understanding of the developments which took place in Cameroun in the period shortly before and following its contact with the European nations which impinged on it through conquest, trade and colonisation. It is possible to adopt a narrower basis for description, which indicates the extent of distinct ethnic blocs in Cameroun and suggests possible links between them and other similar groups according to linguistic or territorial criteria. Thus Le Vine[9] distinguishes the following groups: Semitic (the Arab, Chadic or Fulani); other northern peoples, known collectively as the Kirdi, who do not fall into the previous category; two groups of Bantu—the Equatorial Bantu of the areas between the Congo basin and the plateau areas, and the Northwest Bantu at the coast and in the coastal hinterland (including the Douala and related tribes on the littoral and those surrounding the inland

9

plateaux); the Southern Nigerians whose closest ties are with the peoples of the present eastern states of Nigeria; the Cameroun highlanders (the Bamiléké and Tikar peoples); the plateau Nigerians, who are closely allied to the non-Fulani groups which inhabited parts of the former British Northern Camerouns; the Eastern Nigritic, many of whom live alongside the Kirdi, though some (e.g. the Chamba and the Bali) form distinct groups whose historical associations are of contact and conflict with the Cameroun Highlanders; and the Pygmies of the forest areas in the southeast, near the Congo basin.

These categories offer only a very rough guide to ethnic linkages. Within almost all of the blocs identified, there are a large number of smaller units. These vary in size, culture, language (or dialect) and history; in their degree of contact with one another, their reaction to the advent of invading groups and alien cultures; and their influence on the unfolding story of the formation of a Cameroun nation. It is only possible to dwell on the characteristics of a few of them, in an effort to point to their significance in present-day Cameroun and the process which led to its creation. In doing so, some attempt will be made to deal with both the historical and the ethnological features of the peoples discussed.

Geographical, historical and ethnic factors coincide to give an importance to the north, which, as already indicated, contains nearly a quarter of the population of modern Cameroun, some two-thirds of whom—around 800,000—are Kirdi. These do not form a unified group, ethnically or in any other way. Even their collective name is Fulani, and is intended to indicate not only their cultural differences from this dominant group but also their non-Muslim religions. The word 'Kirdi' is Fulani for pagan. There are more than twenty-five such groups, and they include Nigritic, Chadic and plateau Nigerian peoples in the classification given above (with the first category being further sub-divided into Eastern Nigritic and Sudano-Nigritic). The largest, like the Masa and the Matakam, have between 70,000 and 90,000 people in them, while others (like the Kapsiki or the Mofu) number between 30,000 and 40,000. Many were driven into isolated communities on the plains or in the mountains by Fulani invasions from the north, and joined others who were already there and had been settled in farming activity for a considerable time. These agricultural communities remained distinct from the Fulani livestock farmers who became their overlords in the area as a whole, both before and during the colonial period.

The isolation may have assisted in preserving Kirdi distinctiveness during the period of overrule; but their separate identity, the social and political distance between them and the Fulani rulers, and their remoteness from the centres of power, have meant that the Kirdi peoples have shared very little of the material progress which has taken place in Cameroun. The areas they inhabit still remain the least developed in the country, and it is only relatively recently that they have begun to enjoy the benefits of medical, educational and economic programmes designed to provide for the north as a whole. As a subordinate, though numerically preponderant group, the Kirdi have had little political influence. They have remained politically tied to the Fulani, and have given their allegiance to Fulani leaders—whether the Lamibe* or Emirs of the colonial era, or the politicians who have led the parties in more recent times.[10]

The Fulani number somewhat more than 400,000. Their presence in northern Cameroun is the result of the establishment of a substantial Fulani empire in the nineteenth century. As part of a holy war (*jihad*) waged by their leader, Uthman dan Fodio, against the Hausa, Fulani rule came to extend over large portions of the interior of present-day Nigeria, Cameroun and the surrounding states. By the time the Fulani arrived, the empire of Bornu had already been in existence for some four centuries; its Muslim rulers had held sway over parts of northern Cameroun, and Islamised states like those of Mandara and Kotoko had been created in the eighteenth century.[11] Dan Fodio succeeded in conquering much of Bornu; he established the headquarters of his own empire in Sokoto, in the north of what is now Nigeria.

The Fulani empire was itself composed of a large number of smaller units, each ruled by an Emir who owed allegiance to Dan Fodio at the centre. One such unit was created by Moddibo Adama, who came from the Benoué river valley and rallied to Dan Fodio's *jihad* in 1806. Using Fulani troops from his own area and Hausa adherents of the Fulani cause, he invaded the areas around the Mandara and Atlantika mountains, and established suzerainty over a substantial area to the south and east during the next three

* This is the plural; Lamido is the singular.

decades or more. By 1841 he had acquired control over the entire area (except for pockets inhabited by dispersed and fleeing tribes- men who took to the mountains or the plains), which was known after him as Adamawa. The capital, Yola, was established in that year as the headquarters of the new emirate. Under the Emir, Lamibe had control of subject areas and peoples. Each Lamido was permitted a high degree of independence in his rule, though all Lamibe paid tribute to the Emir at Yola.

The Fulani are believed to have originated from the Senegal valley at the western extremity of Africa; they are not ethnically related to the Hausas of Nigeria, or the peoples of the Nigerian plateau, the Chad region or the Nigritic groups over whom they came to dominate. In Adamawa, they settled along the Benoué valley, and still predominate in towns such as Garoua, Maroua and Ngaoundéré which formed the extremities of the emirate. Their hierarchical, centralised power structure was subordinated to colonial government by Britain and France; but the Emir and the Lamibe were able to retain a great deal of their authority under both colonial systems, and remained key figures in the systems of indirect rule which persisted until foreign control was very nearly at an end.

A similar set of developments occurred in the remainder of the northern parts of Cameroun. Those areas of the Bornu empire which had not been conquered by the Fulani underwent reform at the hands of the Kanembu, a cattle-keeping people who were from Kanem. Their leader, el Kanemi, defeated the Fulani, but took control of the Bornu empire and created a ruling dynasty. El Kanemi's son, Omar, had gained complete command by 1846, but less than fifty years later he was in turn displaced by a Sudanese conqueror, Rabeh. By 1896, Rabeh had made his capital at Dikwa and was in the process of instituting administrative reforms similar to those of the Fulani governmental system when his pro- gress was checked by the intervention of colonial powers—France, Britain and Germany. Rabeh himself was killed in 1900, in battle against the French who had come to an agreement with the British on the division of large areas of land between them. Subsequent rulers were established by the French in Dikwa, and later by the Germans. All were taken from members of the Kanemi dynasty, and they too were allowed to administer the areas of conquest, under the ultimate authority of the conqueror but left relatively free to govern through lesser officials in the hierarchy of traditional administration.

Among the many consequences of the Fulani invasions which took place with increasing intensity from the seventeenth until the first half of the nineteenth century was the pressure brought to bear on the Tikar peoples. These migrated southwards from as far afield as Ngaoundéré, and may even have originated as far north as Bornu itself.[12]

The name Tikar is an omnibus term. It is used to designate a great number of small, ethnically related tribal units, whose languages, in general, form part of a common linguistic stock, but are not necessarily mutually intelligible. They have been classified as belonging to the Benoué-Cross-River group of semi-Bantu languages; but this is a categorisation *grosso modo*, which is subject to a number of exceptions (e.g. the Bali, Bafut and Ndop tribes are said to speak Bantu languages). Vernacular *lingae francae* do exist which enable a high degree of intercommunication between the different units, and a pidgin English is also commonly used as a means of overcoming language barriers.

The language link between different Tikar groups is, on the whole, perhaps less important than their physical location. Most reside in the highlands of Cameroun, in both the eastern and western federated states of the Federal Republic. But this is a large area, and notwithstanding distinct similarities in the traditional political organisation of the Tikar tribes and in their economic activities, larger groupings have tended to develop separately in more recent times, on either side of the borders established before unification.

When estimating the political significance of the Tikar tribes, it is possible to exaggerate both their fragmentary character and the degree of political solidarity built up between them. The position is further complicated because they need to be considered in relation to the internal political situation of West Cameroun as well as in respect of the movement for unification of the two parts of Cameroun. Many of the tribal units have maintained a discrete traditional political organisation, with the Bafut and the Nsaw manifesting a strong internal cohesiveness and the Kom likewise retaining traditional distinctions between them and their neighbours. To a certain extent, these divisions were reinforced under British rule through the creation of administrative units based on them. Historically, there is a hostility between Tikar peoples and some of the other large ethnic groups in the highlands, like the Bali and the Widekum, who are themselves traditional enemies with a history of wars in the nineteenth century and the early part of the twentieth.[13]

Yet grassland peoples as a whole—many of them Tikar in the generic sense used by anthropologists—did form one of the bases on which political support was obtained by party leaders in the British trust territory of the Southern Cameroons from the mid-1950s onwards for dissociation from Nigeria and unification with French Cameroun. The difficulty lies not so much in distinguishing the ethnic basis of the support but in deciding why it was given. By this late period, traditional or ethnic identity had been overlaid by economic and political ties and animosities created during the period of alien rule. Ethnically different from the peoples of the coastal and forest areas in the Southern Cameroons, the grasslanders had also been left largely at an economic disadvantage through the more extensive development of ports and plantations at the coast and in its immediate hinterland. But if economic development in the context of the modern economy led to closer relations between similar ethnic groups across the international frontier in the south of Cameroun, there is little evidence that this occurred to a significant extent in the interior. In any event, the overwhelming majority of the Tikar peoples (nearly 300,000) are in West Cameroun, while a much smaller number—fewer than 20,000—are in the francophone part of the country.

None the less, there are ties between the Tikar peoples and other ethnic units in East Cameroun. The Bamoun, for instance, are formed from two ethnic groups—a Sudanic people who broke away from the Tikar at Rifum some 250 years ago, and the Bamiléké peoples whom they conquered.[14] They thus provide an ethnic bridge between the Tikar of West Cameroun and the Bamiléké of East Cameroun. Wars fought by Bamoun kings to amalgamate the smaller chiefdoms among the Tikar and Bamiléké succeeded in unifying the state. In the early part of the nineteenth century it was able to withstand the Fulani invasion, and later was to try and extend its influence over the Nsaw and other Tikar groups. The campaign against the Nsaw was unsuccessful, and Nsangu (the Bamoun king or Mfon) was killed in one of the battles in 1888.

Shortly afterwards, Njoya came to the throne. From 1895, he was able to consolidate Bamoun power, and he established the position of the state in relation to neighbouring tribes as well as the German colonisers and their French successors. Despite their ethnic links with the Bamiléké and the Tikar, the Bamoun maintain a distinct position in Cameroun society, based partly on the strong centralised kingdom created by Njoya around the capital at Foumban. Njoya was converted to Islam early in his reign, and the spread of the religion has much to do with the high degree of cohesiveness exhibited by his people in relation to peoples in the surrounding areas. The separate Bamoun culture was further reinforced by the invention of a written script for the Bamoun language.[15]

Religious and cultural solidarity have set the Bamoun apart from the Bamiléké in particular, and have also meant that the Bamoun were little influenced by missionary activity during the periods of German and French rule. Politically, Njoya was at loggerheads with the colonial administration and was ultimately deposed by the French, though the Bamoun were able to retain their political system within the overall context of French rule. More recently, the Bamoun have allied themselves with northern Muslims; they supported Ahidjo's *Union Camérounaise* and have provided Ministers in his governments. At no stage did they exhibit sympathy with the Bamiléké politicians, either electorally or in relation to the insurrection which took place in Bamiléké areas in the period before the Federal Republic was created.[16] Nevertheless, the choice of Foumban as the site of the constitutional negotiations between leaders of the two sections of Cameroun in 1961 was based not only on considerations of geographical convenience. There was at least an element of symbolism in the selection, which sought to stress Foumban's importance as a cultural if not also a political meeting-point for the new country, as well as emphasise the role allegedly played by the Sultan[17] of Foumban in the process of unification.[18]

Of all the peoples in the Cameroun highlands, the most populous are the Bamiléké. They number nearly 750,000, and most live in the plateau areas to the south and the east of the Bamboutos range of mountains. Like the Tikar, they are a complex of small tribes rather than a single ethnic unit, and are also fragmented into small chiefdoms, of which there are more than 100.[19] These are situated in five main areas, around Dschang, Mbouda, Bafang, Bafoussam and Bangangte. The largest chiefdom has more than 30,000 inhabitants; the others have mostly less than 5,000, with a dozen or so numbering between 12,000 and 20,000, and the smaller ones having only a few hundred members.[20]

The name Bamiléké is, apparently, a Bali creation chosen by the Germans who came into contact with the Bali early on in their colonisation, and it is not used by the Bamiléké themselves traditionally. Ethnically and linguistically,[21] the Bamiléké have proved difficult to classify and appear to have arrived in their present location in a series of five waves, starting at the beginning of the eighteenth century. Their fragmentary character is reflected as much in the seventeen or more languages and dialects used by Bamiléké as it is in the existence of their many chiefdoms.[22]

The traditional political system of the Bamiléké involved the rule of a Fon (chief), but although the chiefs were autonomous in their chiefdoms they often ruled through sub-chiefs who were of varying importance depending on whether they owed their position to conquest, voluntary allegiance or administrative usefulness. A chief was usually assisted by an hereditary council of notables, the *kamveu*, whose duty it was to advise on matters of importance, and by a number of officials. Bamiléké society also contained a variety of associations which were of great political significance within the traditional system, and were created originally for religious, military, occupational or age groups.[23] The chief was not an autocratic ruler, though it is not clear to what extent his power was curtailed or diffused as a result of the existence of these groups. As the chief during the period of French administration came to acquire more power as an agent of the government, so he was able to rely less on other traditional institutions. This tendency towards autocratic rule is alleged to be one of the bases for later discontent among the Bamiléké.[24]

Another source of dissatisfaction was the overpopulation of the area. As the population grew from about 360,000 in 1939 to an estimated 460,000 in 1956 and was moving towards 600,000 at the end of the 1950s,[25] pressure on the land became intense. This was exacerbated to an extent by a traditional system of inheritance which provided for the succession of a single heir to family land and left other males with a less than adequate source of income. The allocation of land to members of a tribe was a matter for the chief; and, as the chiefs were decreasingly subject to traditional restraints, opportunities for abuse grew. Large numbers of Bamiléké migrated and settled further south in the Moungo valley or sought employment in the towns, which grew rapidly as economic development occurred. But the vast majority remained where they were and witnessed the growth of disaffection.

Politically, the Bamiléké were deeply involved with the rebellion which took place in the late 1950s, and played a leading role in the political party which advocated the use of violent means to achieve independence and unification, the *Union des Populations du Cameroun* (UPC). Both urban and rural Bamiléké participated in the revolt, but they were not able to draw upon traditional institutions. In the 1940s an attempt was made to found an allegedly traditional pan-Bamiléké organisation, the *Kumze*. There was no historical basis for the association, but it did provide a vehicle for the unity of some Bamiléké outside the framework of the chiefdoms. As it became clear that its bias was anti-traditional, it lost the support of the chiefs, and dwindled in significance. For the most part, support for the revolt came from urban areas, where the Bamiléké exhibited a high degree of solidarity as they took jobs which might have been occupied by people from tribes in the areas surrounding the towns, and from those elements who wished to break the power of the traditional chiefs. In any event, as the Bamiléké came to be associated increasingly with violent resistance, they were rejected by the rather more moderate politicians of the British trust territory and those who supported them.

None the less, the Bamiléké have acted as a political unit, at least in East Cameroun. After the proscription of the UPC in 1955, they elected a bloc of deputies who continued to act together and, for a long time, in opposition to Ahidjo and his party, though they were later integrated into the single party that has held sway in the state more recently.

A large and politically important ethnic group which is in no way directly related to those already mentioned is the Beti-Pahouin group of Bantu who inhabit the central part of the southern area of francophone Cameroun. In all they number nearly 700,000 people. The largest tribe is the Ewondo, in reality a group of tribes speaking the same language, who live in the area around Yaoundé, and with the nearby Eton total about half a million. Grouped with them are the Boulou, another Bantu language people with some 150,000 members, and the rather less significant Fang who make up the remaining 50,000 in the ethnic complex.

This is the group of people who, of all those situated in the interior, were most widely subjected to the influence of Christian missions. As a result, a segmentary pattern of traditional political organisation based upon a loose-knit and non-hierarchical clan structure[26] underwent substantial modification during the period of French rule. Chiefs were integrated into the system of government, and became functionaries of the system. The extensive mission activity led to a relatively high literacy rate, and to the spread of Catholic influence, particularly among the Ewondo and the Eton; the Boulou were converted by Presbyterian missionaries, as were the Bassa further south.[27]

As economic progress was made under the Germans and under the French, large numbers from these groups were recruited to work on roads, railways and public works. They were among the first to take up active participation in nationalist politics, and the Beti in particular gave expression to their political views through the largely Catholic centre party of *Démocrates*—which later opposed the Ahidjo government—while the Boulou tended to lend their support to another early nationalist party, the *Action Nationale* of Charles Assalé, which also later turned against Ahidjo. In both cases, however, leaders of these parties were effectively integrated into Ahidjo's single party.

Not so the leaders of the Bassa-Bakoko, another Bantu language ethnic unit, whose ties are ethnically closer to the peoples of the coast. They number some 200,000, and came, as already indicated, under missionary influence early on through the activities of the Presbyterians. Traditionally, there had been a history of conflict between them and the Boulou, but the more decisive influence on their political involvement in modern Cameroun was the impact of economic changes brought about by forced labour, first under the Germans and later through the system of prestation introduced by the French in the period after 1920. Social and economic disruption was experienced yet again when France set about the creation of a large hydro-electric and aluminium-smelting complex at Edea towards the end of the 1940s and in the 1950s. The spread of education and religion under missionary influence, and the social and economic dislocation of the traditional system, all contributed in some measure to the success with which the violent

18

political methods of the UPC took hold among the Bassa after 1955. They were aided by the fact that one of the first nationalist leaders of Cameroun and a leading figure in the UPC, Reuben Um Nyobe, was Bassa; he and a close colleague, Theodore Mayi Matip, were able to use traditional Bassa clan organisation as part of their underground opposition, and in order to galvanise political support against the candidates at elections who favoured Ahidjo.

If the north of Cameroun provides one major point of focus in the country's history, the other is to be found in the south, at the coast, and is the result of the long history of contact between the peoples of the area and European traders, missionaries and colonisers. Ethnically, the coastal region is composed of three groups of tribes all of whom speak Bantu languages.[28] They are the Kpe-Mboko group, which includes the Kpe or Bakweri, the Mboko, the Isuwu and the Wovea, all of whom are situated in West Cameroun; the Douala-Limba group, which embraces the Douala,[29] Mongo (or Moungo), Pongo, Oli (or Wouri), Bodiman, Kolle and Limba, of whom only the Moungo traditionally straddle the boundary between the two states, with the remainder coming from the francophone area; and the Tanga-Yassa group, a small group which inhabits parts of the area to the south of the country from Kribi to the border with Rio Muni. Because of the history of contact between the first two groups, along the mouths of the Wouri and Moungo rivers, and as workers in ports and on plantations, it is difficult to isolate the members of any one tribe and provide an exact figure (or even a rough estimate) of its number. The Kpe-Mboko group probably now number about 50,000, of whom roughly half are immigrants from other parts of the country; the same is true of the Douala-Limba group, who total around 90,000, though the Douala themselves are not much more than 25,000, and the total of the indigenous population is only about 45,000.[30] There is a high population density—the result of the alienation of land for towns, factories, ports and plantations; for the Bakweri (Kpe-Mboko) group, it is as high as 300 per square mile, while in the town of Douala and the villages surrounding it, at more than 550 per square mile, it is even higher.

The peoples at the coast were the first to become involved with Europeans. There are suggestions that Mount Cameroun may have been sighted as early as the first voyage to Africa recorded in European history, that of Hanno of Carthage in the fifth century BC, and that it was this active volcano that he described as the 'Chariot of the Gods'.[31] It was another 2,000 years before the area was again described by Europeans. The Portuguese reached the Bight of Biafra in 1472 in the reign of King Alphonso V, and during the next twenty years established a settlement on the island of Fernando Po, about twenty miles off the coast.

Although they did not settle at the coast, the Portuguese traded in ivory and in slaves with the peoples they encountered there, whom they named the Ambos, or Ambozi.[32] The name Cameroun is in fact derived from the Portuguese word *Camarões*, after the name given to the Wouri river, the *Rio dos Camarões*.* In the seventeenth century, the Dutch succeeded in displacing the Portuguese, and established trading posts along the Bights of Benin and Biafra in the course of developing commerce with the Calabar and Efik peoples near the Rio del Rey. Over the course of the next century and a half, a lucrative trade was built up in goods and people, and contact was made with the people at Douala, Bimbia and Malimba whose chiefs became wealthy as they came to participate more and more as middlemen.

The Dutch were succeeded by the British as the principal European power on the coast at the beginning of the nineteenth century. By this time, the slave-trade had become illegal in Britain, and in 1807 British ships were prevented from engaging in it. British boats nevertheless traded in the other commodities provided by the tribes at the Cameroun coast, and were in almost continuous contact with the Douala. These people, originally ruled as part of a coastal dominion by a single king, known as Bele (corrupted to Bell), came to be governed in a number of separate entities as trade increased and lesser rulers came to compete for wealth. Sometimes referred to later as towns, these chiefdoms were ruled by members of the ruling Douala dynasty who broke away from the domination of Bell. The first of these was Akwa; he was followed by Priso or Joss (a corruption of the English nickname George or Joss), and Ebele, who established himself at Bonabela and was known as Dido. All three kingdoms

---

* The word refers to prawns discovered at the Wouri estuary, though the variety actually found are apparently more correctly described as a form of crayfish.

* *

were situated on the eastern side of the Wouri, and the names associated with them survive today—Manga and Bell, Priso and Akwa. A fourth kingdom was established on the western bank at Bonaberi, a town which still exists under that name, but which was for a time known as Hickory. Some measure of Douala unity was achieved in later years, despite these divisions, through the creation of a council in which the chiefs met. Known as the Ngondo, this survived to play a part in more recent history.

European penetration of the coast began in earnest in the third decade of the nineteenth century and early explorations of the interior were begun by British officers. Britain obtained permission from Spain, which had acquired Fernando Po from Portugal, to establish a small settlement on this island in 1827. While this continued to be concerned mainly with trade in palm oil and ivory, official British activity was concentrated on policing the area with gun-boats, from the Niger Delta southwards, in an effort to eliminate the slave-trade; and on signing treaties with chiefs in order to legitimise trade, secure British influence and exclude (or at any rate pre-empt) competition from the agents of other nations. Numerous treaties of this kind were entered into between British consuls and representatives of the indigenous populations, including one with two Douala chiefs in 1842.

At about the same time, missionary influence came to be felt. A small mission settlement had been set up on Fernando Po, and this was extended in 1844 by the Baptist Missionary Society which brought volunteers from England and Jamaica. An early settlement was established at Bimbia in that year, but did not last more than five years. In 1858, however, a more determined move to establish a permanent settlement was made by Alfred Saker of the Baptist Missionary Society, whose followers had come under pressure to leave Fernando Po as a result of Spanish Catholic disapproval of their Protestant presence. Saker founded his mission station at Ambas Bay, on land purchased from King William (originally Bile or Billy) of Bimbia, and thus started the town of Victoria—the first to be settled by Europeans on the coast of Cameroun—and was responsible for its administration.

Britain made no formal attempt to colonise either the coast or the interior. She continued to police the area with her navy, and retained informal control of parts of it as a result of the agreements reached with the coastal chiefs for the suppression of the (now clandestine) slave-trade and for the promotion of trade. British consular officials kept a watchful eye on developments at the coast with a view to seeing that British humanitarian and commercial aims were not thwarted, and a British Court of Equity was established at Douala to settle disputes between the traders of different nations.[33]

The Douala people meanwhile came into contact with German trading companies and their representatives, and other posts were established further south by French commercial interests. The competition between the traders of these three nations for the products sold at the coast by the Douala was, by the 1880s, to develop into a scramble for control over the entire area—a process which led to the colonisation of Cameroun by Germany in 1884.

2. Conquest and Division: German Rule and its Aftermath

INTRODUCTION

German rule in Cameroun lasted only thirty years, from 1884 to 1914. This is a short period by any standard, even that of colonial Africa; but it was one which is as instructive about the process of colonisation in Africa as it was important for the immense effect it had on the country itself, both while it lasted and afterwards. The circumstances in which Germany came to control the Cameroun coast are bound up with the rush by the major European powers to establish colonies in Africa during the latter half of the nineteenth century. They illustrate all too clearly the atmosphere of commercial rivalry and competition for areas of economic and, possibly, strategic importance which surrounded the determination of these nations to divide Africa between them.

The extension of German control into the interior and the manner in which it was accomplished, as well as the thoroughness with which it was maintained, combined to alter the fabric of life in the country and the future of its institutions for all time. Its international boundaries were fixed, the foundations of its modern economic structure were laid, most of its towns were established, and its network of roads and railways were begun during the period of German sovereignty. A system of government was introduced which altered the laws, and either incorporated or subordinated traditional rulers, but in both cases made them dependent on the colonial power for their authority. Even the world war which brought German rule to an end profoundly affected the future of Cameroun. By the division of the country between Britain and France, the basis for the establishment of two cultural and political traditions was created. These took firm root during the forty-seven years which preceded reunification, and have yet to be resolved finally within the context of the Federal Republic of Cameroun.

GERMAN COLONISATION AND EXPANSION

Germany was a late-comer to colonial rule in Africa and, at the beginning at any rate, an unenthusiastic one. Even German traders were slow to get started on the west coast of Africa. The Hamburg firms of Woermann and Jantzen & Thormaehlen first established trading centres near Douala and Victoria late in the 1860s. By this time, British traders and missionaries had been active in the area for more than forty years. Numerous treaties had been signed with Cameroun kings and chiefs,[1] and a British 'Court of Equity' had been in existence for more than a decade. Representatives of the German firms had participated in the court and worked alongside their British counterparts, although in their trade with the Cameroun tribes they continued to compete with one another for new markets and influence.

France had also begun to show an interest in this part of the coast. In the 1870s a French company had opened a trading station at Malimba, and others at Big Batanga and Campo; and in 1883 they established themselves more firmly through a treaty with King Mukoko ('Pass-All'), which was signed in April of that year.

Germany still showed little interest in acquiring colonies in this part of Africa. Bismarck, the German Chancellor, had apparently remained unmoved by pressure from commercial interests as well by the arguments of the advocates (in the Reichstag and outside) of a general move towards colonial expansion.

Right up to the beginning of the 1880s, the German Chancellor maintained his opposition to the acquisition of colonies, and reiterated his lack of desire for overseas possessions. Then, in 1883, he changed his mind. Why he did so remains uncertain,[2] but the speed with which the change occurred caught Britain off guard and enabled Germany to take advantage of the British government's hesitancy over whether or not to acquire Cameroun as a colony.

Once they realised that the presence of rival groups of traders from different nations would make a choice necessary, the Cameroun kings and chiefs expressed a clear preference for British rule. No doubt with the encouragement of British traders,[3] letters and petitions were addressed to the British government inviting British annexation. One of the earliest of these was addressed to Queen Victoria in 1879 in the following terms:

'Dearest Madam,
We your servants have join together and thoughts it better to write to you a nice loving letter which will tell you about all our wishes. We wish to have your laws in our towns. We want to have every fashion altered, also we will do according to your consuls word. Plenty wars here in our country. Plenty murder and plenty idol worshippers. Perhaps these lines of our writing will look to you as an idle tale. We have spoken to the English Consul plenty times about having an English government here. We never have answer from you, so we wish to write ourselves. When we heard about Calabar River, how they have all English laws in their towns, and how they have put away all their superstitions, oh we shall be very glad to be like Calabar now.'[4]

This was followed by other letters to Hewett, the British Consul for the Gulf of Guinea, and to the British Prime Minister, Gladstone, in 1881 which stated explicitly, 'we want our country governed by British Government'. In March 1882, Gladstone replied that his government was not prepared to assume authority for the country, though he did promise to give the matter further consideration.[5]

It would be wrong to give the impression that the desire for British annexation only came from the Cameroun kings and their councillors. There was also constant pressure from the British traders themselves, from their head offices in England, and from Hewett, the Consul. Even the German merchants appear to have told the British representatives that they wanted British sovereignty to be established along the coast,[6] though in view of their activities among the chiefs and their efforts to persuade Bismarck to establish German control such statements must be taken to have cloaked their real intentions.

Despite all this, Britain still delayed. What finally moved the British government to action was, apparently, the fear that the French were becoming too closely involved with coastal chiefs. In November 1883, the Cabinet reached a decision, but nothing was done until May of the following year. Hewett was then sent out and instructed to create a 'floating consulate' with authority over the coast from Nigeria to Cameroun, and to sign treaties

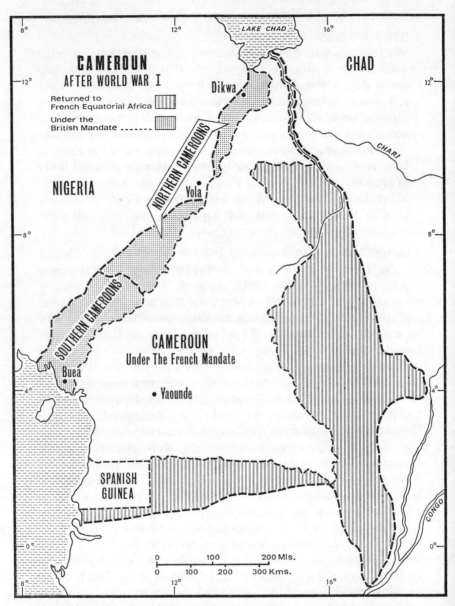

3. Cameroun after World War I (*after Mveng, op. cit., p. 360*)

with the chiefs which would prevent them from ceding territory to any other power without the consent of Her Majesty's government.[7] No attention was paid to the possibility that Germany, too, might be interested in acquiring the area, and the British were apparently unaware of any change in German colonial policy. But Bismarck's policy *had* already been reversed. In the same month that the British Cabinet finally decided to send a mission to Cameroun, he succumbed to pressure from Woermann and others, and decided to further trade by sending out consuls and a warship patrol, and to authorise the signing of trade treaties with the chiefs. Annexation had not yet been authorised.[8]

In February 1884, however, the explorer Eugen Nachtigal was sent to the west coast of Africa to make a preliminary investigation of the prospects for German occupation. In April— while Britain was told that the purpose of the voyage was 'to complete the information now in the possession of the German Foreign Office at Berlin on the state of German commerce on that coast', and accordingly instructed her representatives to help the Germans in whatever way they could[9]—Nachtigal was ordered to acquire the coast for Germany.

Thus Germany and Britain were literally involved in a scramble for the colonisation of Cameroun. The outcome was decided by a narrow margin. The British, still more concerned about the French, divided their expedition: one half, under Captain Brooke, set off to sign treaties with the chiefs at Big Batanga and Malimba in the French 'sphere'; the other, under Hewett, moved eastward from Lagos towards Cameroun, but was also establishing agreements with chiefs at Bonny and in the Niger delta. Brooke passed some German boats and became suspicious; he dispatched an officer, Captain Moore, to reach Douala before Hewett was expected to arrive. But he was already too late. The Germans had been there since July 1, conducting meetings and preparing the way for a treaty that was signed on July 12. Moore was only able to come to an agreement with one Douala king, Bell, who agreed to wait one week for Hewett. Nachtigal, aided by Schultze, the German Consul, Schmidt, the Woermann agent, and Voss who represented Jantzen & Thormaehlen, had completed all the work for Germany by the time Hewett arrived on board *The Flirt* on

July 18. The German flag had been hoisted over Cameroun on July 14.

The treaty signed on July 12 with the Douala kings read:

'We the undersigned, Kings and Chiefs of the territory named Cameroun, situated along the River Cameroun between the Rivers Bimbia in the north and Kwakwa in the south, and as far as longitude 4° 10′ north* have voluntarily decided, during the course of an assembly held at the German factory on the banks of King Akwa['s territory], that:

We are today abandoning totally all our rights relating to sovereignty, legislation and administration of our territory to Messrs Edouard Schmidt, agent of the firm C. Woermann and Johannes Voss, agent of the firm Jantzen and Thormahlen, both of Hamburg and merchants for many years among these rivers.

We have transferred our rights of sovereignty, of legislation and of administration in our territory to the above-mentioned firms, with the following reservations:

1. The territory may not be ceded to a third party.
2. All the treaties of friendship and commerce which have been concluded with other foreign governments shall remain fully valid.
3. The lands cultivated by us, and the sites on which villages are situated, shall remain the property of the present possessors and their descendants.
4. The payments shall be made annually, as in the past, to Kings and Chiefs.
5. During the initial period of the establishment of an administration here, our local customs and usages shall be respected.

Signed: Ed. Woermann.   Signed: King Akwa.
Witnesses:

O. Busch, Endene Akwa, Ed. Schmidt, Coffee Angwa, John Angwa, Manga Akwa, Scott Jost, Lorten Akwa, Ned Akwa, David Meatom, Joh. Voss, King Bell, Joe Garner Akwa, Big Jim Akwa, William Akwa, Jim Joss, Matt Joss, David Joss, Jacco Esqre, London Bell, Barrow Peter, Elame Joss, Lookingglass Bell.'[10]

* This should read 'latitude 4° 10′ north'.

The reservation of rights by the chiefs were to be of some importance later, during the period of German rule, when subsequent Douala chiefs attempted to secure adequate compensation for land that had been expropriated. It is also worth noting that one important reservation, contained in a memorandum submitted by the kings and chiefs, was not included in the treaty: the Douala, as experienced traders and important middlemen, had sought to establish their right to continue their role as go-between, by stating: 'Our wishes is that white men should not go up and trade with the Bushmen, nothing to do with our markets, they must stay here in this river and they give us trust* so that we will trade with our Bushmen'. This was a forlorn hope. It was a principal aim of the German annexation that the 'middleman monopoly' of the Douala should be broken, or at least circumvented. So far as Woermann was concerned, this was the most important way in which trade could be made more profitable, while additional advantage was to be obtained from the establishment of plantations and speculation in land.[11]

Strictly construed, the treaty with the chiefs was made with two German companies; but Nachtigal took it as conferring rights over Cameroun[12] on the German Empire, a procedure not uncommon in the history of African colonisation and one which was not surprising in view of the instructions he had received from Bismarck. The Germans spent the next few years extending their control over the coastal areas, by consolidating their conquest of the chiefs and securing the withdrawal of the British and other European representatives.

The first major incident in this process involved a military exercise against two recalcitrant Douala towns, Joss Town and Hickory Town (Bonaberi) in December 1884.[13] The first of these challenged the authority of Kings Bell and Akwa, claiming that it had not received a share of the 'dash' (bribe, or, more charitably, present or price) paid by the German agents to the kings for signing the treaty. In the case of Hickory Town, the objection was political: Lock Priso, the chief, was opposed to the treaty with Germany, would not regard himself as bound by the signatures of the kings, and subsequently signed a treaty of his own with Hewett, the British Consul. Bell and the Germans treated this as a form of rebellion, and, apparently at Bell's request, the local

* i.e. credit.

German agent called in aid from Admiral Knorr who landed a force of marines and subjugated Joss and Hickory. Both towns were bombarded and levelled to the ground, and a British mission station was destroyed. Four German lives were lost.

As this incident shows, the British were not inactive after the Nachtigal treaty. In the latter part of 1884 and the first months of 1885 agents were busily signing treaties for Britain on the Cameroun coast; there was a good deal of rivalry between the representatives of Germany and a Pole in British employ named Rogozinski, who went as far as to establish himself as Commissioner for Victoria, after making thirty-five 'temporary' treaties with local chiefs.

Nevertheless, the British government, under pressure from the other powers at the Berlin Conference, called at the end of 1884 to resolve the disputes between the rival colonial powers in the 'scramble for Africa', had decided to consolidate its position in Nigeria and to abandon any further attempts to assert a claim to Cameroun. Accordingly, in May 1885 Britain and Germany agreed to define the border between Nigeria and Cameroun, though Britain still reserved its rights in respect of Victoria and Ambas Bay.[14] These, too, were soon to be transferred to Germany, after protracted negotiations involving compensation for the mission land (fixed at £4,000, although only £2,750 was paid in the end). German suzerainty over the Cameroun coast was finally established at the end of January 1887.

In the meanwhile, Bismarck's initial hopes that the colony could be administered by the merchants and at no expense to his treasury were being overtaken by events. The suppression of the recalcitrant Douala in 1884, and the abolition of the Court of Equity the following year, began the process which led to the first appropriation of funds for a colonial administration in Cameroun in 1885 and the dispatch of the first governor, von Soden, shortly afterwards. Bismarck's reluctant colonialism was the product of continued pressure from Woermann, and the obvious failure of the local traders to manage the possessions without military backing. His lack of enthusiasm for assuming the burdens of colonial expenditure was shared by the left and centre parties in the Reichstag, who remained watchful over the activities of the colonial governors and critical of colonial administration throughout the period of German rule in Cameroun. A by-product of these attitudes, however, was the failure to establish a metropolitan Colonial Office. Up till 1907, well after Bismarck's demise, Cameroun, along with other German possessions, continued to be administered by a division of the Foreign Office.

The administrative and economic structure established for Cameroun by von Soden and his successors will be described below. For the moment, it is necessary to concentrate on the way in which German control was extended beyond the coast and into the interior of the country.

Although von Soden is credited with having been an advocate of gradual penetration,[15] a considerable number of conquests and explorations took place during his governorship (which lasted until 1895). Initially, there was the matter of tidying up the treaty situation at the coast and ensuring that rights conceded to the British were ceded to Germany. Thus Rogozinski's treaties with the Kpe people (Bakweri) around Gbea (Buea) were replaced, and sovereignty was acquired over the area surrounding Mount Cameroun. This proved to be fertile land, suitable for the establishment of plantations, and ultimately, because of its climate, Buea was to become the capital of the German colony. But the Kpe were also subjugated militarily: an expedition under von Gravenreuth in 1891 failed to overcome their resistance at Soppo after an incident in which a missionary had complained that they were taking the law into their own hands by using ordeals to carry out a death sentence; but a further expedition in 1894 put an end to their opposition. Their lands were appropriated and substantial fines imposed which had to be paid with wages received from working on plantations.[16]

Between 1892 and 1895 the Bassa and Bakoko people were also conquered by expeditions mounted from Douala, which followed the Sanaga and Kwakwa rivers; the Bassa in particular proved difficult to overcome. The occupation of their territory, and the use of their men as labourers on the Douala-Yaoundé railway was a constant source of friction, which lasted throughout the period of German rule and aroused a hostile attitude to colonial government. In 1887 earlier moves to expand from the coast into the interior had begun from Big Batanga and Kribi in the south. Under two officers, in the company of zoologists and botanists, these moves started as an attempt to explore the Nyong river to its junction.[17] In the process, Yaoundé was settled, after the Ewondo had been

31

overcome. Other settlements were established at Ebolowa in 1895, and four years later came a major military exercise against the Boulou who attempted to defend their monopoly of interior trade, and in the course of doing so nearly destroyed Kribi. They were finally subdued in 1901, after considerable loss of life on both sides.

Meanwhile, there had been some effort at penetration in the east, where there was strong resistance by the forest peoples, who were defeated only in 1907. Starting in 1888 a series of exploratory expeditions led by Zintgraff in the north resulted in campaigns against the Tikar and Bamiléké peoples, as well as the Bali and their neighbours.[18] These were followed by a series of campaigns organised by Hirtler which led to the occupation of areas towards the centre, and after overcoming the Tibati the Germans reached Foumban. In these operations, the Germans began to encounter the organised military apparatus of the northern peoples under their Lamibe, and they developed the technique of subordinating these leaders within their administration or imposing new Lamibe where existing leaders proved unco-operative—the beginning of 'indirect rule' in northern areas of Cameroun. But the establishment of German domination of the north did not take place without a series of hard-fought battles. Led at first by Morgen and von Stetten who started from Yaoundé and moved northwards, and later by Dominik using a northern route in the Adamawa region, they successfully overcame resistance in Tibati, and in the period up to 1902 followed the route along the Benoué to take Garoua, and then moved first south to conquer the areas to the south around Ngaoundéré and then north as far as Maroua. Although fighting continued on and off until the end of the first decade of the twentieth century, these campaigns established the essential geographical limits of German control over Cameroun.

None of these expeditions would have succeeded without government support—one of von Soden's successors, von Puttkamer, participated in several of them—but it remains true that they were not the result of any major imperial thrust by Germany. The soldiers and the explorers involved were relatively minor figures in the colonial establishment; no great German general was ever sent out to Cameroun, and no imperial army was dispatched to overrun its people. German resources, limited as they were by a parsimonious and watchful Reichstag, were concentrated more on building the country's economic base and securing a profitable return from the colony.

THE GERMAN ADMINISTRATION

The head of the German administration in Cameroun was the Governor, who was initially responsible to the Chancellor, but later to the Colonial Office. The Governor was empowered to legislate for the country, to collect and levy taxes, and to administer the courts and the military forces. Although, at the beginning, the Governor was required to consult an advisory council, this institution was abandoned early on and was only revived in 1904 after considerable agitation by local merchants and in the Reichstag.

The number of colonial officials in German Cameroun—including those in local administrative districts—was never large, though it was to increase as more territory was conquered and economic development occurred. An initial staff of a Chancellor and two secretaries to assist the Governor had grown by 1890 to include customs, police and medical officers, teachers and the like, but still only numbered about a dozen officials. The addition of harbour masters, engineers to supervise the building of roads and bridges, botanists and zoologists, and a growing number of officers in charge of the hinterland had raised the number to 70 by 1900. Five years later there were 110, and in 1912, towards the end of German rule, the total reached 238.[19] These figures do not include police or troops, who were supervised by German officers. In 1914 there were a mere 1,200 police, with 30 white officers. The soldiers—most of whom came from Dahomey—only numbered 1,550 in the same year, though they were in the charge of 185 German officers.[20]

Two sets of courts were established by the Germans, one for the whites and one for Camerounians. For the former, a court of first instance was established in each administrative district (*Bezirksgericht*), presided over by a judge who was aided by two or four lay assistants (*Beisitzer*). German civil and criminal law, and procedure, was applied, and there was an appeal to an *Obergericht*, situated in Cameroun, but which also acted as a court of appeal for Togo. Later, a court of appeal for all the colonies was established in Germany (the *Kolonialgerichtshof*), to deal with cases involving whites only. Punishments were seldom severe

33

for whites. Rudin points out that there were few gaol sentences, and that those over six months were served in Germany; incarceration with Africans was considered an affront to the dignity of the white criminal.[21]

For Africans, a separate system of courts under the presidency of chiefs dealt with civil cases involving less than 100 marks, and criminal cases for which the sentence did not exceed 300 marks or imprisonment of more than six months, but they could not try any case involving the death penalty, or murder or manslaughter. The Governor or his representative could attend their sessions and there was an appeal either to the Governor or to the *Oberrichtre* established by him.

There was a marked difference between the types of punishment prescribed for Camerounians and those meted out to whites. Whipping was by far the most common sentence for Africans. It was, according to Rudin: 'strongly disliked by them, much criticised by the Reichstag, carefully regulated by the Government, and highly recommended by the colonialists as the only way of teaching the natives that some things were wrong.' [22] Despite the control exercised over (and perhaps by) the government, the number of floggings rose from 351 in 1900–01 to 4,800 in 1912–13. Prison sentences of more than six months rose from 73 to 584 over the same period, while those under six months increased from 442 to 4,147, and fines from 133 to 943. The total number of Africans punished for offences against the colonial laws grew from 773 in 1900–01 to 11,229 in 1912–13.[23] Death sentences were not common, though thirty or more people were executed in three of the years between 1901 and 1913. These figures may be contrasted with the largest number of cases involving whites for any one year of German rule. In 1909–10, for instance, 114 were heard, though there is no record of the number of convictions. Rudin says that habitually 'a rather large number' of whites were acquitted.[24]

Local administration throughout the southern portion of Cameroun was in the hands of officers, who were at first placed in charge of small stations garrisoned by a small force, but who later came to administer large districts known as *Bezirke* (the officials in charge were *Bezirksamtmänner*). These officers exercised both administrative and judicial functions in the areas under their control, though whites were always to be tried by the Chancellor at the centre, and death sentences required the Governor's

34

approval. Administrative duties involved the establishment and maintenance of good relations with Cameroun chiefs in the area, and the supervision of such services as might be available to deal with roads, health, education and missions, as well as the promotion of commerce and agricultural products, and the study of climatic conditions. Administrative officers were given wide discretion to administer laws and collect taxes, and were often able to exercise their powers without much curtailment from the capital.

In the north of the country, Germany pursued a policy of indirect rule through the sixty or so Lamibe who were the traditional rulers of the Fulani (Fulbe) in the area. These maintained administrative control over their areas, and were subject to only the most tenuous supervision by two German Commissioners who resided in the region. The principal aims of these resident commissioners was to secure the loyalty to Germany of the Fulani rulers. Beyond this, they were to act as 'advisers', to settle disputes between rival claimants for a Lamidate, and to attempt some economic development.

ECONOMIC DEVELOPMENT UNDER THE GERMANS

One of the reasons why Germany had acquired Cameroun was because Woermann and the other merchants wanted to add other economic activities to the trade they had already established with the Douala. During the thirty years of her rule in Cameroun, this objective was accomplished: not only was trade extended to other parts of the country, but new products were developed for export to Germany, plantations were established for the supply of raw materials and a market was created for the importation of German goods. In the process, roads and railways were started, an educational system begun and health services provided.

In order to stimulate trade, and increase private capital investment for agricultural development, Germany granted large tracts of land—amounting to nearly half the entire country—to two chartered companies. The *Gesellschaft Nord-West Kamerun* was given some 100,000 square kilometres (nearly two and a half million acres) of land covering a wide area from the Nigerian border to the interior in the centre of the southern part of the country in 1898; and, in the following year, the *Gesellschaft*

35

Sud-Kamerun received 80,000 square kilometres bordering on what is now Gabon and the Central African Republic. In return for a virtual monopoly of all trade in products discovered within their areas, the companies were required to explore the land assigned to them, to construct roads and bridges, and to encourage settlement. In fact, they did little more than was absolutely necessary for their own trading purposes, and their assumption that they had absolute rights to exclude other traders caused much dissatisfaction among the trading community. Although both discovered and exploited vast quantities of rubber, ivory, timber and other raw materials, and established factories for the processing of some of these, neither company was a very great success. The *Gesellschaft Nord-West Kamerun* only declared a profit in five of the fourteen years of its operations, while the *Gesellschaft Sud-Kamerun* lost nearly 2·5 million marks during the course of its existence. Nevertheless, both companies represented a major means for the injection of capital into Cameroun and, between them, contributed just under a fifth of the total of nearly 96 million marks which was invested in the country during the period of German rule.[25]

Germany also invested in the establishment of plantations in the south, particularly those around Buea and Victoria. Traders were always more numerous than planters, but the number of plantations grew rapidly between 1890 and 1900 under the partnership of the Woermann and Jantzen & Thormaehlen firms. By 1913, 195 whites were engaged in work on 58 plantations which employed 17,827 African workers. In the area surrounding Mount Cameroun alone, plantations accounted for more than 400 square miles (100,000 hectares approximately, of which 83,000 had been taken from the Kpe (Bakweri) without any compensation).[26]

The growth of exploration companies and of the plantations led to improved transportation facilities. Traders had always complained that their activities were restricted by the inaccessibility of so many of the richer areas in the interior. Although the great charter companies fulfilled only a very small part of their original commitment to build roads, the government was able to do a good deal in this regard, and private investment resulted in the building of a serviceable network of railways. Much of the development of roads and bridges was left to Camerounians. The plantations constructed private roads of their own, but the responsibility for building most of the public roads in the south of the country from 1900 onwards was that of villages and tribes through whose areas they ran, and they were also charged with maintenance. At first, these duties were imposed after conquest as the price to be paid for defeat; later, after the institution of a general tax of six marks a year for every adult male in 1908, it became possible to commute the tax into thirty days labour on public works[27] such as road-building. In 1913 there were 500 kilometres of roads suitable for automobile traffic, a total which the traders did not regard as adequate, and which still left them heavily dependent on human porterage. On the Kribi-Yaoundé route alone, something like 85,000 porters (men, women and children) were employed. By law no carrier was supposed to bear a load of more than 30 kilo-grammes (66 lb). The distance covered by the route was 280 kilo-metres (175 miles, approximately).

But the most important development occurred in the field of railways. Although projects for railway construction had been discussed from 1901, early moves were made only in respect of a small, narrow-guage track to serve the private interests of the plantations for the carriage of goods. In 1906, the Reichstag agreed to provide loan facilities for the construction of a 160-kilometre (100-mile) track from Bonaberi, near Douala, to Nkongsamba. Known as the *Nordbahn,* the railway line was put into service from 1911, and, as late as 1969, was still the only railway in the south-west of Cameroun. The line was privately owned and operated at a profit in 1912 and 1913. The government built another railway, known as the *Mittellandbahn,* intended to run for a distance of 360 kilometres, from Douala to the Nyong river town of Wide-menge; only 150 kilometres were completed by 1913, but this rail-way also provided the basis for the country's main form of inland transport, which the French administration was later to extend as far as Yaoundé.[28]

All these economic activities—trade, plantations, and the development of transport—involved competition for Camerounian labour. At the start labourers proved difficult to obtain; and, when persuasion (often by missionaries) failed, forced labour was obtained by conquest and through taxation. From 1902 onwards, the government attempted to regulate recruiting procedures, so as to avoid abuses both in the treatment of workers—some of whom had been tied together en route to their destinations—and in the contracts they were made to enter into.[29] The average wage received by labourers was 8–9 marks per month for those who undertook contracts of twelve to eighteen months, and 6 marks a month for those agreeing to work for six months. Workers were not given their wages in full: 50 per cent was withheld until the end of the contract period, so as to keep them from running away.[30] Health conditions, particularly on the plantations, were appalling. Workers recruited from the malaria-free interior were brought south to disease-infested areas, with devastating results. No over-all figures on the subject were kept by the colonial government but the extent of the deaths among recruited workers can be gauged from early reports from administrators that between half and two-thirds of labourers from their districts never returned. In 1902, it was reported that on one Victoria plantation the death-rate was 20 per cent; and, in 1904, a plantation with what was regarded as an 'excellent' health record recorded the death of $7\frac{1}{2}$ per cent of its workers in the first nine months of the year. Even towards the end of the German administration, the situation was much the same. Records for one plantation covering the period 1909–13 reflect an average death-rate of 7·93 per cent.[31]

Throughout the colony, some attempt was made by the government to combat disease, and overcome the more widespread varieties, like malaria, leprosy, smallpox, sleeping sickness, falariasis and dysentry. However, in 1912, of the twenty-nine German doctors in Cameroun, fifteen were attached to the military, and only nine to the civil administration. Five had been specially brought in to deal with sleeping sickness.

Education was promoted largely by missions during the period of German rule, though it was closely regulated by the government, particularly in the last three or four years. Care was taken to ensure that only German was taught as a second (foreign) language. The government also provided some initiative in the establishment of agricultural schools at Victoria, Dschang and Yaoundé, and attempted to get a school started in the north at Garoua. In 1913 the government operated four schools—at Douala, Victoria, Yaoundé and Garoua—with a total enrolment of 833 pupils. By contrast, there were 631 mission schools (more than half of them run by the Basle Mission), with some 40,000 pupils.

German policy with regard to the acquisition of land was a distinct source of friction between the government and the colonists on the one hand, and the Camerounians on the other. Early government policy stipulated that all unoccupied land was crown land. Later, some attempt was made to regulate the sale of land, and a land commission was established in 1902 to provide detailed regulations on the subject. The upshot was a not very successful attempt to create reservations for Africans, with a minimum holding per family, and to limit the rights which could be purchased by whites from the government in crown land to leaseholds. The reservation policy proved difficult to enforce as the Africans declined to be confined to the areas set aside for them; the government modified its policy, and to raise revenue, sold freeholds to whites; and, for its own purposes, the administration reserved rights to appropriate large tracts for railways, roads and other public works as well as for urban development.

One such act of appropriation led to sustained objections from the Douala people in the last three years of German rule, and provided the basis for long-lasting grievances and political disaffection. In order to limit land speculation and to combat the spread of disease in the fast-growing town (its population increased from 63,600 in 1910 to nearly 92,000 in 1913),[32] the government proposed to appropriate 280 hectares of valuable land along the river front. The Douala objected that their land was protected by the terms of the 1884 treaty, and that they would be made to move to areas where they could not fish and to less fertile land. There was also the suspicion—shared by traders and missionaries—that the government only proposed to appropriate the land in order to resell it for 'development' to private interests at high prices. The protests lodged with the local government were of no avail, and the removal of the population was commenced in 1912.

Rudolph Douala Manga Bell, the Douala king, continued his campaign however, which included petitions and protests to the Reichstag, and the employment first of a Hamburg lawyer and then the dispatch of their own representative, Ngoso Dinh, to argue their case. The German government remained adamant, took reprisals against Manga Bell (who was dismissed from his government post), resisted Reichstag opposition, and tried to prevent consideration of the matter by suppressing or delaying telegrams from Cameroun.

Douala Manga Bell was ultimately forced to take more drastic measures. He attempted to enlist the support of Sultan Njoya of

Foumban, and, shortly before war broke out, attempted to contact the British and French governments to secure their aid. For these acts, he and Ngoso Dinh were charged with treason in 1914, convicted and—despite strong protests—executed.[33] The question of compensation for the Douala land was not settled for another thirty-eight years,[34] but the bitterness of the Douala, the martyrdom of their two representatives, and the alliances they had forged with other Cameroun leaders were to contribute to the beginnings of Cameroun nationalism.[35]

NEW FRONTIERS

Shortly before the end of the German administration, the frontiers of Cameroun were extended considerably, principally at the expense of French possessions in Equatorial Africa and of Spain. In the elaborate colonial shuffle that took place in the first decade of the twentieth century, France had abandoned any pretensions towards Egypt, and in turn had acquired suzerainty over Morocco. German and Spanish claims to those areas were compensated in 1906 at the Algeciras conference by awards in Equatorial Africa, but in 1911 a further foray by Germany into Morocco brought about new negotiations with France, which resulted in a further award. Germany received 275,000 square kilometres of territory which was formerly part of the French Congo. This increased the size of German Cameroun by more than half, added something like a million inhabitants to the area under its control, and provided access to the Congo. The southern boundary of the country now enclosed Spanish Rio Muni.[36] In return, Germany ceded a small area in the north between the Shari and Longone rivers, known as the 'duck-bill', to France. Occupation of the new territory took place in two stages, in October 1912 and February 1913, which meant that German control had little real effect before war occurred and yet another territorial settlement had to be made at the instance of Britain and France.

THE GERMAN IMPACT ON CAMEROUN

Germany's administration of Cameroun produced considerable benefits for herself and bequeathed a not inconsiderable legacy of development to the country. Although the number of German residents in Cameroun increased substantially over the years (from 65 in 1890 to 1,643 in 1913),[37] there was never any question of settlement in the colony by large numbers of people from the metropolis. Germany's benefits consisted of the prestige she derived from being a colonial power, and from the opportunities Cameroun offered for trade. During the period 1891–1912, Cameroun exported more than 200 million marks worth of goods to Germany, and was an outlet for German exports to the tune of a further 281 million, a good deal of which consisted of capital goods. The cost of administering the territory was never great: in 1912 it was a little over 13 million marks, and for the twenty-one years up to 1912 it only just exceeded 71 million. Cameroun contributed more than a quarter of all colonial trade in 1911, and received more than four-fifths of its imports from Germany in the same year.[38]

For Cameroun, profound results flowed from the German occupation. In material terms, there was the infrastructure of roads, railways, ports and bridges; the development of the economy; the start of the educational system; and the introduction of new crops, techniques and services. Le Vine lists a number of less tangible benefits such as the introduction of an exchange economy, wage-labour, new forms of land-ownership, urbanisation, the encouragement of an 'African social stratum capable of mediating between the Europeans and the African Camerounians of the hinterland', as well as the inculcation of habits of obedience and deference to authority.[39] Some of these may be regarded as of arguable value—to Camerounians as distinct from their subsequent foreign rulers—but Le Vine's conclusion that 'on the whole, German rule in Kamerun was strict, often harsh, but usually just' [40] seems to be shared by most other writers about the country, including those from Cameroun like Fr Mveng and l'Abbé Ketchoua.

It is interesting to note that most views of the German adminis-tration have tended to gloss over the less pleasant incidents—such as the treatment of the Douala, forced labour, and military conquest—and to have emphasised the more positive German contributions to modern Cameroun. Many of these judgements were made retrospectively, after the country had experienced other alien administrations, and as the German control of a single Cameroun came to be viewed as a symbol of the unity for which nationalist movements under the British and the French governments strove in later years.[41]

WAR AND THE DIVISION OF CAMEROUN

The First World War involved considerable fighting in Cameroun. From its beginning in August 1914 until February 1916, the British and French forces mounted an attack on the German possession. In the south a force under General Aymerich advanced from the French Congo and another took Douala and then moved northwards, while a third moved from the northern part of Nigeria into northern Cameroun. Despite severe losses and several setbacks, the allies were able to defeat the German armies and they jointly assumed responsibility for the territory under a condominium in 1915.

Shortly after the cessation of hostilities, in March 1916, the allied governments reached agreement on the return to France of that part of her equatorial African possessions which had been ceded to Germany in 1911, and on a division of the remainder of Cameroun between them. France received four-fifths of the country, and Britain two separate areas bordering on Nigeria amounting to some 53,000 square kilometres and not wider at any point than about fifty miles. Each country at once proceeded to establish an administrative structure for the territory newly placed under its authority, which conformed closely to that which it operated in its adjacent colonies.

In 1919, however, at the Versailles peace conference, the new system of mandates was established to deal with conquered colonies and place them under a system of international supervision. It was decided that both the parts of Cameroun occupied by the allies should be subject to this regime, and France and Britain were required to submit proposals in this regard. France at first resisted any suggestion that Cameroun should be dealt with other than as a colony of hers, but later modified her position by proposing an intermediate arrangement which would reduce the international obligations incumbent upon a mandatory power, and ultimately agreed in 1922 to undertake the administration as a mandate from the League of Nations.[42]

The details of the operation of the mandate system as it applied

to Cameroun will be described in the two succeeding chapters.*
Here it suffices to point out that the division of Cameroun which
took place soon after the beginning of the war in 1914 was to
become the major feature of the country's history for nearly half a
century, and resulted in deep-rooted differences between two
sections of the country in every aspect of the cultural, political and
economic lives of its peoples. It was only after the passing of
British and French control in 1961 that a start could be made on
forging some measure of unity between them again.

* The text of the mandate appears as Appendix 1.

3. From Tutelage to Autonomy under the French

FRANCE RULED the greater part of Cameroun for more than forty years. For most of that period, it did so subject to a system of international supervision of varying intensity, first under the League of Nations while Cameroun was still a mandated territory, and later under the auspices of the United Nations in terms of the trusteeship system established after the Second World War. At no stage did France seek to incorporate the territory into any of its colonies; it always maintained a formal distinction between the status of Cameroun and that of the rest of French Africa, and Cameroun was provided with a separate administrative structure outside the two large complexes of French West Africa and French Equatorial Africa.

But French colonial policy was applied to Cameroun in very much the same form as it was elsewhere in France's African empire. This policy was designed from the start to create deep cultural and economic ties with the metropolis, and was not directed towards the attainment of any degree of independence by the colonies. There were, however, several changes in emphasis in France's attitude to her African possessions over the years. Most of these took place during or after the Second World War, when the main impact of the earlier policy had already been felt. Later, the growth of nationalism in other parts of the French empire—the Far East, and particularly North Africa—had a considerable influence, as did the presence of African politicians in the parliamentary institutions and governments of metropolitan France. Gradually, France came to accept the need for a greater measure of local participation and control in each of her African possessions, and ultimately she was to concede independence to them.

Developments in French Cameroun were very much the result of these changes in policy. They influenced the administrative structure and the institutions of government in the territory, which in turn affected the course of politics in the country. But

44

there were also special factors at work throughout the period of French rule. To start with, there was the aftermath of German colonial activity, and, later, the revival of German interest in her former protectorate. These combined to have their effect on early African political movements, and also provided some stimulus for economic development undertaken by France. Secondly, there was the fact that Cameroun had been divided between France and Britain. For all the differences that were to become entrenched in the cultural and economic ties of the two mandated territories, the political demand for their reunification became an important constituent of Cameroun nationalism. Thirdly, the impact of rapid economic change combined with powerful nationalist feeling to produce a violent reaction against French control, which lasted even after government was in the hands of Camerounians. Fourthly, there was the continuous awareness, on the part of both the French administration and the Cameroun nationalists, that the country was an international trust whose future could be influenced by the active interest in its affairs displayed by the organs of the League of Nations and, after it, by the United Nations.

INTERNATIONAL SUPERVISION

The system set up by the League of Nations for the administration of the German colonies did not provide machinery for international control over the territories concerned. Rather, each territory was placed in the charge of a European power which was entitled to apply its own policies there, subject to the terms of an agreement with the League. The object was not to prepare the mandated territories like Cameroun for political advancement so much as to eliminate some of the worst abuses of the colonial system. Thus Articles 22 and 23 of the League Charter, which set up the mandate system, sought to prohibit traffic in slaves, forced labour, the sale of alcohol and of arms to the local populations. They also laid down that the mandatory power was to ensure the 'moral and material well-being' of the peoples in the mandated territories, including their freedom of religion and conscience, and declared that this duty was a 'sacred trust of civilisation'.

To secure adherence to these precepts, the League created a Permanent Mandates Commission, whose task it was to follow the activities of the mandatory authorities through the receipt

45

of annual reports on the progress of each territory. The Commission had no power to enforce policies in the mandated areas; its position was further weakened by the fact that it was composed not of representatives of League members (i.e. governments), but of individuals appointed for their special knowledge and qualifications regarding colonial matters. Despite its lack of power, it would be wrong to underestimate the influence of the Commission during the period between the two world wars. Its members took an active interest in the detailed affairs of the mandates; they were vigilant in questioning the mandatory powers on their policies, and frequently criticised them for failings revealed in the reports submitted or the oral examination of the colonial administrators who were called upon to defend the actions of the governments concerned.[1] There is no doubt that, in this way, the Commission averted some colonial malpractices and mitigated the effect of others, if only by exposing them to international scrutiny.

The trusteeship system created by the United Nations after the Second World War introduced several new elements into the process of international supervision.[2] These arose principally because, in the changed international environment of the post-war period, an opportunity was given to both colonial and anti-colonial powers* to exert an influence within the UN. One result was that the new system was geared to a more extensive and somewhat more explicit set of goals, which included political advancement. Thus the UN charter provided that trusteeship existed in order to

> promote the political, economic, social, and educational advancement of the inhabitants of the trust territories, and their progressive development towards self-government or independence as may be appropriate to the particular circumstances of each territory and its peoples and the freely expressed wishes of the peoples concerned . . .[3]

The phrasing of this provision is far from clear; it is cautious and ambiguous, not least in its reference to 'self-government or independence' as alternatives without specifying which was to be the ultimate product of the trusteeship. (Gardinier points out that the ambiguity was further compounded by the use of the term

---

* Including not only former colonies, in increasing numbers after 1946, but also the USSR and its supporters.

'self-administration' (*s'administrer eux-mêmes*) in the French text; he also suggests that the vagueness in the Article, and the balance in the composition of the Trusteeship Council were both products of a compromise between anti-colonial and colonial powers.[4]) But it did provide the basis for more rigorous supervision of the way in which the trust territories were administered. Supervision itself was to be the responsibility of the Trusteeship Council, a body which consisted of government representatives, but whose membership was equally divided between administering and non-administering (i.e. those not charged with the administration of trust territories) powers. This attempt at balance within the Trusteeship Council was in fact to the disadvantage of the anti-colonial powers, since it enabled the administering governments to coalesce with other colonial (but non-administering) powers to defeat them. The grouping did manage to inhibit the investigatory powers of the Council, for instance by refusing to allow oral petitions and representations by the inhabitants of trust territories to be entertained by the Council.

Despite these imperfections and limitations, the trusteeship system was effective in bringing pressure to bear on the administering authorities, in Cameroun as elsewhere. It involved the submission of annual reports on each territory as under the League's mandate system, but these could now be debated in the Council, and the administering powers not just questioned but taken to task over their policies. It also involved on-the-spot investigations by visiting missions elected at the UN. On four occasions between 1949 and 1958, such missions were sent to Cameroun to examine the manner in which both Britain and France were carrying out their obligations under the trust agreements which they had undertaken. The missions received detailed submissions and petitions from individuals and political parties in Cameroun seeking relief in respect of specific grievances, or commenting generally on the political future of the country. Even the limitation on the presentation of petitions to the Trusteeship Council was ultimately overcome: in the 1950s, when the anti-colonial nations were numerous enough, they were able to bypass the Council and hear representatives from Cameroun (among other territories) in the Fourth Committee of the UN (the Committee on Trusteeship and Non-Self-Governing Territories).

Thus international surveillance of Cameroun under French

administration was of considerable significance throughout the period of the mandate and of trusteeship. The influence of the trusteeship organisation on political developments in Cameroun will be mentioned later in this chapter. The considerable part it played in the process which led to the independence of French Cameroun and its subsequent unification with the British trust territory will be discussed in Chapter 5.

FRENCH POLICIES AND THE INTERNAL ADMINISTRATION OF CAMEROUN: FROM MANDATE TO SELF-GOVERNMENT

French colonial policy in Africa is said to have oscillated between the two poles of assimilation and association, the former being identified with the libertarian views stemming from the French Revolution of the eighteenth century and the latter from the authoritarian views that gained ground during the period of imperial expansion in the nineteenth century. Both tendencies are observable, but it is doubtful whether any clear-cut distinction between them can be seen in the unfolding of colonial policy in Cameroun. Assimilation emphasised the political and cultural objectives of France's 'civilising mission' by laying stress on the ability, indeed the right, of anyone who acquired the French language and habits of life to be treated just as any other French citizen. It also, by the same token, dismissed the political desirability of any divorce between France and those in the colonies who could be regarded as Frenchmen (known as *assimilés* or, more commonly, *évolués*); and, at the same time, relegated those not yet at this stage to a different category in the body politic.

Association, on the other hand, involved a greater degree of paternalism—that is, an assumption that most Africans either could not or should not be treated as citizens on an equal basis— and accordingly stressed the more traditional colonial objectives of bringing 'peace, order and good government' as well as economic development to the overseas dependencies.

In fact, assimilation was never applied widely, and only really operated fully in a few small areas of what is now Senegal. To absorb all the inhabitants of the French African possessions into a common citizenship with French nationals would have involved vast expenditure, and could, in theory, have reduced metropolitan France to a position of impotence within the French empire if it had succeeded. France had neither the resources to accomplish the former nor the desire to effect the latter.

Instead, aspects of the two policies were combined, in Cameroun as elsewhere in French West Africa and French Equatorial Africa. The assimilationist view contributed to the maintenance of a distinction between French citizenship, which was conferred on the *évolués* as a gallicised élite, and the vast mass of the coloured population, who were regarded as *indigènes*. The fact that the *indigènes* (or *administrés*) were not given the benefit of rights under the French legal system and were subject to a separate legal regime known as the *indigénat*, made the assimilationist view all the easier to reconcile with the associationist principle of differentiation. The policy of assimilation was also used to buttress the notion that France and her empire were one and indivisible; this harmonised well with the absence of any desire by the advocates of association to provide for the eventual independence of the colonies. Both groups advocated direct rule. The absence of adequate funds made it necessary to make use of traditional rulers who were seen as instruments of colonial policy and were treated as subordinate to the centralised administrative structure required for the efficient administration of the territories. Economic development was a major part of the policy of association, but it was seen as a necessary aspect of the joint progress of both France and her colonies in the symbiotic relationship favoured by the advocates of assimilation.[5]

The institutions created by France for the administration of Cameroun under the mandate reflect clearly the emphasis on centralised government and a modified form of direct rule. At the head of the system established in 1921 was a Commissioner who was responsible to the Minister of the Colonies. The Commissioner was advised by a *Conseil d'Administration* which consisted of the heads of central government departments in Yaoundé and, initially, nominated European residents (known as *notables*), with no representation for Camerounians. In 1927, however, two Camerounian *notables* were appointed to the body, and in 1942 the composition was again altered to embrace four nominated Europeans and four Camerounians in addition to the departmental heads and chief administrative officers from the regions. A further advisory body, the Financial and Economic Council, was created in 1942, and included six Camerounians in addition to members of

49

the administration and representatives of the Christian missions.[6]
Other bodies advised on agriculture and hygiene.

Local administration was in the hands of officials known as
chefs de circonscription, of whom there were initially fourteen and
later seventeen. In 1935 the *circonscription* was replaced as the
unit of administration by the region, but the same number of
units was retained. The *chefs de circonscription*, and the *chefs de
subdivision* under them, were assisted by *Conseils de Notables* at
each level. These councils were composed of Camerounian chiefs
or other representatives of each ethnic group in a district—on the
basis of one for every 5,000 inhabitants—who were chosen by the
chef de circonscription from a list of suitably qualified persons
from the area (qualifications included ownership of property,
possession of a good income, and absence of any criminal convictions[7]); they were presided over by the *chef de circonscription*, and
had to be consulted on matters such as taxation, labour levies and
the construction of public works, but there was no obligation to
follow their advice. Although these were the main avenues for
participation by Camerounians in government until after the end
of the mandate, there was no pretence that they were representative.[8] They were there to carry out government policy and to
assist the administration in doing so.

A similar attitude was adopted to the chiefs, whose power was
reduced and whose authority came to rest on government appointment, not traditional office. They became government servants
who were paid salaries or commissions on tax collected, and were
there to serve the administration. Even in the north and centre
of the territory, where some attempt was made to incorporate
the Muslim Lamibe and other traditional leaders in a form of
indirect rule, the French administration was quite prepared to
depose those who showed any sign of deviating from its policy.
Thus, after a sustained dispute with Sultan Njoya of Bamoun
over who had the authority to appoint sub-chiefs, Njoya was
deposed in 1931 by the Commissioner and exiled to Yaoundé
with a pension.[9] Nevertheless, the chiefs remained key functionaries in the system of administration, and were accountable for
administering the affairs of a subdivision, village or group of
villages.

A dual judicial system was also introduced by the French
administration. For French citizens, a set of courts applied the

codes applicable in France, as modified in French West and Equatorial Africa. For Africans, a separate system of courts came into existence in 1921, and was modified in 1927. Chiefs, whose judicial powers were abolished, were given powers to conciliate civil matters in an effort to settle them before they reached a court. But a hierarchy of courts was created at subdivisional and regional level, presided over by the appropriate administrative official (who was assisted by African assessors). These courts dealt with both civil and criminal cases. In civil matters, they were often dependent on the opinions of chiefs or the assessors who provided a description of the law to be applied, namely the customary law in so far as it did not conflict with the 'principles of French civilisation'. In criminal cases, the courts at subdivisional level had restricted jurisdiction, but those at regional level could try virtually all offences, including those which carried the death penalty. Objections to this system of justice revolved around the ambiguous part played by court interpreters upon whom the courts' officers relied and who often misrepresented evidence, particularly where cases involved chiefs who were their employers. But far more important was the complaint that, for most Africans, offences could be tried by an administrative rather than a judicial officer. It was only at the top of the hierarchy of separate courts, in the *Chambre de Homologation*, that a professional *magistrat* was involved, and then he was assisted by one European and one African assessor in reviewing the decisions of the courts below.[10]

By far the most deeply resented facet of the differential treatment of *citoyens* and *sujets* under French policy was the *indigénat*. This created an entirely separate set of offences for all but the very small category of Africans who were exempted from its application. Punishment was the prerogative of the administrative officers in regions or subdivisions, and took place without trial, although an appeal was possible to the Commissioner. The system was used to restrict civil liberties, including rights of association and movement; to enforce conscripted labour to build roads and other public works. It placed virtually unchecked discretionary power in the hands of administrative officials, and caused humiliation and hardship. Le Vine sums up the bitterness felt by most Camerounians by describing the system thus:

The *indigénat* was used in the Cameroons to punish natives who failed to cultivate their gardens or work on the railway, who failed to pay their taxes within three months of its levy, who failed to take off their caps in the presence of the local administrator, who spat on the floor of a government office, who had not kept an appointment with the local *chef de subdivision*, who had come late to work on a works project, and so on.[11]

It is small wonder that, when reforms came to be considered after the end of the world war, the *indigénat* was among the first of the colonial laws to be abolished.[12]

The major changes in French policy date from the Brazzaville conference of 1944, held at the instance of General de Gaulle and presided over by the Governor of Chad, Felix Eboué. Cameroun had played a significant part in the Free French war effort. Douala was the first of the overseas territories which had received General de Gaulle in 1940, and, although there was no actual fighting on Cameroun soil, Cameroun, along with the other African dependencies, had contributed soldiers to the French forces.

The Brazzaville conference was designed to reshape French relations with the African possessions, by permitting a measure of decentralisation through the creation of representative assemblies with limited powers in each territory. But there was no question of independence for any of them. Any idea of autonomy or evolution outside the French empire was specifically excluded, and even eventual self-government was explicitly rejected.[13]

The changes envisaged at Brazzaville were implemented in a series of reforms initiated at the constituent assembly which adopted a new constitution for France under the Fourth Republic in 1946. These were strongly assimilationist in character. They included the abolition of the *indigénat*, prestation, and the distinction that had hitherto existed between *citoyens* and *sujets*. The inhabitants of all the overseas possessions were placed on the same footing as French citizens, at least in regard to their enjoyment of civil liberties and the fact that they were subject to the French criminal codes. (In civil matters they continued to use customary law.) They were not, however, given equal voting rights with the citizens of metropolitan France.

The constitution created a number of new political institutions and enabled the Africans to participate in all of them. At the centre, the dependencies were given the right to elect a total of 41 deputies out of 627 to the French National Assembly. Of these, 32 were elected to represent African possessions, which also elected 34 of the senators in the Council of the Republic. The constitution also created the 'French Union', a body comprising (1) all the French dependencies in North Africa and Indo-China, together with (2) the French Republic (of which the other African countries were members as the 'Overseas Territories'), and (3) the 'Associated Territories of the French Union' which were the former mandated territories of Cameroun and Togo.

This complex structure was established partly in order to overcome French reservations about the trusteeship system only recently instituted by the United Nations. France had first declined the UN's invitation to enter into trusteeship agreements concerning her African mandates, since she wished to administer them as integral parts of France. In line with the decisions at Brazzaville, she saw their future as *self-administering* (not self-governing) parts of France. As a result of pressure from the anti-colonial nations in the UN, the French government reversed its earlier decision and agreed to submit them to the trusteeship system.[14] But, in order to pursue her original goal, France agreed only to administer Cameroun as 'an integral part of French territory', and proceeded to draw a careful distinction in the constitution between the Overseas Territories—which were an integral part of the French Republic—and the Associated Territories of the French Union, which were not.[15] In practice, there was virtually no difference in the way Cameroun participated in the new institutions of the Republic. However, French recognition that Cameroun was not an inseparable constituent of France was to be a useful lever in the hands of nationalist leaders who later sought independence.

For the present, independence was not even contemplated. Cameroun elected three deputies and three senators to the French parliament in 1946. Two of these were elected by the 38,000 African voters who were qualified to vote on the basis of a restricted suffrage, and one represented 4,000 or so Frenchmen living in the territory.[16] Cameroun was also granted a Representative Assembly of forty members, with power to decide the territorial budget and other fiscal and economic matters, subject to the metropolitan *Conseil d'état*'s power of veto; and the right to be consulted

3—C * *

53

on government proposals concerning public land, education, labour conditions and economic development.[17] Of the members in the Assembly (known as ARCAM), sixteen were Europeans and twenty-four Africans.

Over the next few years, the suffrage was extended for Africans, so that by 1951 more than half a million were eligible to vote, and the number increased steadily thereafter.[18] In 1952, the composition and the title of the assembly were altered, but not its powers. It was named the Territorial Assembly (ATCAM) and enlarged to fifty members, thirty-two of whom were elected by the 'second college', that is, Africans, and eighteen by the French of the 'first college'.

By this time nationalist pressure for more radical reforms was building up in Cameroun, among both the more moderate political parties led by Paul Soppo Priso, Jules Ninine, Charles Okala, Charles Assalé and Andre-Marie Mbida, as well as by the more militant *Union des Populations du Cameroun* under Reuben Um Nyobe. In the next four years, the campaign for change was mounted even more strongly. By 1956, the UPC had been proscribed after a major outburst of violence in Douala and other towns, and was in exile; the other political parties were demanding immediate reform of the territory's status. A resolution had already been passed in ATCAM calling for the end of the trusteeship system. What is more, developments in North Africa and the Far East had made France realise that some alterations in her colonial system were necessary, and pressure from the United Nations as a result of developments in Togoland caused her to move even more purposefully.

In 1956, the *loi cadre* was enacted by the French Assembly. This was an enabling law, providing certain blanket provisions which were applicable to all the overseas possessions, such as the abolition of the two-college system and the introduction of universal suffrage, and leaving the territorial institutions for each dependency to be specified separately. Initially Cameroun was not catered for separately, but pressure from the Cameroun members in the French National Assembly made the French government seek the advice of ATCAM in drafting a new constitution for the territory. This came into force in April 1957, after the first elections based on universal suffrage had been held the previous

December and had involved nearly a million voters, who elected seventy members to the Territorial Assembly.

The new Statute of Cameroun[19] converted the existing Assembly into a body with considerably more power, although France still remained responsible for matters such as defence, external affairs, currency and civil liberties, as well as education (above primary level), the courts and security forces. It did, however, clearly indicate that France was prepared to foresee the end of trusteeship, though Cameroun was still to be represented in the French parliament. It also provided for the creation of a government of Cameroun, and, leading a coalition party, Mbida became the first Prime Minister.

THE DEVELOPMENT OF A MODERN ECONOMY

When the French assumed control over Cameroun, considerable advances had already been made—especially in the south and centre of the territory—in the direction of a modern economic structure. Long contact with European traders had established a money economy, and production was of surpluses for sale rather than crops solely for consumption. The plantations and the public works undertaken by the Germans had made further inroads into traditional economic activities and techniques, through the appropriation of land, the employment of labour and the introduction of taxation. Exports were in demand, and the colonial economy which sought to establish the close nexus between metropolitan needs and overseas products, was effectively in operation.

France built on this basis, energetically promoting the development of a modern economy. *Mise en valeur* ('economic development' is a free translation, though the phrase connotes a dynamic concept involving transformation and realisation of potential into viability and profitability) was an important constituent of French colonial policy in the 'association' period before the Second World War, and the French desire to secure the economic interdependence of Cameroun and France went along with a need to substitute French values, markets, products, techniques and personnel for the German, so as to alter the country's allegiance for all time. In the early period—given the generally low level of economic activity in Europe, the depression of the 1920s and

55

1930s, and an emphasis on trade in raw materials rather than aid for the production of manufactured goods—most effort went into improving the infrastructure, increasing the agricultural production of peasants and plantations, and extending commercial activity. After the war, there was substantial aid, from both government and private sources in France, for industrial expansion and more sophisticated methods of stepping up agricultural output.

Within a few years after the creation of the mandate, the French administration had secured the removal of most Germans from economic involvement with Cameroun. The state pre-empted a considerable number of German properties from private individuals or firms, and assumed ownership of most of those previously run by the German colonial authorities. Of the remainder more than two hundred were sold by auction, mostly to French nationals or Camerounians, with a few going to English and other expatriates.[20]

Production of cocoa, bananas, palm products and rubber was greatly increased on the plantations; timber began to be exploited on a large scale, with more than 200,000 hectares of forests being used for commercial purposes by 1936; and agricultural research enabled coffee to become an important export commodity with production of an indigenous strain of the arabica variety, largely in the hands of Camerounian peasants and small-holders, many from the Bamiléké areas. The results were impressive. Cameroun's foreign trade increased by nearly 500 per cent during the interwar years, from 96 million francs in 1922 to 467 million francs in 1938.[21]

Improvements were also made in the social services, with the expansion of educational and medical facilities. By 1938, there were 102,000 pupils in primary schools (although 90 per cent were still enrolled in those run by voluntary agencies), and some small effort had been made at introducing state-operated secondary schools.[22] A sustained campaign had been undertaken under Dr Jamot to eradicate sleeping sickness, and government expenditure in the medical field increased more than six-fold, resulting in the building of public hospitals in the bigger towns, and the provision of mobile medical services in rural areas.[23]

Roads and railways were also extended. The French administration had acquired the German *Nordbahn* and *Mittellandbahn* lines by expropriation and they linked the latter to Makak and Yaoundé, a distance of more than 130 kilometres. Similar construction work was undertaken on the roads during the mandate period. But a great deal of the work on these projects was done by forced or conscript labour, a practice which the French took over from the Germans, although the mandate specifically prohibited it. Conditions of work did not differ greatly from those under German rule which had produced a high death-rate among tens of thousands of labourers who worked without adequate pay or medical supervision, and the Permanent Mandates Commission was highly critical of this aspect of French administration.

As under German rule, the system of labour was linked to taxation.[24] Known as prestation, it involved compulsory service on public works for at least ten days per annum, and thereafter work was paid at a low rate. In theory, the labour could be commuted by the payment of two francs a day, but this was seldom allowed in fact. Recruitment was by government officials or chiefs, who often used a proportion of the workers on private farms and plantations, and was enforced by resort to the *indigénat*, with little attention to the human requirements of personal dignity, family life or subsequent health. Fr Mveng says that there are few even among the present generation who do not recall the emotion-charged occasions during the nights when 'mysterious agents, come from one knew not where, descended on villages, removed the able-bodied men from their homes, and led them to an unknown destination'. All too often, because of inadequate medical supervision and hard labour for long periods in unhygienic conditions, the destination was death. Official estimates always suggested only a low death-rate (less than 0·1 per cent) but other observers—including those of the Permanent Mandates Commission—put the figure at nearer to sixty or seventy per thousand.[25] Constant criticism from the PMC led to a revision of many of the more objectionable features of the system, but it remained a corollary of the distinction between *indigènes* and *évolués* until that form of differentiation was abolished in 1946.

Economic development was stimulated during the last war by demand for Cameroun's products, but the real thrust took place after the war. The port at Douala was enlarged, new roads built, railways improved, air services introduced and telecommunications extended into a territory-wide network. Education was greatly increased at all levels, with the government schools increasing in number throughout the period up to independence in 1960. Thus primary school enrolment rose from 113,000 in 1947 to nearly 331,000 in 1958, and the number of state schools shot up from the pre-war figure of 76 to reach 650 by 1958. Secondary schooling increased even more dramatically over the same period, rising from 136 pupils to more than 7,500; while teacher-training, vocational and technical education, which had barely existed before the war, occupied rather fewer than 500 students in 1947, but more than 8,500 in 1958.[26] By the end of the period, all university training still took place abroad—in Dakar or in France—but the number of students increased from 45 to more than 300 in 1957, with the total number of students in all forms of higher education outside the country reaching 1,155 in the same year.[27]

The new relationship established between France and her overseas possessions from 1946 produced a series of economic plans for Cameroun, which concentrated capital expenditure on social and physical infrastructure. Industrial activity followed the harnessing of hydro-electric power at Edea, and the establishment of an aluminium smelting complex there. In all, a total of nearly 500 million dollars is estimated to have been invested in Cameroun up to 1959, with about half supplied by French aid funds (principally the *Fonds d'Investissement pour le Développement Economique et Sociale des Territoires d'Outre-Mer*—FIDES), though more than a fifth also came from private sources, and about 15 per cent through the collaboration of the private and public sectors in joint enterprises. Foreign trade increased enormously, imports in particular going up by 700 per cent, while the volume of exports rose from 164,000 tons in 1938 to 426,000 in 1959.[28]

One consequence of the economic spurt after 1946 was the rapid urbanisation of the country. This occurred, for the most part, in the south in towns like Edea, Yaoundé, Mbalmayo, Ebolowa, Eséka, Nksongsamba, Dschang and Foumban. Each showed a sharp rise in population as industries and government departments grew. The most spectacular rise took place in Douala which had a population of less than 40,000 in 1945 but had reached 124,000 by 1957. In the big towns, like Douala and Yaoundé, population growth was accompanied by pressure on housing and amenities and by price inflation. It also saw the emergence of a substantial number of unemployed, which grew rapidly throughout the 1950s, as the greater prosperity in the towns caused an ever-increasing influx of immigrants from the rural areas. Thus Douala was estimated to have 5,000 unemployed in 1954 (in a population of 110,000), but this rose to 12,000 in 1957 (nearly 10 per cent of the inhabitants) and had grown to 25,000 by 1960.[29]

At the same time, the rural exodus led to the influx of large numbers of Camerounians who were not indigenous to the big towns. In Douala, for instance, the Douala people already represented less than half the population of the town by 1947 (46 per cent), but by 1955 they were reduced to a fraction over 20 per cent. More important still was the displacement of the indigenous population in key areas of employment. The Bamiléké gained especially from this set of changes. Some 100,000 of them emigrated from the Bamiléké areas in the twenty-five years after 1931. Their number in Douala rose from just over 8,000 in 1947 to 29,650 in 1956, by which time they outnumbered the Douala people, and were only slightly less numerous than the members of the next three ethnic groups put together.[30] They also had the greatest number of employees in the administration, banking, commerce, transport, secondary industry and the extractive industries. Perhaps even more significantly, they constituted nearly 30 per cent of the unemployed. In Yaoundé and Ebolowa, they were more than 10 per cent of the population in 1957, and, again, concentrated their efforts in commerce, industry and transport.[31]

The Bamiléké people were not the only group to undergo social upheaval—the industrialisation around Edea produced similar disruption among the Bassa,[32] and the rapid growth of Yaoundé made for great changes among the Ewondo. But the total effect of the population pressure, land laws, and resistance to traditional rulers' abuses in the Bamiléké areas, together with overcrowding and unemployment in the towns, contributed greatly to their political disaffection during the 1950s and their espousal of violent resistance during the period of revolt at the end of the decade.

POLITICS: PARTICIPATION, ALIENATION AND VIOLENCE

There was little political activity in Cameroun in the period between the wars. Some opposition to the regime on the part of traditional rulers like Sultan Njoya was accompanied by a measure

59

of political involvement by the followers of Lotin Samé and his United Native Church in the 1920s. Building on the religious fervour of his supporters, Samé was able to combine an embryonic black nationalism, of the kind advocated by Marcus Garvey in the United States, with some political campaigning directed at eliminating the injustices under the French administration; but the movement for religious separatism from which it originated was short-lived, and its political impact was negligible.

The other continuing source of political opposition to the French under the mandate was the sustained attempt by the Douala and their leaders to obtain adequate redress for their confiscated lands. A preliminary disavowal by the French of any responsibility for the alleged misdeeds of the Germans was succeeded in the mid-1920s by a French offer to provide compensation on the same scale as the Germans had proposed, and for the sale of all unused land for the benefit of re-housed Douala. This was followed by an agreement in 1926 under which the government set aside 500,000 francs for compensation on condition that alternative land was taken up by dispossessed Douala. In fact, only 40 of the 330 prospective beneficiaries accepted the offer, and discontent continued to be voiced at public meetings. From 1927, the Douala chiefs took to petitioning the League of Nations concerning their grievances, but without success. In 1931, however, their case was taken up by Vincent Ganty, a non-Camerounian resident in Paris, who had the backing of the Douala leaders and who submitted numerous memoranda and petitions to the League, dealing not only with the land issue but with other failings of the mandate administration such as the systems of justice, education, taxation and labour—indeed, the whole colonial system. Ganty, whose organisation was estimated to have obtained from the Douala annual subscriptions amounting to 100,000 francs, even requested the League to establish a Cameroun Republic.[33]

The movement may have been on the way to developing into a strong anti-colonial political force, but its influence waned and it was superseded by more moderate and pro-French organisations, as German colonial pretensions, which involved the recovery of Cameroun, came to the fore in the 1930s. The *Union Camérounaise* comprising a group of Camerounian *évolués* was set up in Douala in 1938, and called the attention of the great powers to its opposition to any policy of appeasement which would return Cameroun to Germany. Much more important—as the real genesis of Cameroun political parties—was *Jeunesse Camérounaise Française* (*Jeucafra*) which was founded in 1938 by Paul Soppo Priso, a Douala who was to play a considerable part in the political development of the country after the reforms of 1946. At this point, however, there was little that *Jeucafra* could do except stress the loyalty of its members to France and their desire to participate more fully in French institutions. It was a discussion group for the Camerounian élite. The *indigénat* effectively prevented any mass involvement in politics even if the élite had desired this; in any event, there were no institutions under the mandate which gave an opportunity to either *évolués* or *administrés* to take an active part in the affairs of government.

This was changed in 1946, with the introduction of the reforms under the Fourth Republic, and the provision for Cameroun's representation in the French National Assembly and Council of the Republic, as well as the creation of the dual-college Representative Assembly (ARCAM). Political parties developed fast, proliferated and indeed outstripped the opportunities available to them for parliamentary activity under the new system. For the next twelve years, politics in Cameroun involved an almost continuous counterpoint, with the themes of progress towards self-rule and unification being taken up alternately outside the party framework and within it; and the focus of political activity moving between parliamentary pressure and extra-parliamentary violence.

Even before the institutions of the Fourth Republic had been set up this dichotomy was evident, though the two elements tended to converge initially in fighting for seats in the bodies established in 1946 and 1947. The extra-parliamentary tendency was first off the mark in 1944, when the Communist-dominated French trade union federation, the *Confédération Générale du Travail* helped found the *Union des Syndicats Confédérés du Cameroun* (USCC) under Charles Assalé. The Union, in common with most other similar bodies in the French colonies, challenged the overseas labour laws. When it met with no success, a series of strikes followed in Douala in September 1945, which led to rioting. Troops were used to suppress the rioters, and there was a death toll of nine, with twenty wounded.

The immediate political repercussions of this episode were to be seen a month later, when Prince Alexandre Douala Manga Bell defeated a candidate favoured by the administration in the election for Cameroun's delegate to the French Constituent Assembly. Bell helped to pass the *Loi Laminé Gueye* in 1946, which reformed labour legislation and abolished the *indigénat*

Bell remained a deputy until late in the 1950s, occupying the seat in the National Assembly from the south (and mainly Douala) part of the territory. He played little part in internal Cameroun politics, however. A picturesque and somewhat effete figure in the National Assembly, he was known for his wealth and pliability in support of French government policies. He represented the French Government at the UN Trusteeship Council and was used to bolster the arguments which countered those of the radical petitioners from the UPC (q.v.).

Dr Louis Ajoulat was the other deputy from Cameroun for much of this period. Elected to represent the French residents, he also became an important figure on the French political scene. A moderate Catholic whose views were more liberal on colonial matters than those of his MRP colleagues, he helped form the *Indépendants d'Outre-Mer* in the National Assembly with Leopold Senghor of Senegal and others. As a member of this group he held government office—particularly as a junior Minister in the Foreign Ministry—for a long period until the mid-1950s.

Meanwhile, Soppo Priso pressed for the implementation of the assimilationist goals formulated at the Brazzaville conference: a territorial assembly for the country, elective councils in the regions, and the appointment of more Camerounians to influential posts in the administration. *Jeucafra* had converted itself into the *Union Camérounaise Française* (*Unicafra*), a name which was intended to symbolise its devotion to France as much as to Camerounian causes. Soppo Priso, as its leader, was elected to the Assembly of the French Union in 1946.

Political parties as such had not yet been formed. Even when they did come into existence, they were not the major influence within the Camerounian institutions in the period up to 1952. The first elections (for the French Parliament, the French Union and ARCAM) took place at the end of 1946, but candidates were not elected on a party basis. Ideological diffierences did play a part in the affiliations of the members elected, but they were the alignments of France, and had little direct bearing on affairs within the territory. The electorate was, as yet, too small to provide the basis for major divisions; and even ethnic or locally-based parties from the regions were slow to form. They only really provided the foundation for party groupings after the reforms of 1956.

This is not to say that the politics of ARCAM were quietist. Although its members concentrated on using and extending the limited powers granted to them under the 1946 reforms they were not slow to criticise both the metropolitan and the local governments. Demands were made for more representative institutions and further legal reforms, including the extension of the franchise. The administration was made to pay attention to ARCAM views on legislation and financial questions, and severely taken to task when it did not. Within the body itself, Camerounians were able to assume authority as the chairmen and *rapporteurs* of committees which were at first held by Europeans.

For all this, Gardinier concludes that 'ARCAM carried on its deliberations as the kind of non-political administrative body that France had intended it to be.'[34] The dynamics—and the drama— of Cameroun politics were created outside the parliamentary framework; and it was there that the ideological content of Cameroun nationalism was developed, initially as a result of the militancy of the trade unions and later by the political parties which grew out of them.

The process started in March 1947, when the USCC made an attempt to take over *Unicafra*. The left-wing trade unionists failed to convince the moderates to adopt their radical policies, which included the use of a general strike; and, after their defeat, established their own political party in April 1947. This was the *Rassemblement Camérounais (Racam)*.[35] It was started by nine members, including Reuben Um Nyobe, Secretary-General of the USCC, and declared its opposition to the assimilationist policies from the start. It also demanded independence for Cameroun. Because of its radical policies, it was forthwith banned by the French administration.[36]

Exactly a year after *Racam's* establishment, Um Nyobe formed another party, again with the backing of the USCC. This was the *Union des Populations du Cameroun* (UPC). Ostensibly, it was started to 'group and unite the inhabitants of the territory in order to permit the most rapid evolution of the peoples and the raising of their standard of living',[37] but, in fact, its principal objective was the independence of Cameroun from France. This switch from the rather inappropriate conventional Marxist aims to the more relevant demands of nationalism proved effective. Um Nyobe and his colleagues in the UPC—Dr Félix-Roland Moumié, Ernest Ouandié, Abel Kingué—were urban-based, French-trained, *évolués*; but they received the support of 'traditional' organisations like the Douala *Ndongo*, the Bamiléké *Kumsze*, and Um Nyobe was able to build upon support he received within his own Bassa area.

The party became the Cameroun affiliate of the RDA, thus retaining the links established through the USCC with the French communists. But its main emphasis was nationalist and anti-colonial. Its outspoken opposition to the continuation of the trusteeship status of the territory led it to make use of the UN Visiting Mission in 1949 to further its policies; and it developed ties with organisations in the British Cameroons, which were also beginning to direct their attention to achieving a greater measure of self-determination. Thus, Um Nyobe and the UPC established contact with the Cameroons National Federation and, later, the Kamerun United National Congress*; and, together with them, developed a policy which aimed at the unification of the two parts of Cameroun. Other factors than the UN's responsibility for both territories helped to underpin the appeal of this unificationist aspect of the nationalist programme, both domestically and abroad. These included ethnic affinities between tribes in the two territories (including those of the Douala and Bamiléké with coastal groups and grasslanders respectively), trade relations that had been built up across the borders and were inhibited by the frontiers, and labour migration at the local level. Internationally, there was the example of the attention focused on Togo because of the division of its Ewe people between the Gold Coast and the French mandated territory of Togo. Above all, from the UPC's point of view, there was the opportunity for hitting at French policy—with its assimilationist emphasis on closeness to France—through an appeal for unity with an area outside the French sphere of influence.

It was thus primarily in order to further the immediate goal of independence from France that the unification policy was first actively pursued by the UPC. Although the party achieved some

* See below, pp. 84-7.

support from the groups mentioned—both among the urban populations of the towns and the rural areas—it was by no means the dominant influence on Cameroun politics yet. Apart from its contacts in the British Cameroons and its representations to the UN Visiting Mission in 1949, it concentrated on building up support through involvement in local disputes, and on establishing a tightly-organised, centralised internal structure, and a series of 'front' and affiliated organisations based on ethnic or interest groups—the most important of which were the youth and student bodies, *Jeunesse Démocratique Camérounaise* (JDC) and UNEK, and the *Union Démocratique des Femmes Camérounaises* (UDFC).[38] The nature of its policies rather than its activities, however, posed a threat to the French authorities, who frustrated it wherever possible. Thus, the UPC was refused the use of public amenities and facilities for meetings, and civil servants who were members were either subjected to pressure directly or transferred to areas where they could be less effective.[39] More important were the attempts to stimulate alternative parties or groups. Thus, a Bassa organisation, *Evolution Sociale Camérounaise (Esocam)*, was started in 1949—about the same time as the Douala *Ndongo* and the Bamiléké *Kumsze* 'became disenchanted' with the UPC.[40]

As the next round of elections came closer, political parties began to play a larger part in Cameroun affairs. The first such party was founded in 1951 by Ajoulat.[41] It was the *Bloc Démocratique Camérounaise* (BDC), which was opposed to the idea of pan-Cameroun unity, but advocated the abolition of the dual college electoral system, an increase in the franchise, and more powers for the local representative assembly. It received support from moderate Camerounians (including Ahidjo and Mbida), and the Catholic church. Campaigning on its platform, Ajoulat was able to win a seat to the French National Assembly in 1951. (The other seats were filled by Douala Manga Bell in the south and Jules Ninine from the north.) In the ATCAM elections of the following March, the BDC was a leading, and the most successful contestant, along with the SFIO and the RPF—the French parties. The UPC only contested four of the nineteen regions, and won no seats; apart from the opposition it encountered from the BDC and the other moderates, it also had to contend with *Esocam* splitting the Bassa vote.

Generally, the period between 1952 and 1956 saw the growth

65

of a surprisingly large number of political or semi-political organisations, each with a local ethnic base, which provided the necessary support for various of the politicians and helped keep the UPC at bay.[42] Ultimately, the local associations and groups were to merge themselves into conglomerates, or form coalitions, in the ALCAM of 1957. On a national level, 1952 also saw Ajoulat trying to break the monolithic trade union power of the USCC by establishing a local branch of the *Confédération des Travailleurs Chrétiens*, an action which had its political outcome when Senator Charles Okala formed the *Union Sociale Camérounaise*, with support from the Socialists, in 1953.

The UPC, meanwhile, was undeterred by its electoral failures or the activities of the other parties. Its representations to the UN had produced some results, in that France conceded in debate that independence for Cameroun was not ruled out. Um Nyobe continued to build his organisation, and, within Cameroun, to stress the goal of unification. At the UN the Fourth Committee had indicated that it was prepared to hear petitioners even if the Trusteeship Council was not, and consequently Um Nyobe made an appearance before it in 1952. There, he stressed the deficiencies of the French administration and the goal of independence rather than unification. His speech was a great success, not only at the UN, but at home, where the text was widely distributed. The influence of the UPC grew once again. Paradoxically, it was the unification issue which made headway elsewhere in the territory at this time. The *Kumsze* and the *Ndongo* once more took up their support for it, other political leaders began to endorse it, and even the BDC gave it a part in the programme it adopted in 1953.[43] Um Nyobe, by contrast, continued his campaign against the administration, addressing meetings throughout the country, distributing tracts and pamphlets, and widening the UPC's support through the publication of the monthly newspaper *La Voix du Peuple du Cameroun* and several other journals. Despite repeated denials by Um Nyobe that either he or the UPC were communist, the impression that the party had close ties with communist supported organisations was allowed to gain ground, and was reinforced by the avowedly Marxist and Maoist approach adopted by Dr Félix-Roland Moumié after his return to the country from Dakar in 1953. Sporadic local violence broke out, and the UPC was held responsible for this too.

If the UPC had gained from its international campaigning, it was also events elsewhere in the world which helped to bring it into direct collision with the French authorities. By 1954, the retirement of Jean Soucadoux as High Commissioner meant that a replacement became necessary. In the somewhat frenzied and frightened atmosphere of French politics caused by the beginning of the major colonial war in Algeria and France's failure in Indo-China, the French government was not inclined to tolerate anti-colonial vociferousness of the UPC variety. Ajoulat—as part of a mounting campaign against the UPC—was able to use his considerable influence in French government circles to secure the appointment of Roland Pré as High Commissioner.[44] Pré adopted a hard line from almost the moment he arrived in Cameroun. This included active attempts to control the UPC and its activities, and a more restrictive view of the scope for representative institutions in general. His simultaneous alienation of the moderates like Soppo Priso and the UPC was later to aid the formation of a more solidly-based nationalist movement of the centre. But the immediate effect was to provoke the UPC to direct and violent action towards the middle of 1955.

The campaign against the UPC was not confined to the administration. Ajoulat inspired other opposition to its activities, which included efforts made by the BDC, his own *Ad Lucem* Catholic organisation, and the Christian trade union federation. The churches also joined in the denunciation of the UPC. The Catholic bishops went to the length of circulating an episcopal letter at Easter services in 1955 specifically denouncing the UPC as communist and 'putting Christians on their guard' against its alleged machinations. This produced an immediate and spirited rejoinder from the UPC at the polemical level. But it also began a long period of open hostility on the part of the UPC to the churches and the missions, which became the focus of many of its most violent attacks in the future.

The UPC had already been subjected to administrative reprisals earlier in the year when Pré had transferred all of the party's civil servant members to Douala, presumably in an attempt to localise their influence. In fact, Douala became the scene of a series of waterfront strikes in March 1955. These were followed in April by a meeting at which the most far-reaching political demands yet were made. The UPC and its affiliates in the trade union field, as well as its youth, women's and student offshoots, asked for the termination of the trust administration, direct supervision by the UN, and the establishment of an independent Cameroun.[45] In May, though, political action was followed by widespread violence and direct action, which took place throughout the country. Thousands of demonstrators attacked police stations and gaols in Douala and Yaoundé; the ATCAM building was stormed; road-blocks were set up; houses, cars and other property were set alight; and people were attacked in an apparently co-ordinated series of outbursts in the last eight days of May. In all 26 people were killed and 189 wounded (about a third police).[46]

The violence was suppressed by the use of police and troops. It resulted in the proscription of the UPC in July, and the arrest of hundreds of its members. Of the leaders, Um Nyobe, Moumié, Kingué and Ouandié fled—initially to the British Cameroons, where they were given refuge by the pro-unification political leaders like Foncha; and later, abroad, where they were to plan further underground action, leading to the extensive violence of the next few years and the campaigns that lasted into 1970.

The activities of the UPC may have been curtailed by the proscription of the party and the enforced exile of the leaders, but its influence on Cameroun politics was, if anything, greater in the eighteen months following the ban than it had been before. Aided by the developments elsewhere in the French possessions, and at the UN, as well as their disapproval of the policies and actions of Pré, the legal parties pressed home the need for reform. Ajoulat was defeated by Mbida in the elections for the deputies to the French National Assembly the following January, and Mbida's colleague in the Assembly, Jules Ninine, joined in influencing the French government to replace Pré. Pierre Messmer, Pré's successor, introduced administrative changes which included the promotion of Camerounians to higher civil service positions for the first time. Charles Okala, also influential as a Socialist Senator, pressed for an amnesty for *Upécistes* and the repeal of the ban on the party. And, in the French parliament as a whole, 1956 saw moves for the liberalisation of the colonial regime generally, which culminated in the passage of the *loi cadre* in May.

Meanwhile, preparations were being made in Cameroun for the elections that were to be held at the end of the year for ATCAM. Soppo Priso, the leader of the *Démocrates Camérounais*, took the

68

initiative in trying to gain a measure of agreement between differing ethnic groups and political tendencies by forming the *Mouvement d'Union Nationale.* Although his minimum pro-gramme—unification of Cameroun, amnesty for those imprisoned in the aftermath of the May events, and creation of a new terri-torial assembly to negotiate independence with France—did not satisfy the UPC underground, it went a long way to adopting the main points of UPC policy. The *Mouvement* did not get very far. It did, however, lead to a split within the *Démocrates*, Mbida rejecting the prospect of co-operation with the UPC, whether legal or illegal; while the northern politicians, led by Ahidjo, also stood aside from the attempted moves towards a rapprochement.

By the time of the elections in December, the French govern-ment had neither acceded to the demand for an amnesty nor removed the ban on the UPC, which could not, therefore, run its own candidates. The legal parties were, in any event, more con-cerned with preparing proposals for the reform of Cameroun's institutions within the framework of the *loi cadre* than in pressing for independence. As a result, Moumié proclaimed the new UPC policy of boycotting the elections, and, what is more, doing so through violence.

The result was an election which took place just before Christmas 1956, against a backdrop of personal violence, sabotage and political assassination, particularly in the Bassa areas of the south-west to which Um Nyobe had returned to lead the *maquis*.[47] The total number of deaths sustained in this period as a result of the UPC's violence and the military force used to suppress or contain it has never been officially given, but estimates range between 300 and 2,000.

The UPC achieved some of its negative aims. Only 22 per cent of those on the electoral roll in Douala and 12·5 per cent in the Bassa home base of the Sanaga-Maritime region voted. But this was the first election under universal suffrage, and there was heavy voting elsewhere in the country; overall participation was 55 per cent.[48]

The new Assembly contained members elected as much for the regional and ethnic support they received as for the policies they advocated. The northern groups which joined to form the *Union Camérounaise* under Ahidjo had the largest number, with 30 seats (34 per cent of the votes); the *Démocrates* of the central-southern

69

portion of the country, led by Mbida, had 20; Soppo Priso's and Assalé's *Action Nationale*, 8; and, a Bamiléké grouping known as the *Paysans Indépendants*, 9.[49]

The immediate business of the new Assembly was the consideration of the proposals for the new Statute of Cameroun, framed to implement the reforms under the *loi cadre*. This produced internal self-government for the territory, of a kind not originally contemplated for Cameroun, but which the new Assembly insisted should apply to them as it had done to Togo. Under the changed constitution, Mbida was installed as Prime Minister in May 1957 as head of a coalition government. The period of self-government which was thus initiated in the strained atmosphere following the UPC violence lasted only a little more than two and a half years. But it was one which was to see violence on an even greater scale, by the underground and by the government, as the country moved first from trusteeship to independence and then on to unification with the British Cameroons.

4. Integration and Devolution in British Nigeria

THE TWO SMALL separated areas which Britain acquired in Cameroun after the First World War were dealt with as part of Nigeria and not as a separate colony. Britain had obtained them for strategic reasons and in order to tidy up her Nigerian boundaries,[1] and decided to take advantage of the terms of the 1922 mandate from the League of Nations which provided that they should be:

> administered in accordance with the laws of the Mandatory as an integral part of his territory . . . The Mandatory shall therefore be at liberty to apply his laws to the territory under the mandate subject to the modifications required by local conditions, and to constitute the territory into a customs, fiscal or administrative union or federation with the adjacent territories under his sovereignty or control, provided always that the measures adopted to that end do not infringe the provisions of this mandate.[2]

There was no change in this underlying attitude when, after the Second World War, Britain administered the territory under the United Nations trusteeship system.

The British decision was to have important consequences for Cameroun. Henceforward, developments in the 'British Cameroons' (as they now came to be called) were to be linked to those in Nigeria for nearly forty years. The separate administrative and economic needs of the areas were catered for, if at all, within the context of that colony,[3] and political progress took place in the framework provided for Nigeria.

British policy was based on the small size of the two parts of Cameroun it had acquired, and on the financial and administrative convenience of considering them as part of Nigeria. In the early years of British rule, both objectives could be achieved within the system of indirect rule which was implemented throughout Nigeria. This policy was to meet with some success

71

in the northern section of the British Cameroons. It was designed to secure the efficient and inexpensive incorporation of the Northern Nigerian emirates into the colonial administrative structure. Since the traditional Fulani rulers had been used in much the same way by the Germans, they fitted well into the British pattern, which linked them to the existing hierarchies in Yola, Bornu and Dikwa.

But the British policy did not work nearly as well elsewhere in Nigeria, or in the southern part of the British Cameroons.[4] In Southern Nigeria it took little account of the ethnic diversity within the different regions, and almost none of the history of the mandated territory which enabled its people to regard themselves as having a common identity, different from their immediate neighbours in the eastern parts of Nigeria.

In the long run, the combination of parsimony and insensitivity which characterised British rule in the southern part of Cameroun was to result in a lack of any firm commitment by the southern Camerounians to remain on in Nigeria. British policy contributed to the growth of the nationalism which aimed at the reunification of the two parts of Cameroun, though it did not stimulate any real opposition to Britain itself. Throughout the period of British administration, there persisted a feeling among Camerounians that their separate identity ought to be acknowledged, and a growing conviction that their interests would be better served by an arrangement which did not subordinate them to those of the contiguous regions of Nigeria. It was in order to gain a better deal for themselves *within* Nigeria that southern Camerounians directed their opposition to Britain as the administering authority; but the growing consciousness of their distinctive needs, and their status as an international trust along with their French-ruled former compatriots made it possible for them to realise the existence of an alternative which involved complete severance from both Britain and Nigeria.

THE CAMEROONS' STATUS AND THE GROWTH OF FEDERAL NIGERIA

There was virtually no significant constitutional advance in Nigeria until after the Second World War. Until then, both the northern and southern sections of the British Cameroons were integrated into the prevailing system of colonial administration, which maintained the separation of the country into two regions—Northern Nigeria and the Southern Provinces—but contained no representative institutions.

The arrangements made after 1922 applied Nigerian law to the British Cameroons[5] and allocated the various parts of the country between the provincial administrations. The Northern Cameroons were placed under the Lieutenant Governor of Northern Nigeria, and Residents serving under him administered those parts of the territory which were allotted to the emirates of Bornu and Dikwa on the one hand and Yola on the other. Later, the Dikwa emirate became part of Bornu province, while the others were administered within Adamawa province. In each case, local administration was conducted by district heads, who were responsible to their superiors (in the traditional as well as the colonial framework) for supplying information on the district, conducting the census, collecting taxes, maintaining peace, enforcing laws and policing the areas under their control. Adamawa proved less receptive to the policy of indirect rule than the Bornu areas; it had a weaker tradition of centralised rule, a more widely dispersed population, and, unlike Dikwa—which had a majority of Muslims—contained inhabitants two-thirds of whom were not followers of Islam. In addition, the non-Muslims lived in smaller, politically fragmented communities; and transport and communication, particularly in the southern portions of the province, were rudimentary.

While British rule brought a measure of stability to the area and eliminated some of the fighting that had occurred between the different communities in the earlier period, peace was largely achieved through the maintenance and the strengthening of traditional Fulani overrule. Little effort was made to develop the Northern Cameroons economically or in any other way. Administrative officers were few; agriculture and animal husbandry were not stimulated, and investment neither encouraged nor obtained; education, largely left to the missions in an era of restricted government activity, was additionally retarded by the resistance of Muslims to the possibility of Christian penetration; even health received scant attention.[6] Until very near the end of the British period, north Cameroun remained a secure but isolated region, poor, dominated by the emirates, and cut off from the nationalism

73

that developed with the growth of modern political institutions in the south.

In the southern part of the British Cameroons, the period before the development of representative government also saw attempts to introduce indirect rule. The area from the Mambila escarpment southward was placed under the authority of the Lieutenant-Governor of the Southern Provinces of Nigeria and a senior Resident ran the affairs of what came to be known as Cameroon Province from Buea; there were four administrative divisions— Victoria, Kumba, Mamfe and Bamenda.* As in the whole of the rest of Southern Nigeria, these areas were made to share the tortuous process whereby the principles of indirect rule were moulded to suit their traditional political structures. It is not possible here to go into the full ramifications of this aspect of the Camerounian colonial experience, but the essential point is easily described. Indirect rule was originally designed by Lord Lugard to harness the northern emirates, with their existing centralised military and bureaucratic regimes, to the needs of a colonial administration which had neither the men nor the funds to control a vast area with a widely dispersed population. In the southern areas, there was an enormous variety of ethnic groups, by no means all of whom had a centralised form of traditional authority; they were, on the whole, small tribes, scattered throughout a densely populated area. The British officials administering Cameroun were aware of the complexities of applying indirect rule to so disparate a group of peoples, but funds were not available for the application of direct rule. As a result, after some years of careful investigation, a number of different local authorities were established, some based on traditional chiefs (the Fons of the grassland areas), others on councils composed of village headmen and other dignatories, and yet others consisting of village chiefs appointed to act as *primus inter pares* among their colleagues in an administrative unit.[7]

While the Cameroons Province never quite endured the practice

* This arrangement continued, with minor modifications and some change in the nomenclature, until 1954. The Southern Provinces were re-named the Eastern Provinces, and later the Eastern Region of Nigeria; while, between 1949 and 1954, Bamenda Division became a province on its own, while the other three were administered together as Cameroon Province.

of creating entirely artificial 'warrant' chieftaincies (officials whose authority derived not from traditional office, but from an official warrant issued by the colonial administration), as did other parts of Southern Nigeria, the whole system caused widespread political dissatisfaction in Nigeria, leading to riots at Warri and Aba in the 1920s. It was ultimately replaced by a more representative system of local government, with some measure of accountability by the authorities to their constituents.[8]

In general, the local authorities were responsible for various aspects of local government, under the control of a District Officer; thus they controlled police, operated courts (particularly those dealing with customary law and minor offences), collected taxes, and dealt with such matters as health, sanitation and roads. They were permitted to retain half of the revenue obtained from taxes and fines imposed by the courts.

Through their participation in these local authorities, the inhabitants of the Cameroons Province were inaugurated into the institutions of an integrated Nigeria, rather as they were initiated into the politics of the country through the growing opposition to this form of government. The post-war changes in the Nigerian constitution saw them enter a new political order. In addition, the Cameroons passed from the status of a mandated to a trust territory, with added opportunities now provided for petitioning both the Trusteeship Council and (later) the Fourth Committee of the United Nations. These factors combined to make it possible for political leaders in the Southern Cameroons to press home with increasing vigour their claims to be regarded as a people with a destiny of their own.

The manner in which they asserted themselves within the Nigerian framework will be described later in this chapter (and in Chapter 5). For the moment it is necessary to outline the successive constitutional arrangements which were introduced for Nigeria between 1946 and 1958, as a prelude to that country's independence.

The first of these was the Richards constitution of 1946 (named after Sir Arthur Richards (now Lord Milverton), Governor of Nigeria 1943–7). It represented a backward step as far as the Southern Cameroons were concerned, by depriving them of representation at the centre. From 1942, they had enjoyed a single

75

representative (Chief Manga Williams of Victoria) in the Legislative Council originally established in 1923 and dominated by
British officials. Attempts had been made to suggest that other
incumbents be nominated for Chief Williams' seat, but these had
been ignored by the British authorities.[9] Now the Richards
constitution abolished all representation for the Southern Cameroons at the centre,[10] although it did provide for the election of
up to thirteen members of the Eastern Regional House of Assembly
by native authorities (two of whom came from the Southern
Cameroons) and for the entire region to be represented in the
country's central Legislative Council.[11] The constitution was not
at all favourably received in Nigeria. Together with four 'obnoxious' pieces of legislation (concerning land, mineral rights and the
appointment of chiefs), it caused widespread protest on the part
of nationalist leaders, particularly those of the National Council
of Nigeria and the Cameroons (NCNC).[12]

Under the Richards constitution the Southern Cameroons
were very far from achieving separate recognition within Nigeria,
but they did benefit rather more from the constitution introduced
in 1951 by Sir John Macpherson to replace that of 1946, although
still as a part of the Eastern Region. Under the new system, the
Eastern Region alone among the regions had a single legislative
chamber, which comprised eighty elected members, together with
six officials and three who were nominated. Of the eighty elected
members, thirteen were allocated to the Southern Cameroons.
For the first time, too, regional Executive Councils were created,
with a majority of officials, presided over by the Lieutenant-
Governor, and a Cameroons' elected member sat in this body.
At the centre, there was a Nigerian House of Representatives
consisting of seven *ex officio* members, six members specially
appointed by the Governor, and 136 members elected by the various
legislatures in all three of the regions from among their number.
A quarter of these came from the Eastern Region, and seven of
them were contributed by the Southern Cameroons.

The crisis in the Eastern Region House of Assembly in 1953
which led to the collapse of the Macpherson constitution and
produced serious divisions among the Southern Cameroons'
representatives also came at a time when pressure was building up
in the trust territory for separate institutions of its own. This was
reflected at the constitutional conferences which were held in

London in August 1953 and again in Lagos in January 1954. The Southern Cameroons was represented at both meetings.

In London, the demand was made for a separate Cameroons region, but the delegation from the Southern Cameroons was divided on the subject.[13] Nevertheless, the Secretary of State for the Colonies agreed that, if the forthcoming elections were won on the basis of an appeal for a separate status for the Southern Cameroons (by Dr Endeley and his Kamerun National Congress, which advocated this policy), the necessary changes would be made.[14] (It is interesting that the Northern Cameroons was also represented at the conferences, but did not press for separation from the Northern Region.) The condition was satisfied when all the seats for the Federal and the Regional legislatures were won by Endeley, and accordingly it was announced at the Lagos conference that the Southern Cameroons would be separated from the Eastern Region, but would remain part of Nigeria as a 'quasi-federal' territory. This meant that both the Federal Legislature and the Federal Executive would retain jurisdiction in the territory with respect to matters within their competence, that legislation would still require the assent of the Governor-General, but that there would be a House of Assembly consisting of: the Commissioner of the Cameroons (as President) and three *ex officio* members; two representatives of special interests (i.e. nominated members); six representatives of the native authorities; and thirteen elected members. The legislature was given power to raise taxes, and to legislate on subjects on the 'concurrent list' (shared with the federal authorities) and residual matters in terms of the Nigerian constitution. The territory was to have an Executive Council consisting of four official and four unofficial members (including the Commissioner, who presided); it was to elect six members to the Nigerian Federal Legislature, and was to have one federal minister.

By 1957 it was clear that Nigeria was moving rapidly towards its independence. The penultimate stage in this process came in 1958, when the constitution was again revised. The powers of the Governor-General to disallow legislation were reduced and regional self-government was introduced. This meant the intro-duction of a ministerial form of government with an unofficial majority in the Executive Council. The Southern Cameroons shared in these reforms, but it was not yet a fully-fledged Region of Nigeria. It became one in 1959, after a resolution had been passed in the territory's legislature in 1958 requesting the implementation of full regional self-government, and after the matter had been discussed at yet another constitutional conference in London in 1959. For the Southern Cameroons, the new arrangements meant that ultimate responsibility for the territory was still to reside in the Governor-General, since he was responsible for the implementation of the trusteeship agreement on behalf of the United Kingdom government; but the Commissioner was no longer to be a member of the Executive Council, which had an unofficial majority and was led by a premier. A bi-cameral system was created for the legislature, with the introduction of a House of Chiefs; and the number of elected members in the lower house was increased to twenty-six. For the first time, elections were to be based on universal adult suffrage. (In the Northern Cameroons, which were also to be a self-governing region from March 1959, suffrage was confined to males only, as it was in Northern Nigeria.) Representation in an enlarged Federal Legislature of 320 members was to be based on one seat for every 100,000 of the population.[15]

When these provisions came into operation, the date for Nigeria's independence had already been set as October 1, 1960, and the Republic of Cameroun was about to be created as an independent state. The UN was already discussing the question of the future status of the two British Cameroons. It was soon to decide that their subsequent position either within Nigeria or as parts of a reunified Cameroun was a matter for their peoples to determine in a plebiscite. Britain, meanwhile, was to introduce other interim constitutional provisions for the transitional period. These developments will be discussed in the next chapter.

THE ECONOMIC INTERREGNUM

Economic development was not a feature of the period during which the Southern Cameroons was administered by the British and formed a part of Nigeria. In the beginning, there was very little government expenditure, either on the social services or on public works, and the economy remained centred around the plantations which had been established under the German regime. Although no figures were kept to indicate the exact revenue from and expenditure on the Southern Cameroons, the territory ran at a deficit throughout the period of the mandate, and required subsidies from the Nigerian budget. This pattern was resumed after the Second World War, and the question of the British Cameroons' economic viability outside the Nigerian structure was an important one as the separatist (and unification) movements grew stronger.

On assuming authority over the Cameroons, Britain confiscated all German plantations and administered them either directly or through the Nigerian government until 1924, when the cost of maintaining them was said to be prohibitive. An attempt was made to dispose of them by auction to British companies in 1922, but without success, and in 1924 they were again put up for sale without any restriction as to the nationality of the purchasers. Most were bought by their former German owners,[16] about one quarter going to British, Dutch and Swiss companies.[17] As a result, until the outbreak of the Second World War, there were always more German expatriates in the Southern Cameroons than those of any other nationality and Germany continued to be the principal importer of Cameroon products and to supply more than half of the territory's imports.[18] The situation only really altered when the plantations were once again commandeered by Britain during the Second World War, and their German owners interned. In 1946 the plantations were acquired for £850,000 from the Custodian of Enemy Property by the Nigerian government, and leased to the Cameroons Development Corporation—a quasi-public body, established by statute, with a board appointed by the government and authority to borrow up to one million pounds at any one time in order to finance its activities.[19]

The plantations, and the Cameroons Development Corporation in particular, were heavily dependent on the Nigerian (and later the Southern Cameroons) government for capital after 1947; and, to an increasing extent, on Britain for their export markets. Total loans to the CDC from Nigeria and the Southern Cameroons amounted to £2 million between 1950 and 1960, and, after debt repayments there was still £1·75 million owing at the time of reunification with the rest of Cameroun, £1 million of which was to be repaid to Nigeria in eighteen equal instalments from 1970.[20] Apart from its role as an employer of more than half the territory's labour, the CDC played a crucial part in the remainder of its economy, contributing something like two-thirds of its export tonnage and more than half of its export earnings in its heyday, and 41 per cent and 28 per cent of each respectively in 1961. It was thus an important contributor to the ports and transport systems—it ran the only railway, the narrow-gauge track originally built by the Germans—as well as to the revenues of the territory, through the taxes it paid to the government. This would have been an even more valuable item in the territory's financial structure if the Corporation had not had so erratic a record of profitability. From a maximum of just over £60,000 in 1953, profits dropped in 1954 to less than a third of that amount, and only exceeded £25,000 twice in the remainder of the period up to 1960.[21] As a result, the Southern Cameroons found it increasingly necessary to seek direct budgetary support from Nigeria.

The shift to Britain as the territory's main importer was the other notable feature of the economy after 1946. By 1958, three-quarters of all exports from the British Cameroons went to Britain, and the banana crop especially was heavily dependent on the Commonwealth preference of £7 10s a ton which it received.

The extent to which the Southern Cameroons was, or could be, self-supporting only received attention after 1954, when it became a separate entity within Nigeria. Before then, the Nigerian government had spent more on the mandated territory than it had received in revenues, and the extent of its subsidy between 1943 and 1949 was estimated at more than £1 million. In 1955, following a report by Sir Louis Chick, the Financial Secretary in the Nigerian government, a formula was established whereby the federal government would guarantee any shortfall in revenue for a three-year period up to the sum of £580,000. In the event, the poor showing made by the CDC meant that this was used, and a contribution of £450,000 was made in the two fiscal years from 1956 to 1958. Thereafter, another formula was substituted on the recommendation of the Raisman Commission, which was based on the proportion estimated to be due to the territory from the import and excise duties imposed by the federal government, as well as receipt of the entire revenue from income tax, mining royalties and certain other sources raised within the territory itself. In addition, debts amounting to £700,000, plus interest to date, which had resulted from the previous subsidies, were written off. Nevertheless, the new territory was still not able to balance its budget, and estimated a deficit of some £200,000 for the first year.[22]

There were also capital grants from Britain and Nigeria during this period, including an annual contribution of about £300,000 from Nigeria between 1955 and 1958, and an expenditure of £1,200,000 on the Bamenda-Victoria road in 1959; and in 1956, the British Colonial Office granted £1·3 million for various aid projects, including roads, education, agriculture and communications. An outright grant of £450,000 was made to the territory in 1958 by Britain to help meet budgetary deficits.[23]

What emerges from this description of the economy is a picture of underdevelopment—with a rather one-sided emphasis on the plantations and very little substantial economic activity elsewhere in the territory at all—and of the need for support on both current and capital accounts. For some time after a separate government was granted for the Southern Cameroons, there remained a feeling that it was not receiving its just share of Nigerian revenues, and that it would do better if it could operate its own finances. This grievance gave some impetus to the advocates of greater political autonomy, but even they did not remain convinced that the territory could stand on its own, and the most ardent separatists were only able to put forward the choice, ultimately, between the economic advantages of assistance from Nigeria and the unspecified benefits to be derived from aid after a link with francophone Cameroun.

Even then, the economic implications of federation with the Cameroun Republic were never really considered. They were not dealt with in the report on the consequences of separation from Nigeria which was prepared in 1959 for the Southern Cameroons' government by Sir Sydney Phillipson. This report vindicated the view that more was being contributed to Nigerian revenues than had been credited to the territory; but it also pointed out that any increase in receipts which might result from financial autochthony would be more than offset by the loss of subsidies from the federal government and the cost of replacing federal services. Capital expenditure would have to be financed from abroad, and expansion of the social services would have to be curtailed in order to balance the budget. The report concluded that, under certain circumstances, the territory might prove to be potentially viable, but that it could not stand on its own as an independent state.[24]

It was clear, then, that the solution to the economic underdevelopment of the Southern Cameroons was not to be found in the country itself. How it was to be solved outside the confines of the territory was a matter not much debated as the nationalist politicians placed increasing emphasis on the need for lessening ties with Nigeria.

THE GROWTH OF NATIONALIST POLITICS IN THE SOUTHERN CAMEROONS

Political activity in the Southern Cameroons after the start of the Second World War evolved at two different levels. One involved participation in the politics of the eastern part (later region) of Nigeria, the other was directed towards the special situation of the territory and its particular needs. These two aspects of the Cameroons' political life were not incompatible in the first ten years of nationalist campaigning, and many of the leading participants took part energetically in both. It was only later, when British rule ceased to be the sole focus of political attention and developments within the Eastern Region gave rise to dissatisfaction, that the nascent Cameroun[25] nationalism turned towards separatism, and still later towards the active pursuit of union between the two trust territories.

It is not possible to account for the divergence in terms of a single cause; several factors contributed to the process, but they acted cumulatively and not individually, over a period of twenty years. There was no sudden break in the political tradition which marked the emergence of a single-minded determination to further Cameroun nationalism to the exclusion of all else, but a gradual change of emphasis, with the final choice between association with Nigeria and unification hotly debated to the end. The details of the campaign which decided that question are given in the next chapter. Here it is worth listing the factors which affected the evolution from one political framework to the other. Among these were (1) the awareness of the territory's special status under the UN trusteeship system; (2) contact established (on the plantations in particular) between employees from the two parts of Cameroun; (3) the emphasis on regional separation in Nigeria, both constitutionally and politically; (4) resentment at Nigerian—and often Ibo—domination in the political and economic fields; (5) sympathy with the anti-colonial and later unity-orientated campaign of the UPC in French Cameroun; (6) international pressure, from and at the UN, especially after the emergence of an interested bloc of African nations there.

None of these influences was felt at the start of politics in the Southern Cameroons. The first activity was conducted in Victoria, by the Cameroon Welfare Union in 1940, and was directed towards securing the replacement of Chief Manga Williams by one of its own nominees as the sole member from the Southern Cameroons in the Nigerian Legislative Council.

The colonial government took no notice of the CWU's representations, and the organisation soon became moribund. A more energetic group of Camerounians resident in Lagos then took over the task of furthering the interests of the territory through the Cameroons Youth League which had been founded in 1939. The CYL was small, but effective. It had an average membership of twenty, mostly students at the Higher College, Yaba; it charged them a monthly subscription of 6d., and published a monthly newsletter. Among its members were P. M. Kale, Dr E. M. L. Endeley and J. N. Foncha, all of whom rose to prominence in the political life of Nigeria and the British Cameroons.[26] They began almost at once to take an active part in both spheres. In 1944, Endeley—then Assistant Medical Officer in Buea—presented evidence to the Elliot Commission on Higher Education, which spelt out in considerable detail the degree to which education had been neglected in the territory, and the restraining effect this had had on the admission of Camerounians to the civil service.[27] In the same year, he and the other CYL members were in at the founding of Azikiwe's National Council of Nigeria and the Cameroons; Kale participated in the constitutional committee which drafted its Organic Law (i.e. constitution).[28]

This was the period of the campaign against the Richards constitution and the four 'obnoxious bills', and the CYL played a leading part in it. Endeley was quick to press home the special features of the bills which affected the Cameroons, while Kale was a member of the delegation which went from the NCNC to London to seek revision of the constitution and repeal of the legislation in an interview with the Colonial Secretary, Arthur Creech Jones. The inadequate representation of the territory under the new constitution was specifically criticised by the delegation, but Creech Jones equivocated in reply, and advised Kale and the NCNC to await the constitutional reform to be undertaken by the newly-appointed Governor, Sir John Macpherson.[29]

Before that constitution was put into effect, there were several developments which had an important effect on politics in the Southern Cameroons.

In 1946, Dr Endeley had been suspended from the Nigerian medical profession. He returned at once to the Victoria area, where he was invited to become General Secretary of the newly-formed CDC Workers' Union, which he proceeded to build into an effective and influential trade union.[30] He also devoted a good deal of energy to organising the Bakweri people politically through ethnic organisations such as the Bakweri Land Claim Committee and the Bakweri Improvement Union. Among his activities on behalf of the former was the presentation of a petition to the UN urging the return of Bakweri lands confiscated by the Germans for the plantations. Endeley also formed a less narrowly confined political discussion group, the Cameroons Federal Union, whose object was to press for a separate regional status for the territory.

It was during the course of these activities that an effort was made to diminish the influence of Ibo immigrants, both as road and plantation workers and as entrepreneurs and small-scale businessmen in the Southern Cameroons.[31] Regional status was seen as a solution to this problem too.

Political activity increased greatly in 1948 and 1949, stimulated by the constitutional review undertaken by Macpherson at grass roots (i.e. Native Authority) level, and by the visit of a UN Mission to investigate the trust territories. Petitions to the latter and the need to exert concerted pressure in the constitutional discussions resulted in the formation of the first territory-wide political organisation, the Cameroons National Federation, in May 1949. This body grouped some twenty ethnic 'Improvement Unions' with the CDC and other trade unions, as well as Land Committees. For the first time, too, it included representatives of the French Camerounians resident in the British trust area; and it endorsed not only the objective of a separate region in Nigeria, but claimed this would enable it to 'work towards unification with its brothers under the French—the dream of every living Cameroonian'.[32] The UN Visiting Mission brought the CNF into close contact with the UPC of the French Cameroun; this event is said to have led to the UPC's intense concern with the question of unification, which had been endorsed by the British Cameroons organisation.[33]

It would be an exaggeration to suggest that unification was a major pre-occupation of the CNF. Although it obviously touched on a profound element in Cameroun nationalist feeling, the principal advocates of unity—both at the CNF Kumba conference in 1949 and afterwards—were French Cameroun workers from Douala. In the Southern Cameroons, the theme of unity was often mentioned, but the main thrust of nationalist activity was towards the achievement of regional separation in Nigeria, a policy which Endeley—as the leading politician in the territory—now urged at the Ibadan conference to review the constitution in 1949.

The new constitution, adopted in 1951, did not give the Southern Cameroons separate regional status as we have seen. But the thirteen seats which were allocated to them in the Eastern Region provided the first opportunity for the emergence of the territory's leaders, albeit as members of the NCNC, in the House of Assembly. Among those elected in 1951 were S. T. Muna and J. N. Foncha from Bamenda, N. N. Mbile from Kumba, Endeley from Victoria. Endeley, Mbile and Muna were also elected to the Lagos House of Representatives. Endeley became Minister without Portfolio (later Minister of Labour) in the Federal Council of Ministers and Muna was made Minister of Works in the Eastern Regional government. From this point on, developments both in the Southern Cameroons and Nigeria become complex, with the themes of Camerounian unity and regional separatism closely interwoven and the leading political figures emphasising one or the other (and sometimes both) in their bids for electoral and parliamentary support.

First came a division in the Southern Cameroons, leading to the creation of the outspokenly unificationist Kamerun United National Congress (KUNC), led by R. J. K. Dibonge and N. N. Mbile. Dibonge was a Douala and a remarkable man, almost the embodiment of Cameroun nationalism. He had been educated in Germany and occupied senior administrative posts in Douala under the Germans, in Buea under the British and was Chief Clerk in Enugu in 1944. He returned to Douala in 1947, but came back to Victoria in 1949.[34] In that year he also established the French Cameroons Welfare Union (FCWU). Dibonge criticised the exclusion of francophone Camerounians from the ballotting

4—C * *

arrangements under the 1951 constitution; when Endeley refused to support him, he formed KUNC. He was supported by Mbile—Endeley's successor as General Secretary of the CDC Workers' Union—and by Foncha. Though the differences were to disappear shortly, and the CNF merged with KUNC to form the Kamerun National Congress (KNC) in 1952, this was the first of several splits which brought Endeley and Foncha onto opposing sides in Southern Cameroons' politics. One other effect of the establishment of KUNC and Dibonge's leadership was the closer contact established during this period with the UPC, particularly immediately before the visit of the second UN Mission in 1952.

Undoubtedly the most significant event in the Southern Cameroons during this period, however, was the Eastern Regional crisis of 1953. This concerned the situation in which the NCNC found itself, both federally and in the Region, involving a challenge to Azikiwe's leadership.[35] The immediate effect of the three-month long crisis—which produced a rift in the NCNC, the resignation of the government, paralysis of the legislative programme and ultimately the dissolution of the House of Assembly—was to split the Southern Cameroons' representatives. Eight (led by Endeley, Muna and Foncha) allied themselves with the NCNC dissidents and pressed for Muna's reinstatement as a Minister. The other five, who included Mbile, joined with the remainder of the NCNC and were expelled from KUNC for voting against Muna; they then formed the Kamerun Peoples' Party (KPP) and maintained an alliance with the NCNC under Azikiwe.

Aside from these divisions, the most important outcome of the crisis was the opportunity it provided for the Southern Cameroons to press its demand for a separate region. The crisis had occurred just before the start of the conferences to revise the constitution yet again. Both the parties were represented at the conferences in London and Lagos which decided the new Nigerian structure, and both pressed for regional status. They were supported by Azikiwe and the NCNC, who also endorsed the aim of Cameroun unity.[36] Regional status was conceded by Britain, though it was made conditional on electoral support for the proposal at the forthcoming elections. It was the KNC, which under Endeley won all thirteen seats on a separatist programme that was markedly anti-Nigerian in its tone.[37]

The next few years were to see further re-shuffles, alliances and splits among the Southern Cameroons parties and their leaders. Cameroun unity was still not in the forefront of any of their policies, and a good deal of the rearrangement took place in the context of the search for power in the territory itself. The most far-reaching division occurred between Endeley and Foncha. This occurred ostensibly because Endeley failed to maintain an attitude of 'benevolent neutrality' in Nigerian politics; his breach with the NCNC—then in coalition with the Northern Nigerian party as the federal government—took him into informal alliance with the opposition Action Group (led by Chief Awolowo). But there is little doubt that ethnic allegiances also played a part in the decision of Foncha, A. N. Jua and their supporters in the grasslands to break away from the KNC and form the Kamerun National Democratic Party (KNDP).

One of the factors which assisted Foncha over the next few years was his uncompromising policy on dissociation from Nigeria —both the other parties were tarnished by their links with the NCNC and the Action Group. Another was his adoption of a 'quasi-left' [38] political stance; and a third was his close ties with the Fons of the grasslands. All three brought him into contact with the UPC, and his personal friendship with Moumié, although short-lived, led to a measure of co-operation between the two parties. The UPC was given a temporary home in the Southern Cameroons soon after it went into exile in 1955, and a committee of co-ordination between the two parties came into existence. Foncha accordingly became an enthusiastic advocate of Cameroun unity, an end to which he remained committed. But disagreement on the speed with which unification was to be achieved and over the question of an intermediate stage of independence, led to a breach with the UPC leaders which was never healed, particularly after they had campaigned against Foncha and the KNDP in the 1957 elections for the House of Assembly.[39] The UPC left behind a remnant in the One Kamerun (OK) Party, which won no seats in the election. The KNC-KPP majority was reduced considerably, however: the KNC won 6 seats, the KPP 2, and the KNDP 5.

The differences between the KNDP and the other two parties crystallised at the two constitutional conferences which preceded the introduction of the 1958 constitution. Both the KNC and the KPP explicitly came out for continued association with Nigeria as a separate region. The KNDP proposed an interim period within Nigeria, but supported the ultimate aim of secession *and* the joining of both the Northern and the Southern Cameroons, as a prelude to ultimate reunification with the French trust territory.[40] The British decision to institute regional self-government for the rest of Nigeria in 1958 favoured the KNC-KPP position, although it was not immediately applied to the Southern Cameroons. Endeley took immediate steps to get parliamentary approval for the introduction of a responsible ministerial government and full regional status. The KNDP protested without success that discussion of the matter should be postponed until the elections for the enlarged House of Assembly, which was to be created in terms of the 1958 reforms, had been held. The elections were in fact held in January 1959. Endeley had, by this time, virtually abandoned any support for unification except as a long-term goal.[41] Foncha campaigned on his qualified, quasi-unificationist policy. He won a bare majority, capturing fourteen of the twenty-six elective seats, mainly as a result of the support he received in the grasslands.

By this time, the United Nations had been under pressure, as a result of the political events in Togo and the French Cameroun, to find a solution to the question of the status of the trust territories once they were allowed to merge from French tutelage. This raised the problem of the future status of the British Cameroons too, since the impending independence of Nigeria meant that they would also have to decide between the alternatives of remaining in an independent Nigeria or joining with an independent Cameroun. Foncha still hoped that this choice could be avoided. He and Endeley left almost immediately after the 1959 elections for New York in order to present their views on the future of the country to the Trusteeship Council and the Fourth Committee of the UN. It was here that the ambiguities implicit in Foncha's programme came to light, as the two leaders searched for a formula which would enable the people of the British Cameroons to decide the matter in the plebiscites which were to be held shortly. The details of those discussions, and of the campaign which revolved around the plebiscites, are given in the next chapter.

5. From Self-Government to Independence and Federation

THE ATTAINMENT of self-government for Nigeria and of regional status for the Southern Cameroons left the party leaders in the British trust territory free to concentrate their attention on the debate over unification. This was not the issue which dominated developments in French Cameroun, where unification was not a matter for dispute: by the time self-government came in 1957, it had been accepted by all parties as the eventual aim of an independent Cameroun. The immediate problem was the achievement of independence.

This was accomplished within the next three years. Cameroun became independent at the beginning of 1960 after a decision had been taken by the United Nations to this effect, and after there had been a major shift in French colonial policy. The UN's decision also made it possible for the two trust territories to unite. But the transition of French Cameroun from trusteeship to independence was effected against a background of mounting political violence and military activity, under a Camerounian government backed by French troops. This period also saw the emergence of a strong government, with Ahmadou Ahidjo and his northern supporters in the *Union Camérounaise* acquiring control over the state and reducing the other parties and their leaders to participation in minor roles either within the structure thus created or in opposition to it.

Once Ahidjo had established his government in an unassailable position of dominance and he had taken steps to overcome the opposition both inside and outside the parliamentary framework, he was able to turn his attention to the question of reunification with the British Cameroons.

CAMEROUN GOVERNMENT: THE FRAMEWORK CHANGES

Three separate sets of factors combined to move Cameroun rapidly from the severely restricted form of self-government

89

which it had obtained in 1957 to the more substantial degree of control it was given over its own affairs from 1959. These were: (1) a constitutional dispute within the territory, which led to the recall of the High Commissioner and precipitated the fall of the Mbida government; (2) the influence of United Nations decisions on the termination of the trusteeship status of Togo, which produced changes of attitude to Cameroun as well on the part of the last French government under the Fourth Republic; and (3) political and constitutional changes in France, which led to a reversal of her previous policies concerning independence for the African countries under her rule.

When Mbida was installed as Prime Minister under the 1957 reforms, he had the backing of all the parties in ALCAM except Assalé's *Action Nationale*, although his own *Démocrates* were a minority in the Assembly. His government was not a popular one. Its policy of tough military repression of the UPC presumably had the support of the *Union Camérounaise* and its leader, Ahidjo, who was Vice-Premier and Minister of the Interior. But Mbida's inability to obtain the French government's assent to an amnesty for political prisoners, and—more important still—his conservative programme for the future advancement of the territory which involved a ten-year period of evolution towards independence, and no mention whatever of unification, reduced his support. One result was the withdrawal of the UC ministers from his government in January 1958.[1] When Mbida attempted to replace them with *Démocrates*, the High Commissioner, Jean Ramadier, declined to make the appointments. This unconstitutional refusal to follow the advice of the Prime Minister led to Ramadier's recall; but it also showed where power lay under the 1957 constitution. The unsatisfactory nature of the constitution and Mbida's own weak policy proposals had the immediate effect of toppling him from power, since he could not muster a majority to defeat a series of motions of censure which were moved in the Assembly. His government fell in February, and Ahidjo took office under a new High Commissioner, Xavier Torré, constructing a government from ministers who were members of the *Action Nationale* and the *Paysans Indépendants* as well as his own party.

Ahidjo thus laid the foundation for a north-south alliance which was to be the mainstay of his power from then on. He had by then, of course, been active in Cameroun politics for a considerable time, and had perceived clearly how power could best be obtained. Although he came from and represented the north in ALCAM, his basis of support was not the conservative northern aristocracy. His brand of conservatism rested on the traditionalist association in Benoué which he had founded in 1948. Until he succeeded in bringing about the merger of the various local, traditional and ethnic groups from the north in the *Union Camérounaise* after the 1956 elections, he had given his support to Ajoulat and the *Démocrates* in the Assembly. Ahidjo is a young man. Born in 1924 at Garoua, he was not yet thirty-four years old when he took office as Prime Minister. He is a Fulani, and a Muslim, but he is not a member of the northern nobility. After finishing secondary schooling in 1941, he entered the administration the following year as a radio-telegraphist, a job he left only in 1953 when he was elected to the Assembly of the French Union.

Ahidjo's political programme has always enabled him to retain the support of the conservatives from the north, though his familiarity with the intricacies of modern government has made it clear that he is not one of them. Since Ahidjo assumed control no observer of developments in Cameroun has been left in any doubt about his great astuteness in handling the affairs of state. But his command over the governmental machine is only one of the characteristics of his political style. Another is the almost total absence of an ideological approach to political issues. This goes together with a preoccupation with the realities of power, at home and abroad, rather than with the superficial trappings of government. The result has been a severely pragmatic set of policies, characterised by cool and careful calculation. Ahidjo has seldom allowed himself to be swayed by purely ideological or theoretical arguments; but his skill in planning policies and anticipating their effects has protected him from allegations of opportunism. It is pragmatism rather than flexibility that impresses most observers as the outstanding feature of Ahidjo's political outlook. His shrewd understanding of the political process in Cameroun has enabled him to continue in power for an uninterrupted period since 1958. But neither this nor his total rejection of the flamboyant have disguised a hard-headed determination to exercise unrestricted control over his country's government and a ruthlessness in dealing with his opponents.

The government which took office in 1958 under Ahidjo had

three main policy aims: reassuring France that close co-operation would follow the achievement of a greater measure of self-rule; the establishment of a time-table for independence; and a search for political harmony, based on the shared objectives of all the political parties, but tough measures against those who threatened the security of the state. Having thus constructed a policy which combined firmness of government with a determination to seek independence, Ahidjo was able to begin negotiations with France within a month of assuming office. In June, he received the backing of ALCAM for a resolution which demanded the termination of trusteeship, Camerounian control over all internal affairs, and an explicit recognition by France that Cameroun would become independent. By the time the resolution was passed, France was already well on the way to making important concessions in her African policy.

At the UN, a decision in 1957 made it clear that independence for Togo would, in all probability, be approved the following year through the termination of the trusteeship status of that territory. Without finally committing herself to the immediate independence of Togo, France attempted in February 1958, to forestall further moves in this direction by agreeing to full internal autonomy for the Republic of Togo, while retaining reserve powers and continuing to be responsible for foreign affairs, defence and the monetary system.

Three months later, France herself underwent a major political upheaval when General de Gaulle came to power. Under his Fifth Republic, France finally abandoned the policy which involved an organic link between the metropolis and the African countries which it ruled. For the rest of French sub-Saharan Africa the new order entailed participation in a referendum on the form of future association with France. In the case of Cameroun, however, the French government simply announced at the UN General Assembly in October 1958 (after agreement had been reached with the Ahidjo government) that it wished Cameroun's trusteeship status to end, and that, from January 1, 1959, the territory would be granted a status and institutions like those provided for Togo.

In Cameroun, meanwhile, ALCAM had passed a resolution[2] adopting the new constitution, and going one stage further by requesting termination of trusteeship and the grant of independ-

ence by January 1, 1960.* The response of the UN was to advise
the forthcoming Visiting Mission of the Trusteeship Council
to the territory to investigate ways and means of implementing
this request, and of ascertaining the views of the people of
Cameroun on the question.[3] But, in Cameroun, the new constitution went into force from the beginning of 1959. Its preamble
contained a clear recognition that the new statute was the final
prelude to the end of trusteeship and independence, as far as the
French government was concerned. For the rest, it transferred
control over internal affairs to the Cameroun government, while
leaving France with jurisdiction in matters of foreign relations,
internal and external security, and the monetary system. There was
no provision for a further general election under the new system;
and none was in fact held until after the adoption of a constitution
for the independent Republic of Cameroun in the first months of
1960.

STRONG GOVERNMENT AND VIOLENT OPPOSITION

Opposition in the Cameroun Legislative Assembly to the short-
lived Mbida government came from the members of Assalé's
Action Nationale (who included Soppo Priso). They adopted a
critical approach to the 1957 Statute of Cameroun, urging a
move to complete independence. When the Mbida regime fell in
1958, they joined the government formed by Ahidjo, leaving the
Démocrates as the opposition party. Mbida himself followed an
increasingly radical line of attack on the new government, and
was eventually to join forces temporarily with the exiled UPC in
Guinea. But his party retained its conservative approach, with the
result that its supporters in the Assembly crossed to the government side in growing numbers.[4] Not for the last time, Ahidjo was
able to take advantage of a weak and divided opposition.[5]

Ahidjo's principal concern over the next two years was not the
parliamentary opposition, however. It was the activities of the
maquis inside the territory, and of the UPC abroad, that his policies
were designed to combat. In dealing with both, he was to deploy
the full array of military forces and political skill at his command—
first, to smash the underground, then to divide and conciliate what
was left of the party in the country.

* It also expressed a desire for unification with the British Cameroons.

He inherited from Mbida a situation which enabled him to pursue his policies with even greater effectiveness. The UPC had been outlawed since 1955. It had set up its first headquarters in Kumba, across the border in British-administered Southern Cameroons. There, Moumié and his exiled *Comité-Directeur* were able to direct the first campaigns of violence in Cameroun. They also established contact with legal parties in the British trust territory and with leaders like Foncha who provided them with refuge. A considerable amount of time was also devoted to building up contact with disaffected leaders of the Bamiléké (whose territory was situated near Kumba, but just across the frontier). These included Pierre Ninyim Kandem, a young Bamiléké chief who had returned from studying in Paris to succeed to traditional office among his people, but who was deposed by the French administration in 1956. In Cameroun itself, the UPC continued to operate through front organisations of various kinds (though its youth and women's sections had also been established in the Kumba exile), and it received some measure of publicity for its policy through newspapers such as *L'Opinion au Cameroun*, run by Dr Marcel Beybey-Eyidi.

After the British had expelled the UPC from Kumba in 1957, there appears to have been a division in its ranks, reflecting a tactical if not an ideological split. The *Comité-Directeur* (Moumié, Ouandié and Kingué) moved to Cairo, where they concentrated on establishing a network of newspapers and radio broadcasts, developed support among African leaders from other parts of the continent, and formulated a systematic programme for organised violence by the *Armée de Libération Nationale Kamérounaise* (ALNK) in the Bamiléké regions of the west and the Moungo region in the south of the territory.

Another wing, under Reuben Um Nyobe, operated within Cameroun exclusively. Um Nyobe never managed to achieve any electoral success, but he clearly possessed both political charisma and political skill. As a result he obtained a hearing and a following throughout the country. The essential constituents of his nationalist policies—independence and reunification—were adopted in the end by all parties. As Mveng says, he is regarded by many Camerounians today as the father of the country's independence.[6] Towards the end of his career, Um Nyobe's elusiveness and fearlessness in organising the underground gave his activities a legendary aura, and he was credited with mythical and magical powers in the best traditions of millenarian heroism.[7]

Initially, Um Nyobe did not engage in violent activity, but spent considerable time and effort organising the *maquis* for future campaigns. At the same time, he showed a willingness to open negotiations with the government. In preparing the underground, he was able to consolidate his base among the Bassa people with the aid of Matip, and to use this in appealing for support to his considerable following elsewhere in the country. Um Nyobe's initial approach to the Mbida government was to press the need for granting an amnesty to all the imprisoned *upécistes*, and to urge it to agree to the goals of independence and reunification. He even suggested a 'moral and political détente'.[8] But Mbida was not receptive to any of these proposals. He was inclined to a very limited view of the country's political future—a policy which was shortly to cause the fall of his government. Besides, amnesty was still a matter for the French National Assembly, which delayed consideration of the proposals which had been before it since 1956.

As a result of Mbida's intransigence, Um Nyobe delivered an ultimatum that he would resort to violence; from mid-1957 until September 1958, he carried out his threat, through his *Comité National d'Organisation*—the body he had set up, especially among the Bassa, to carry out his revolutionary goals. An attempt by the Catholic Bishop of Douala, Mgr Mongo, to mediate in September failed because neither side was willing to compromise. Um Nyobe's response to the mediation attempt was to increase his demands on the government, by asking for the immediate dissolution of ALCAM, new elections, a general amnesty and immediate independence. Violence occurred on an unprecedented scale, mainly in the Sanaga-Maritime region but also in the Bamiléké and Moungo areas of the south. The action included attacks on plantations, missions and government offices; the killing of chiefs, officials and missionaries and the kidnapping and wounding of others. It also involved the assassination of one of the Bamiléké deputies in ALCAM.[9]

The Mbida government responded by declaring a *Zone de Pacification* in the Sanaga-Maritime and by moving in troop reinforcements obtained from France. It also armed the local population, and relocated large numbers of them in strategic

95

areas to contain rebel activity, while using the military to conduct searches of forests and villages for rebel bases.[10]

Ahidjo continued this policy after he came to power, even more vigorously and with devastating effect. In a period of little more than a year (from September 1957 to October 1958), 371 rebels were killed, 104 wounded and 882 arrested.[11] But he was also able to make use of the amnesty which had at last been passed by the French Parliament in January, to drive a wedge between the UPC and several hundred of its former supporters who were pardoned for offences committed before 1956.

The rebels lost a good deal of support in 1958 as well, after France had adopted its new course. The promise to end trusteeship and the explicit acknowledgement of the independence that was to follow made the arguments for revolt less convincing. Thus the combination of military force and political skill which Ahidjo had brought to bear on the underground went a long way to breaking its hold in the country. He was able to take this a stage further after Um Nyobe had been surprised in an ambush and killed on September 13 at Boumnyebel, his home village in the Bassa area.

Um Nyobe's death was used to strengthen the government's position in several ways. The dead leader was acclaimed as a national hero: he was widely mourned throughout the territory and praised for his dedication and honesty by Ministers and other politicians who had been his bitter foes while he was alive.[12] Even today, he is revered by many of his former critics and opponents as the founder of Cameroun nationalism.[13] Ahidjo also drew a retrospective distinction between Um Nyobe's policies and those of the old UPC underground leaders, particularly Moumié and his colleagues in the *Comité-Directeur*, who were branded as extremists.[14] The amnesty was also extended to include all who were now prepared to abandon the *maquis*. Weakened by the death of Um Nyobe and by the surrender of Matip a week later, many of the rebels did in fact relinquish their campaign. In the last three months of 1958, more than 1,200 are reported to have given themselves up to the government forces.[15]

In the ensuing months Ahidjo was able to go even further in promoting his policy of dividing the opposition by permitting the ex-UPC supporters in the territory to participate in open political activity. He did not yet go as far as to legalise the UPC, but he allowed Matip to organise his followers into a coherent political faction, known colloquially as the *rallié* UPC. In April 1959, they were given the opportunity of taking part in by-elections for ALCAM seats. In a gesture which pointed all the more effectively to the conversion of the *ralliés* from violent resistance to legal activity and away from Moumié's brand of unremitting rebellion, Matip and five others were left free to contest seats left vacant by the assassinations of 1956 and 1957 in the Sanaga-Maritime and Nyong-et-Sanaga regions (which were Bassa strongholds), and in the Bamiléké area. All seats were won by the former rebels, who joined ALCAM as a group of independents.

During this period, the Moumié faction of the UPC had been consolidating its influence in the Bamiléké areas, but the main thrust of its opposition to Ahidjo took place outside the country, mainly at the UN. The *Comité-Directeur* had transferred its activities from Cairo to Conakry in Guinea in 1958, and was able to gain the support of both the Ghana and the Guinea governments for its campaign against Ahidjo. The UN had received a report from the 1958 Visiting Mission which recommended the termination of trusteeship, and independence by January 1, 1960, without any necessity for elections in the territory beforehand. The Trusteeship Council accepted the report and approved the recommendations after a debate in the Fourth Committee.

The debate turned out to be the most serious challenge Ahidjo had to face from the UPC and its African allies, as well as from the remainder of the anti-colonial bloc. Moumié (supported by fourteen other petitioners) argued that the Assembly which had elected the Ahidjo government was unrepresentative because the UPC had not been allowed to take part in the 1956 general election, and that new elections should be held, under UN supervision, before independence. The African states which backed him—Ghana, Guinea, the UAR, Libya, Morocco, the Sudan, Tunisia and Liberia—supported measures for the revocation of the ban on the UPC, and for new elections. They were joined by the USSR and a considerable number of the anti-colonial nations, but were defeated after an able defence of the territory's desire for independence had been voiced by Ahidjo, the ALCAM President, Kemajou, and representatives of the other parties.[16] The General Assembly of the UN accordingly resolved on March 13, 1959, that from January 1, 1960, Cameroun was no longer to be a trust territory and would become the independent Republic of Cameroun on that date.[17]

97

The UPC did not cease activity after it had been defeated at the UN. Outside the country, it continued to use the good offices of Ghana and Guinea to seek reconciliation with the Cameroun government—but on its own terms, namely the legalisation of the party and the holding of new elections. After a joint declaration issued to this end in May by Presidents Nkrumah and Touré had not achieved any success, the exiled leaders turned their attention once again to violence in the territory. Towards the end of June, the first attacks took place in Douala and Yaoundé, where the guerrillas killed half a dozen or more people, and then spread rapidly to the centre of the country, where raids were made on posts manned by police and gendarmes. But the main burden of the rebel offensive was felt in the Bamiléké areas and those parts of the Moungo inhabited by large numbers of immigrant Bamiléké. Here, the attacks occurred with mounting frequency, causing widespread damage and destruction of homes, buildings, crops, government services, roads and communications.

The revolt was conducted under the auspices of the ALNK, and was led by Martin Singap and Paul Momo. There is no reliable evidence of the total number of people involved on the side of the rebels,[18] but the guerrillas appear to have operated in bands of thirty to forty people. Sabotage and arson were the principal methods used by the insurgents, but they did not stop at killing on a substantial scale, razing whole villages to the ground on occasion. However, it seems clear that they only had small arms at their disposal, and that even these were not available to them in large quantities.[19] There is some doubt about the degree of control that was exercised over the rebels by the UPC *Comité-Directeur*. Relations between the leaders in the territory and the exiled party became strained; the guerrilla bands operated to an increasing extent on their own initiative, and several of their leaders (including Paul Momo) were later disowned by Moumié.[20] Nevertheless, the rebels held sway in most of the south and centre of the territory, and one authority claims that towards the end of 1959 they 'roamed freely over two-thirds of the Bamiléké *region* and extended their attacks into the larger towns of the south, including Douala and Yaoundé with their large Bamiléké populations'.[21] This was in fact the Bamiléké revolt. It has its origins in the kind of over-crowding in the towns and dissatisfaction among urban Bamiléké which have been referred to earlier. But it was based even more on the overpopulation in the Bamiléké areas themselves, and on abuses of power by the chiefs. Under French rule chiefs had been appointed to administer local government affairs, sometimes without any claim to traditional office. Others—like Pierre Ninyim Kandem—had been excluded despite their rightful claims to a chieftainship. Opposition to actions of this kind was exploited by the rebels, but there was also growing resentment at the autocratic manner in which incumbent chiefs, kept in power by the administration, used their powers to operate land distribution, succession and marriage laws to their own advantage. Grievances also arose because of the tendency of the chiefs to rely on support from the administration rather than on the traditional councils which may have acted as a restraining influence on them under the customary system.

The upshot was that Ninyim Kandem became a leading UPC activist and the underground was able to use the strong ethnic ties and loyalties among dissatisfied urban Bamiléké to strengthen their organisation and spread it to the towns. The fact that the Bamiléké there were a displaced but dynamic minority gave them not only cohesion but a cause to fight for, outside the political arena when they were unable to do so within it.

The government set about ruthlessly crushing the Bamiléké revolt as it had done the rebellions which preceded it. This time it used not only French troops and special units of local citizenry, but it also imposed a strict curfew and control through roadblocks maintained by the *gendarmerie* over all movement of people and traffic between the towns. Special courts were set up to administer summary justice under military supervision. The continuation of the revolt until well after independence provided Ahidjo with a pretext for obtaining military aid from France, and enabled him to maintain a strong internal security and defence force long after it had been effectively crushed.

The UPC, however, continued to press abroad for some form of recognition. They were joined in January 1959 by Mbida, who belatedly found common cause with his former enemies as independence approached. In August, Mbida issued a statement with the Conakry exiles urging Ahidjo to call a round table conference in order to effect a reconciliation between government and opposition; he was supported in this by the governments of Ghana and Guinea, and in Cameroun it was taken up by the *rallié* UPC and

99

the *Démocrates*, as well as by Soppo Priso and others. It even led to the resignation of Ahidjo's Vice-Premier.[22] But Ahidjo himself took little notice of the Conakry appeals especially since they were coupled with demands for elections before independence. By October, with independence only a little more than two months away, he was more concerned with arranging the future constitution so as to legitimise the continued rule of the UC over Cameroun and his own power in the independent state which was shortly to come into existence. At the last session of ALCAM, in October, he introduced a package of measures designed to secure his position. This included a general amnesty for political offences which had been committed in the Bassa areas but not for those which could be attributed to the activities of the Bamiléké insurgents. It also made clear the absence of any intention to provide a constitution before independence, though a 42-man advisory committee was established to assist the government with the drafting of one for the new Republic and report back at a later date. And it provided for the exercise of legislative powers by decree, without reference to elective institutions, for a period of six months during which the new proposals were to be formulated. The debate on the last two measures provoked a major onslaught on Ahidjo in the Assembly by Soppo Priso and the *rallié* UPC, who accused him of acting illegally and of trying to create a dictatorship. The opposition was of no avail.[23] The measures were passed, and Cameroun became independent with no new constitution in force and with all power in the hands of the government.

When the constitution did emerge, in February 1960, it was strikingly similar in many respects to that of France under the Fifth Republic. It started with an affirmation (in the name of the people of Cameroun) of a number of fundamental rights and liberties; provided for a President to be elected indirectly by an electoral college comprising members of the legislature and various local elective officials, and for a national Assembly of 100 members. The Prime Minister was to be appointed by the President and was responsible to him, although he could be removed by a special vote of no confidence in the Assembly. The President, in addition to being Head of State and Head of the Army, was given power to declare a state of emergency after consultation with the President of the National Assembly and the Council of Ministers; once this was done, he could assume responsibility for governing the country. He also had the power to proclaim a state of 'urgency' in which he could exercise any powers conferred on him in the proclamation which established this form of rule.[24]

The constitution contained no reference to a set of secret agreements between France and the Cameroun government which had been signed in December 1959. These provided for cultural, diplomatic, fiscal, monetary and economic co-operation between the two countries, including both financial and military assistance by France to the Cameroun government.

On February 22, 1960, the constitution was submitted to a referendum. Soppo Priso and the *Démocrates* had earlier declared their opposition to it, proposing that a new constitution be drawn up by a constituent assembly. Other opposition came from the trade unions and from the Catholic hierarchy as well as from the unofficial UPC *ralliés* and the Bamiléké representatives in ALCAM. Despite the attempt by the underground UPC to organise a boycott of the polls, three-quarters of the electorate did vote, and the constitution was approved by 60 per cent of them; the bulk of support came from the north of the country, but there was a heavy adverse vote in nearly all southern areas.[25] The referendum was followed by an announcement that a general election would be held for the new National Assembly in April, and by the legalisation of the UPC so that it could put up candidates at the election. Moumié and the exiles did not return to take part in the campaign, but Matip led the *ralliés* who participated for the first time under the formal label of the UPC. All the other parties also ran candidates, and so did a number of independent groups.

About 69 per cent of the electorate voted for some 365 candidates. The result was a victory for Ahidjo's *Union Camérounaise*, which received 45 per cent of the votes but fifty-one of the hundred seats. The UPC obtained thirteen seats, though their five Bamiléké deputies left to join the newly formed grouping of Bamiléké members, the *Front Populaire pour l'Unité et la Paix* which then had eighteen members. The *Démocrates* under Mbida, who returned to fight the election in yet another change of line, obtained eleven seats, while Assalé's *Action Nationale* and Okala's *Socialistes* joined to form a ten-member group known as the *Progressistes*. There were two independents, Dr Marcel Beybey-Eyidi, and Doula Manga Bell who defeated Soppo Priso for the Wouri seat.[26]

In May, Ahidjo was the only candidate in the election for President, and received eighty-nine votes in the Assembly. He formed a coalition government which included representatives of the *Démocrates*, the *Progressistes* and the Bamiléké FPUP. Assalé was appointed the first Prime Minister, and Okala the Foreign Minister. There was still considerable opposition to Ahidjo and his government, in the Assembly as well as underground in the country and abroad. Over the next few years, Ahidjo was able to whittle away the parliamentary opposition; and he struck hard at the *maquis* in the country, using funds and troops made available by France. As his position became more powerful within the Republic, so the impact of the exiled UPC became less noticeable. With the death of Moumié at the end of 1960,* it lost its most forceful leader. Moumié was a medical doctor who had returned from study in France and Senegal to join the UPC leadership in 1955. A convinced Marxist, he was responsible for the ideological trend towards a left-wing policy, at least within the *Comité-Directeur* which he controlled in exile. An able organiser and debater, as well as a polemicist of great skill, he was also instrumental in establishing links between the UPC and the countries of the Soviet bloc and China, as well as with the African governments with more radical leanings. After his death, the UPC did not give up its attempts at dislodging Ahidjo, nor relinquish its propaganda campaign against the Cameroun government or its contacts with the underground. But without Moumié's drive and single-mindedness in the pursuit of the rebel cause, its influence dwindled as the number of its failures mounted. Even Ghana and the UAR, which had been among the UPC's staunchest supporters abroad, recognised and exchanged diplomats with the Ahidjo government shortly after independence. Russia, too, sent an official mission, and an official statement was made indicating that diplomatic relations would be entered into by the Cameroun government if the USSR ceased to give official support to the UPC.

Ahidjo had succeeded in outflanking the UPC by achieving independence, granting an amnesty and holding elections. Only one item remained—reunification with the British Cameroons. By the time he was installed as President, this was well on the way to being achieved as a result of decisions taken at the UN.

* Moumié was poisoned in Switzerland on November 3, 1960, allegedly by an agent of the French secret service.[27]

THE BRITISH CAMEROONS AND THE POLITICS OF REUNIFICATION

At the 1959 debate on Cameroun at the UN, it was not only the situation in the French trust territory that had been discussed. The Trusteeship Council and the General Assembly also considered the question of the future status of the British Cameroons. The matter to be decided was what was to become of the territories under British trusteeship once the Cameroun Republic became independent on January 1, 1960, and Nigeria achieved full sovereign statehood on October 1 of the same year. But, if the issue appeared straightforward, the solution was far from clear.

The Northern Cameroons had not been the scene of any public discussions on the subject. The UN Visiting Mission of 1958 had sought the advice of the Consultative Committee for the Northern Cameroons, which had been in existence since 1955. It consisted of six members chosen by local councils; the territory's members in the Northern Region and Federal Nigerian legislatures; the Lamido of Adamawa and the Emir of Dikwa—a total of 12 members. The Committee had taken the view that integration with Nigeria was the wish of the overwhelming majority of the people of the territory, and the Mission had accordingly suggested that it was not even necessary to hold a formal consultation on the question.[28] In the Southern Cameroons the political situation had changed since the Mission's visit, with the election of the KNDP to power under Foncha early in 1959. But Foncha's majority for dissociation from Nigeria had been small, and his own attitude to the choice between a further period of trusteeship, independence or federation with francophone Cameroun was by no means free from obscurity. The Mission recommended a plebiscite in the Southern Cameroons to decide the matter.

When the report of the Visiting Mission was debated by the Fourth Committee, the recommendations concerning the Northern Cameroons were not accepted. The Committee also paid no heed to the representations of Mallam Abdullai Dan Buram Jadda, who spoke on behalf of the territory and declared its desire to remain within Nigeria after he had rejected the other suggestions—that it become part of Cameroun or join with the Southern Cameroons alone to form a separate state. The UN decided instead that there should be a plebiscite in Northern Cameroons before the end of

November 1959. The question to be put to the northern electorate was whether it wished to remain part of the Northern Region of Nigeria or whether it wished to postpone a final decision on its future to a later (but unspecified) date.

The Southern Cameroons' position was considerably more complex. Only the One Kamerun Party, represented by Ndeh Ntumazah, advocated reunification with Cameroun completely and without qualification. Dr Endeley, on behalf of the KNC, supported the idea of a plebiscite to decide whether the territory should remain part of an independent Nigeria or federate with the Cameroun Republic. Foncha advocated federation with Cameroun, but he did not want the plebiscite question framed in the way Endeley had put it: he wished the electorate to decide only between the alternatives of continued association with Nigeria or complete severance from that country. Behind the differences between Endeley and Foncha lay tactical considerations. Endeley was confident that, given a choice between the violence-ridden Cameroun Republic with its authoritarian government and Nigeria, the electorate would never choose the first. Foncha wanted to avoid putting the question before the electorate in a way which would enable Endeley to take advantage of it by harping on the alien character of the francophone regime and its political record.

Faced with the inability of the Southern Cameroons' leaders to agree on a specific set of proposals, the UN accepted an interim solution. This provided (1) for separate plebiscites to be held in the Northern and Southern Cameroons; (2) a tentative date for the Southern Cameroons' plebiscite as somewhere between December 1959 and April 1960; and (3) postponement of the decision on the exact nature of the proposition to be put to the Southern Cameroons' voters until its next session, in September 1959.[29]

Between March and September 1959, the politicians in the Southern Cameroons tried to reach agreement, but they succeeded only in shifting their positions without greatly clarifying the issue. Nor did a conference of all the Southern Cameroons' political parties held in August at Mamfe come up with a solution; indeed, further variations on the existing attitudes came to light there. Kale, who had by now formed his own Kamerun United Party (KUP), urged independence for the British Cameroons as the sole objective of the plebiscite, while the KPP under Mbile continued to be the most outspokenly pro-Nigerian group. Endeley and Foncha produced subtle policy distinctions: the former suggested that the territory ought to see association with Nigeria as the first step towards the creation of yet a larger federation which should aim to include Ahidjo's Cameroun within its framework as well; while Foncha argued that independence from Nigeria was the *sine qua non* of reunification with Cameroun and ought to be achieved first.

All of these proposals were canvassed at the UN session in September, and the KPP came up with yet another formula in an attempt to reach a compromise. It suggested that those areas which voted for federation with Cameroun at the plebiscite should be permitted to join, while the others should be allowed to remain in Nigeria. This met with no success either. Foncha and Endeley then took refuge in a proposal to postpone the plebiscite until 1962 (with the territory continuing under trusteeship until then), and an agreement on separation from Nigeria which would come into operation from the date of that country's independence.[30] Although this suggestion met with general approval in the territory, it proved unacceptable to the anti-colonial bloc, particularly the radical 'Casablanca' group of African nations (i.e. Ghana, Guinea, Mali, Libya, Morocco, Tunisia, the UAR, Sudan and Liberia) who feared the 'balkanisation' of African states in general and were resistant to a suggestion which might strengthen the position of Britain in the short term and Nigeria in the long run. In the end, a further compromise was reached, which specified that a plebiscite should be held between September 30, 1960 and March 1961; provided that separation from Nigeria must be effected not later than October 1, 1960; and stated that the choice for the voters of the Southern Cameroons at the plebiscite should be between joining an independent Nigeria and an independent Cameroun.

The last point involved a major concession by Foncha, and one that was not much liked by his supporters at home. Jua, who was deputising for Foncha in his absence, cabled his disagreement; it is suggested that the KNDP even considered removing Foncha as leader.[31] Their objections were based on the political awkwardness of having to face the electorate with a choice between the familiar if disagreeable association with Nigeria and the unknown effects of joining with a country whose imported culture and language were alien, whose system of government was foreign, and whose recent grim political history was unsettling. Foncha was able to allay these fears, satisfied that his earlier formula for political success—grassfields ethnic support, anti-Ibo sentiment and the nationalist appeal of reunification—would win the plebiscite for him, and retain power for his party.

In the Northern Cameroons, the plebiscite was held on November 7, after a perfunctory campaign in which it was widely assumed that the decision would favour continuation as a part of Nigeria. This proved not to be the case. Despite the influence of the NPC and the Fulani rulers among the all-male voters, the result of the plebiscite was:

For integration with Nigeria 42,797
For continued trusteeship and postponement of the
decision 70,401

The outcome was attributed to a protest vote against the local government system of the territory, to the activities of the Nigerian opposition parties and to the support obtained by the newly-formed Northern Kamerun Democratic Party (NKDP) among non-Fulani groups, especially the Chamba. The result angered the Nigerian Prime Minister, who blamed it on the machinations of the British officials who had conducted the plebiscite. From the UN's point of view, it meant that the territory would have another plebiscite at the same time as the Southern Cameroons and on the same terms. In relation to the Southern Cameroons, it represented a victory for Foncha, and rather more of a setback for Endeley, who was no longer able to point to the northern attachment to Nigeria or continue to propagate his policy of support for an independent, or quasi-independent, British Cameroons, with anything like the degree of conviction he had earlier mustered.

An immediate effect of the plebiscite vote was the reform of the local administration system for the Northern Cameroons, mainly as a result of UN pressure for the separation of the territory from Nigeria and the introduction of a more representative form of local government. The territory was made a separate province of Northern Nigeria under trusteeship administration and was divided into four districts, which made it possible for minority ethnic groups to elect their own local authorities. The form of suffrage was still to be that which prevailed elsewhere in the

Northern Region, namely male adult suffrage, but the local authorities were to contain a majority of elected members. The purpose of the reforms seems to have been to meet the objections of the Northern Cameroons' people to the existing pattern of Nigerian government and thus to provide the basis for reversing the 1959 plebiscite decision when the second plebiscite was held.

There were also reforms for the Southern Cameroons, which came about as a result of the need to satisfy the UN resolution requiring a separate administration to be set up for the territory by the time of Nigeria's independence. Accordingly, a new constitution was devised and came into force as the Southern Cameroons Constitution Order in Council, on October 1, 1960. The new constitution did little to alter the governmental institutions of the territory. It retained the form and the size of the two legislative houses; re-established the form of responsible government, under a Prime Minister, which had existed since 1958; and kept the Commissioner as head of the administration, subordinate to the British government as the body accountable to the UN while the territory remained under trusteeship. But it did initiate a new and separate judiciary for the Southern Cameroons, give the territory control over police and other territorial affairs, and introduce a set of fundamental rights and liberties which were justiciable before the courts. In substance, these were virtually identical with those which had been applicable in the British Cameroons under the Nigerian constitution, and which were also contained in the new Nigerian constitution. The arrangements were interim in character, intended only to tide the territory over the period before a final decision was taken on its future at the plebiscite, rather than to provide it with the apparatus of an independent state.

The date for the plebiscites had been set at February 11, 1961, but the Southern Cameroons' parties were still jockeying for position until well after the new constitution came into force. Foncha had further discussions with Ahidjo late in 1959, and on four occasions in 1960. No agreement had been reached between them on the details of any future form of state after reunification, but this was probably as much to Foncha's advantage as to his disadvantage. He could not be held to a specific set of proposals, and was free to pursue his alternate—and conflicting, not to say confusing—policies of support for an independent Southern

Cameroons while advocating unification. In other words, he was able to lay more emphasis on anti-Nigerian aspects of his policy than on any positive elements concerning reunification, beyond an appeal to the desire to sweep away the 'artificial' boundaries of the period of alien rule.

Towards the end of 1960 the political situation began to crystallise. In November, the Cameroun National Assembly, at Ahidjo's urging, expressed unanimous approval of a resolution calling upon the government to set in motion measures to effect reunification. At the same time, Foncha finally accepted the fact that he would have to campaign on the definite alternative of reunification with Cameroun and not a period of intervening independence. He had tried to persuade the British government at a conference in London to agree to interpret a vote in favour of unification with Cameroun as one which implied a preparatory period of independence. The Colonial Secretary declined to do so, supporting Endeley's view that the choice must be clear at the plebiscite. The UN, shortly afterwards, authorised the production and distribution of an official leaflet setting out *The Two Alternatives* to the electorate.

Endeley did not alter his position greatly. He clearly believed that he could rest his arguments on the lack of information concerning the 'Cameroun alternative', and the unwholesome record of both government and opposition in the francophone state. It is by no means certain that he perceived the danger to his chances of success that arose from Foncha's grassfields support and the anti-Ibo and anti-Nigerian policies of the KNDP. To the extent that he was aware of the strength of these aspects of Foncha's programme, he attempted to counter their effect by falling back on the earlier KPP proposal that those electoral divisions supporting reunification should join with Cameroun and leave those favouring Nigeria to remain in the federation. He was apparently confident that his newly-formed Cameroon Peoples National Congress—the product of a merger in March of the KNC and the KPP—would hold the coastal areas around Victoria, and Mbile's stronghold of Kumba as well as substantial parts of the Nkambe division.

Foncha's programme, as it was put to the electorate, contained the well-rehearsed mixture of Ibophobia,[32] fear of a general swamping of the tiny Cameroons population within Nigeria, and the old grievances over previous Nigerian neglect of the territory. Endeley, on other other hand, took his stand on a preference for the known over the unknown; harped on ethnic and cultural differences between the Southern Cameroons and Cameroun; stressed the degree of French influence in the Cameroun Republic; and played on the calm and secure atmosphere within Nigeria as compared to the traumas of political life under Ahidjo's government. Johnson adds that Foncha was able to use his prestige as Prime Minister and that of the KNDP as the party in power.[33] The complexity of the proposals contained in *The Two Alternatives* also probably helped him among the large number of relatively unsophisticated members of the electorate.

In the Northern Cameroons, the same issues were canvassed, but in a different context. The NPC, after its two defeats in 1959, had already tried to make amends by introducing the reforms of July 1960. In the plebiscite campaign it was able to exert its influence as the governing party in the Northern Region and the party of the Federal Nigerian Prime Minister. The low literacy rate in the territory made for a far greater reliance on oral communication of the different party policies and meant that the superior organisation of the NPC could be used against the small, ethnically-limited parties campaigning for Cameroun.

The result of the plebiscite was a clear victory for Foncha's programme in the south, and a decision in favour of Nigeria in the north. The voting was as follows:

	For Nigeria	For Cameroun
Southern Cameroons	97,741	233,571
Northern Cameroons	146,296	97,659

Ahidjo's government registered a strong protest against the northern decision and claimed that it was the result of electoral malpractice, perfidy and undue influence on the part of the British who had administered the plebiscite. There was an attempt to set aside the decision, and to contest the validity of the plebiscite at the UN and at the International Court of Justice, but neither succeeded. Northern Nigeria reabsorbed the northern part of the British Cameroons.

In the south, the plebiscite showed that Foncha had the support of most of the voters in the Victoria, Mamfe, Bamenda and Wum divisions, with the electorate in Kumba and Nkambe much more evenly divided than had been expected. It remained only for the triumphant Foncha to begin serious negotiations for reunification.

6. The Character of Camerounian Federalism

THE ADOPTION OF THE FEDERAL CONSTITUTION

The plebiscites which took place in February 1961 did not establish the content of the constitution of what was to become the Federal Republic of Cameroun. They decided that a single, reunified Cameroun would come into being; that it would be composed of only two parts (the former Southern Cameroons trust territory and the Cameroun Republic); and that the new state would be a federation. No decision was made about the nature of that federation, and very little was put before the voters by way of specific information which would have enabled them to decide this question. It is not that the matter had been overlooked. Both President Ahidjo and Prime Minister Foncha had separately considered the question and formulated their own ideas. Foncha and the KNDP had a knowledge of federal institutions and a familiarity with the machinery of federal government which derived from their experience within Nigeria. Ahidjo was perhaps less conscious of the intricate workings of federations, but he had only recently been engaged in constructing a new system of government for the Cameroun Republic, and was ready with definite proposals which were designed to retain this, with suitable modifications, in the altered context made necessary by the projected federal framework. In the year preceding the plebiscites, discussions had taken place between Ahidjo and Foncha on no fewer than five occasions in an attempt to arrive at a satisfactory agreed basis for the constitution of the future state, but without success.[1]

The Southern Cameroons' leader favoured a loose federal structure. Proposals for a union along these lines were submitted to Ahidjo, but he rejected them as incompatible with the highly centralised constitution he advocated. There was, however, a clear and urgent need to provide the voters at the forthcoming plebiscites with some concrete indication of what was to be involved in the reunification of Cameroun, particularly since the implications of continuing as a part of Nigeria were already known. This need was met by the publication of two short communiqués, which outlined some of the attributes of the new system in general terms, and enabled the Administering Authority to present them to the electorate. Among other things, a list was provided which gave the minimum number of matters which would be the subject of federal control, and a pledge was given that the unified Cameroun would not form part of either the French Union or the Commonwealth. An overall impression was created that the federation would be a loose one.[2] As a result, the extent of the differences between the two approaches to federation was obscured, at least temporarily, and discussion of the details of the new constitution could be postponed until after the plebiscites had been held.

In the event, dicussion was further delayed, and only really began in earnest some five months later, when unification had been decided and was little more than three months away. Towards the end of June, the Southern Cameroons' political leaders met in Bamenda to draft a comprehensive set of proposals as a basis for negotiation with representatives of the Cameroun Republic. Even at this stage, for reasons which are not clear, the degree of divergence between the two opposed conceptions of federation was not known to the conferees at Bamenda, and they were not made aware of the specific alternative with which they would be confronted. The upshot was that the Bamenda proposals for a loose federation, devolution and the safeguarding of the powers of the states as against the central authorities,[3] were greatly at variance with the format that was to emanate from the Ahidjo government; little scope remained for negotiation and compromise between the two sets of views when the opportunity finally presented itself at Foumban early in July.

The Southern Cameroons' proposals included a ceremonial rather than an executive head of state; a bi-cameral federal legislature; a governor as head of each state, with a prime minister as head of a responsible government in each of the component states; separate state and federal citizenship; the allocation of a wide range of legislative powers to the states, particularly in the early stages after union, though with an acknowledgement that, at a later date, some of these could be transferred to the central government; the entrenchment of a large number of provisions by a procedure which would make amendment difficult, and dependent on the consent of a two-thirds majority in the legislature of each state, or on approval in separate state referenda; specific provision for the protection of fundamental human rights; the power of the President to veto legislation considered detrimental to the rights of states, or of minorities within them, as well as matters of more particular concern to the Southern Cameroons itself, such as the maintenance of the general legal system of the state, the retention of the House of Chiefs, and safeguards for the continued existence of the customary court system. Other suggestions included those for the placing of the federal capital in Douala, the introduction of a transitional period for the transfer of powers to the new federal institutions, and the election of the President by popular vote rather than by members of the legislature.[4]

By no means all of these proposals were dismissed at the Foumban conference, or at the subsequent discussions in Yaoundé which decided the final content of the federal constitution. Several were accepted as they stood (e.g. the last two, though the transitional period was shortened considerably; and the specific provisions concerning customary courts and the House of Chiefs[5]). Others produced modifications in some of the Ahidjo proposals so as to accommodate the wishes of the Southern Cameroons' representatives (e.g. the state legislatures were given control over primary education, and provision was made for the continuation of a separate police force in the western state). But others were simply rejected or ignored. And there can be little doubt that the more important proposals—those which reflected the underlying differences in principle, and were concerned with the structure of the new state, the organs of federal and state government, and their relation to one another—were overridden. They proved to be wholly incompatible with both the objects and the terms of the draft constitution submitted by Ahidjo to the conference.

The constitutional arrangements which were actually adopted for the Federal Republic will be discussed in greater detail later in this chapter. Here it is only necessary to stress the major considerations which lay behind them, and which made certain the rejection of the alternatives advanced by Foncha and the other delegates from Southern Cameroons. In his draft, Ahidjo sought, in the first place, to establish a clear preponderance of federal over state institutions. This was no doubt in line with his general preference for strong government. It also represented the continuation of the centralised administration which had been embodied in the system of government created by the 1960 constitution of the Cameroun Republic. Thus, any arrangement which sought to distribute power or share it between the central government and the states would have involved a detraction from the considerable authority and power already enjoyed by Ahidjo and the UC, which expected to retain control over the eastern state and acquire it in respect of the federation. In order to ensure this control, the Ahidjo proposals therefore contained provisions for a very wide range of matters which were to come within the federal sphere of competence under the new regime, and only a vague reference to the powers of the states. The draft also eliminated any form of control by state governments over federal institutions, though it did provide a means whereby the state representatives at the federal level might be able to exert some measure of restraint over the federal government.*

Secondly, the Ahidjo draft sought not merely to consolidate existing power at the centre, but to enhance the power of the federal executive in relation to all other organs of government, whether at the federal or state levels. Here the intention was to change the existing parliamentary pattern of government that had been allowed to develop in the Cameroun Republic into a presidential system. Thus, it would be possible to establish the pre-eminence of the President within the federal system, and, by making the state governments dependent on the President, secure continued control over the government of the eastern state.[6] These objectives were accomplished in different ways: by providing for extensive presidential powers in regard to governmental, judicial and civil service appointments; by including measures which gave the President power to act either exclusively, or concurrently with the legislature; by eliminating the institution of a responsible ministry at the federal level; and by emphasising the role of the President in the appointment and dismissal of the Prime Ministers and governments of the states.

What emerges from this consideration of the east Cameroun constitutional proposals is that Ahidjo and the UC had well-defined political objectives as well as a clear underlying concept of the

* See below, p. 116.

state which they were in the process of constructing. There was nothing like this degree of coherence in the suggestions which emanated from the Southern Cameroons parties,[7] and their problems were not lightened by their ignorance of both the principles and the details of the Ahidjo constitution. Added to these difficulties, there was the fact that, at Foumban, they were presented with a complete draft to contrast with their own outline measures, and that time was against them. Johnson points out that the need to formulate a set of agreed responses among themselves to the draft that confronted them took up nearly all of the five days set aside for discussion. The delegations from the two states only met one another for ninety-five minutes in formal session, the rest of the time being devoted to meetings of the Southern Cameroons' party representatives.[8]

It is not surprising that the overall framework of the federal constitution followed the model presented by Ahidjo. Most of the efforts of Foncha and his colleagues at Foumban and at the subsequent meeting in Yaoundé were devoted to obtaining alterations which would mitigate the full impact of Ahidjo's new (and in many ways highly original) centralised regime on the existing institutions of the future western state. They were not altogether unsuccessful in this respect, as already indicated, though the number of actual concessions made was small, and did not affect either the structure of the federation or significantly advance the powers of the west Cameroun government within it. The degree to which the west's institutions were to be preserved, and western influence felt within the federation, was made dependent not on the constitution but on the ability of the state and its leaders to participate in the political and administrative apparatus which emerged in the new federal state.

THE FEDERAL CONSTITUTION

A federal system is one which involves an institutionalised division of the powers of government between those organs of the state which exercise authority over the entire country and its inhabitants (the federal government) and those whose competence is limited to only a part of the country and its population (the state governments). There is no single formula for federal systems. Their precise character will depend on the manner in which these powers are distributed, and the relative importance accorded to the federal and the state governments. A degree of confusion arises over the distinction between federal and confederal arrangements. In a strict sense, the latter do not exist as a separate category of constitutions. But, where a constitution emphasises the component states to the detriment of the federal government, a constitution will be said to exhibit confederal characteristics.

Many of the noteworthy features of the Cameroun federal constitution arise in relation to the distribution of power between the federal government at the centre and the federated states of East and West Cameroun.[9] Because the former is so markedly dominant within the system, it will be examined first, but in the process of outlining the features of the federal institutions mention will also be made of other significant constitutional arrangements which have been framed to meet the particular demands of the Cameroun political and social system.

The Federal Government

Article 4 of the constitution defines the federal authority as inhering in the President and the Federal National Assembly. It is they who exercise, between them, the powers enumerated in the constitution. The precise powers of the federated states are not defined. The states are free to act in regard to matters not specified as falling within the competence of either of the two federal authorities. They are also permitted to deal with certain specified matters where the federal authorities do not choose to do so.[10]

The Federal National Assembly

In framing the constitution, the proposal for a bi-cameral legislature was rejected, and a unicameral system was adopted. The choice was justified on the grounds of economy and efficiency.[11] But it is doubtful whether these were the only reasons for turning down the two-chamber system. The functions of a second legislative chamber are normally to provide for further representation of states at the centre—often on an equal rather than a proportionate basis—and for further debate and an opportunity for reconsideration of legislation. The Ahidjo government representatives at Foumban may thus have seen the proposal as a threat to the centralised character of the constitution as well as a means of inhibiting the federal government.

The federal National Assembly comprises fifty members, elected by direct, universal suffrage in a secret ballot.[12] The first National Assembly was not, however, constituted in this way; an interim arrangement permitted the members for each federated state to be selected by the legislatures of each state, a device which gave the dominant party in each sector sole representation in the federal Assembly. The first election for this body was held in 1964. The constitution specified the life of the Assembly as five years, but the election scheduled for 1969 was postponed for fifteen months to make its term co-extensive with those of the President and Vice-President.

Representation of the federated states in the federal Assembly is proportionate to the population of each state, and each member is to represent 80,000 citizens. On the basis of the figures given in the constitution, there are fifty seats in the Assembly, forty of which represent East Cameroun and ten West Cameroun. Political parties and groups are permitted by the constitution to participate in elections, and they did so in 1964 on the basis of a single list of candidates for each of the electoral districts and not in respect of single-member constituencies.[13] In the light of subsequent developments leading to the formation of a single national party,[14] this provision has become redundant, but it has not been deleted from the constitution.

Both the number and the duration of the Assembly's sessions are limited by the constitution: it must meet at least twice a year for sessions which may not exceed thirty days, although it may also be convened for an extraordinary session of not more than fifteen days by request of the President or two-thirds of its members. Legislation passed by the Assembly must normally receive the assent of the President within fifteen days, but it may become law without his assent in certain circumstances.

An important limitation on the powers of the Assembly is contained in Article 18 of the constitution, which deals with the right to delay legislation by a 'second reading'. This is a feature unique to Cameroun, and also represents one of the few respects in which the constitution envisages curtailment of the powers of a central authority through the actions of state representatives. It creates a procedure whereby the President may of his own accord or at the request of the Prime Minister of either federated state request a bill to be read a second time. At the second reading, the bill must receive the approval of a majority of the members of the National Assembly from each federated state.

Much has been claimed for this provision, though it has not been used to date. It has been described as introducing the notion of a 'concurrent majority' and as an indication of the 'confederal nature' of the constitution, as well as being 'the only precise and specific check and balance' between the federated states at a central level.[15] The basis for such claims is the fact that it is possible, on a second reading, for as few as five members of the Assembly from West Cameroun (or twenty from the eastern state) to prevent the passage of legislation. This is seen as a major concession to the protection of both state and minority interests.

The extent of the concession is, however, rather less than has been claimed for it, as a closer examination of the provision (and of the political context in which it operates) shows. With the advent of a single party for both East and West Cameroun, it is clear that the likelihood of a dissident majority within either of the state delegations is remote. But, more important from a constitutional point of view, is the extent to which the President is given control over the procedure for the second reading. It is noteworthy, in the first place, that the power to request a second reading which is given to the Prime Ministers of the federated states is matched by a similar opportunity which is given to the President himself. Secondly, though, it would seem that the President is in a far stronger position in this regard than the Prime Ministers. The test of Article 18 states that the second reading *may* be requested by the President 'either of his own motion or at the request of either of the Prime Ministers of the Federated States'.[16] In other words, the President's decision to ask for a second reading rests entirely on his discretion, and he is not obliged to act on a request for one by either of the Prime Ministers.

There is a much more explicit limitation on the powers of the legislature in respect of *amendments to the constitution*.[17] Here, again, a procedure is prescribed which is very similar to that involved in the second reading. The President and members of the Assembly may propose amendments, but both are subject to restrictions. In the case of members, a constitutional amendment may only be proposed if the proposal bears the signatures of one-third of the total membership of the Assembly, that is, supported by at least seventeen members.[18] This means that no such

117

amendment could emanate from West Cameroun representatives alone; they would need at least seven East Camerounian supporters for an amendment even to be considered. In the case of the President, however, the only requirement is that, before proposing an amendment, he must have consulted the 'Prime Ministers of the Federated States'. The wording here suggests that it is necessary for both Prime Ministers to be consulted; but it is only consultation that is required, and the provision does not oblige the President to act on their advice or with their prior consent.

Once introduced (whether by the President or by members) an amendment to the constitution may be passed by a simple majority of the National Assembly, but that majority must consist of a majority of the representatives of each federated state.[19] The minimum number of votes which is required for a constitutional amendment is therefore twenty-seven (twenty-one from East Cameroun and six from West Cameroun).

There is no doubt that the latter provision contains the more significant of the two forms in which the federated states are able to exercise restraint over the central government, if only because it applies equally to measures proposed by the President and those advanced by members of the National Assembly. It represents, in fact, the only case in which the wish of the President may be frustrated by the votes of a minority amounting to no more than ten per cent of the membership of the legislature (i.e. five deputies from West Cameroun).

One other limitation applies to all constitution amendments, whatever their source. There is an absolute prohibition on the passage of any amendment which would 'tend to impair the unity and integrity of the federation'[20]—an exceedingly vague phrase, but one which, no doubt, reflected an attempt to prevent any move towards secession by either state.

The *powers of the legislature* are dealt with in the constitution, but it is not clear to what extent the federal National Assembly is confined to dealing with only a limited number of topics. Articles 5 and 6 of the constitution provide a long list of matters which fall within the federal area of competence. Article 6 makes it clear that although the federated states may legislate in regard to some of the subjects, their power to do so only lasts so long as the federal authorities do not exercise any of these functions.[21] This means that, although in theory the states have wide residuary powers to legislate on all matters which are not set out in the constitution, they are in fact excluded from a very great number of areas absolutely by Article 5 of the constitution; and they can, at any time, be superseded in respect of the substantial number of matters named in the next Article if there is a decision by the federal government to assume power over any of them. Thus the dominant position of the federal authorities, and the dependent position of the state governments and legislatures, is established in the constitution.

But it is the federal authorities as a whole—the legislature and the President—which enjoy this superior position. The role of the legislature within the framework of federal power is both limited and diluted by the constitution. It is limited to the extent that specific powers are conferred on the President, and these will be indicated more fully presently. It is diluted to the extent that the President is able to exercise powers concurrently with the legislature on those subjects which are not reserved by the constitution exclusively for the attention of the National Assembly. It is not easy to tell exactly where the dividing line is drawn, though an examination of the two lists shows that there is a considerable number of matters which are not said to be within the sole province of the legislature.

Federal Subjects [22]	*Reserved for Legislature* [23]
Nationality	Fundamental rights and duties of the citizen:
Status of Aliens	
Regulations concerning conflict of laws	protection of the freedom of the individual; public liberties; labour and trade union legislation; the duties and obligations of the citizen in respect of national defence
National Defence	
Foreign Affairs	
The internal and external security of the Federal State, Immigration and Emigration	The law of persons and property: the law of personal and real property; the law of civil and commercial obligations
Development planning, guidance of the economy, statistics, the control and organisation of credit, external economic relations (including trade agreements)	Political, administrative and judicial organisation with respect to: the electoral system of the Federal Assembly; the general rules relating to the organisation of national defence; the definition of crimes and offences not triable summarily, and the establishment
The monetary system, the preparation of the Federal Budget and the establishment of taxes and revenues of all kinds to meet federal expenditure	

Federal Subjects[22]	*Reserved for Legislature*[23]

Higher education and scientific research

Information services and radio

Foreign technical and financial assistance

Postal services and telecommunications

Aviation and meteorology, mining and geological research, and the geographical survey of the national territory

Regulations governing the Federal Civil Service and Judiciary

The organisation and functioning of the Federal Court of Justice

The territorial boundaries of the federated states

Public liberties*

The law of persons and property*

The law of obligations and contracts in civil and commercial matters*

Judicial organisation, including the rules of procedure and jurisdiction of all courts (with the exception of the Customary Courts of West Cameroun, save as regards appeals from the decisions of such courts)*

Criminal law*

Transport of federal concern (roads, railways, rivers, maritime and air transport) and ports*

Prison administration*

Legislation relating to state lands*

Public health*

Secondary and technical education*

Administrative organisation*

Weights and measures*

of penalties of any kind, criminal procedure, civil procedure, means of enforcement, amnesty and the creation of new classes of courts

The following questions of finance and public property:

the system of currency; the Federal Budget; the imposition, assessment and rates of federal taxes and dues of all kinds; legislation relating to public property

The aims of economic and social policy within the framework of the laws relating to such policy

The educational system.

The language used in these provisions is obscure, and not easy to interpret. Any attempt at a clear distinction between the areas of

* Denotes matters specified in Article 6 of the constitution, which may be dealt with by state authorities until such time as the federal authorities assume powers in respect of them.

competence of the two federal authorities is made even more difficult by the draftsman's use of different terminology in the constitution to define the general powers and those conferred on the National Assembly, even where the subject matter is similar (e.g. 'secondary and technical educational' and 'higher education and scientific research' appear in the first list, but they are not the same as 'the educational system' which appears in the second). Again, 'currency' and 'the monetary system' are not identical. These are but two instances of confusing language, which make it almost impossible to determine where the line is to be drawn between the powers of the two authorities.

It should also be noted that in relation to two of the topics given over to the exclusive competence of the legislature—political, administrative and judicial organisation; and finance and public property—the jurisdiction of the National Assembly is narrowly confined to the subjects specified under each heading. Similar topics which are listed as being within the competence of all federal authorities are not so constricted, and could be expanded beyond the extent of the matters mentioned in the other list.

Quite apart from these discrepancies and limitations, it is clear that there are several important subjects that can be dealt with outside the legislature. Thus foreign affairs, immigration and emigration, foreign aid, control over the press and the radio, the appointment of civil service and judicial officers, and a whole range of economic activities and services can be regulated by executive acts and measures in which the legislature may have no say.

What emerges, then, is that the President may not legislate within the areas set aside as the exclusive prerogative of the National Assembly by Article 24, and that, because of the broad language used in that provision, the Assembly's powers may be more extensive than appears at first glance. But it is difficult to agree with Dr Enonchong's conclusion that 'it is doubtful whether the President of the Republic can validly legislate on any subject under Articles 5 and 6 without the consent of the federal legislature'.[24] If anything, the language and the spirit of the constitution seem more to uphold Professor Gonidec's view that 'for those matters not enumerated [in Article 24] the President has his own legislative powers, the only limitation being respect for the constitution, international conventions and the powers [*compétences*] of the federated states'.[25]

The Federal President

Shortly after the enactment of the federal constitution, Le Vine wrote that it had created 'a hybrid President who combines the attributes of a British-style Governor-General, a Fifth Republic President, and an American chief executive. This new type of presidency does not appear to have parallels in present or past constitutional practice'. While this description rightly emphasises the originality and resourcefulness of Ahidjo and those who framed the constitution, it overlooks the definite preference expressed by Ahidjo and maintained at Foumban for a powerful executive rather than a ceremonial head of state. There is, in fact, very little about the Camerounian presidency which resembles the rather nominal powers enjoyed by a Governor-General in an independent Commonwealth country. Enonchong is almost certainly nearer to the mark when he attributes the character of the office to the joint influence of the American presidency and the wide powers enjoyed by General de Gaulle under the 1958 French constitution.[27] This combination points to both the popular support enjoyed by an elective president, and the vesting of preponderant authority in the holder of that office.

Although the interim arrangements for the application of the constitution made it possible for Ahidjo and Foncha to assume office as President and Vice-President immediately (because they were President of the Cameroun Republic and Prime Minister of Southern Cameroons respectively), both offices are elective.

The President and the Vice-President are elected for five-year terms and may be re-elected. Elections, in which the nation as a whole voted as a single constituency, were in fact held for the first time in 1965, and took place again in 1970. The constitution makes it clear that candidates for both offices must be elected on a single list—that is, candidates for both offices must run together— but they may not be natives of the same state.[28]

The fact that the President is elected by direct popular vote has enabled Ahidjo to lay emphasis on the role of his office as a symbol of the unity of the nation, and to stress the reciprocal bond created between the President and the people through the ballot box.[29] It has, by the same token, given the President a source of legitimacy which equals that of the National Assembly. The constitutional requirement that the President and the Vice-President must come from different states reflects one of the 'federal' aspects of the constitution. It ensures that each of the federated states participates in the executive branch of the federal government. But, at the same time, it has secured Ahidjo's position as President, and it has made it certain that, for the foreseeable future, the dominant role in government will be accorded to a President from East Cameroun.

A constitutional attempt to secure the separation of office at the federal level from other positions of power—at the state or national levels—has not proved successful. While the constitution laid down the rule that both the Presidency and the Vice-Presidency were 'incompatible with other office', it also recognised right from the start that Foncha was entitled to continue as Prime Minister of West Cameroun.[30] He had relinquished the latter office at the time of the first Vice-Presidential election and the provision was thus in force throughout the next five years, but it was allowed to lapse again in 1970, when S. T. Muna was re-appointed Prime Minister of the western state after he had been elected federal Vice-President.

The evident desire of each of the successive Vice-Presidents to retain influence at the state level is an indication of the relative insignificance of the federal office. The subordinate position of the Vice-President is made very clear by the constitution. Like the Vice-President of the United States, he has considerable *potential* power—he succeeds to the presidency automatically when that office becomes vacant for whatever reason, although he may only remain in office until a new President is elected not more than fifty days later. He is not given any specific powers of his own. For the rest, the constitution merely provides that the President shall be assisted by the Vice-President.

There is no such reticence over the position of the President. Mention has already been made of the authority he derives from direct election, and it is clear that he enjoys considerable power in regard to legislation as well. Although the nature of the division of legislative responsibilities between the Assembly and the executive has already been discussed, it is worth elaborating briefly on the extent of the President's powers here, before going on to deal with other aspects of his office.

The President may initiate bills in the legislature on subjects which are within the spheres specifically reserved for the Assembly in terms of Article 24, and receive priority treatment for the measures he introduces; he may also inhibit the passage of legislation by invoking the 'second reading' procedure. But, more important perhaps than either of these is his power to legislate directly on matters which are not clearly reserved for the National Assembly. As a result, in great areas of federal authority he may promulgate decrees and other enactments which have the full force of law. These may take the form of *décrets* or *arrêtés*. There does not appear to be a clear distinction between the two, both of which are administrative in origin, as distinct from *lois*, which emanate from the legislature. In general, *décrets* are presidential, while *arrêtés* are ministerial (along with *décisions* and *ordinances*). Both are subject to review by the courts.[31]

One incidental result of these presidential powers is that, within the area of his legislative as well as his executive competence, the President can determine when the government of a federated state must cease to exercise responsibility over any matter which it controls.[32] The President can not only assume direct authority for legislating in any appropriate field, but may also take over the administration of any state department which operates within the federal area.[33] This is by no means the only way in which the President, as distinct even from the other federal authorities, has a decisive influence, if not actual control, over the affairs of the states. The extent of this control may be seen in the fact that it is the President who appoints the Prime Ministers and the members of the governments (the Secretaries of State for the various departments) of each state. In the case of the Prime Ministers, he does so on his own initiative.[34] The requirement that the Prime Ministers must be confirmed in office by the state legislatures is obviously of reduced significance in a single party state; the President's position is, if anything, made stronger by his power to dissolve a state legislature if it is in 'persistent discord' with its government.[35] In the case of the Secretaries of State, appointments are made on the proposal of the appropriate Prime Minister, but at least one authority takes the view that he may reject nominations[36] and there do not appear to be any conventions limiting the President's powers in this respect (as is the case in Commonwealth constitutional practice).

It should be noticed, too, that no bill passed by a federated state may become law unless it is promulgated by the President, who may delay its enforcement by referring it back to the state legislature or to the Federal Court for a ruling.

In the executive sphere, the President is virtually supreme, reflecting most clearly his position as head of state as well as head of government and head of the army. As one of the two repositories of federal authority—the other being the National Assembly—he is responsible for the conduct of the affairs of the Federal Republic, and is not accountable to the legislature for his actions. Apart from his purely formal functions—such as representing the federation in all public activities or accrediting foreign representatives—he exercises the prerogative of clemency, and has extensive treaty-making powers. It is he alone who may conclude such treaties, which only need ratification if they concern the matters defined as falling within the province of the National Assembly by Article 24.[37] Given the wide range of matters that falls outside this area, this provision considerably increases the capacity of the President to act of his own accord, without any need to consult either the federal legislature or the authorities of either of the federated states. So long as he does not step beyond the limits of federal competence[38] in making any such treaty, his actions require no prior authorisation or subsequent approval.

In his capacity as chief executive, the President not only carries out the terms of legislation enacted by the National Assembly, but is also empowered to 'establish, organise and direct' all administrative services which are necessary for this task (and others that may arise as a result of actions of the state governments). He may make all appointments to the federal civil service and military posts. He is also given specific authority to 'ensure the internal and external security of the federal republic'; the National Assembly's role in such matters is much more restricted.[39]

In addition to this compendium of power and control over the affairs of the nation, the President is accorded plenary powers to deal with a State of Emergency or a State of Siege (a state of Special Emergency), in terms of Article 15 of the constitution, a provision which is derived from a very similar article in the constitution of the French Fifth Republic. There is no restriction on the President's power to declare a state of emergency; the only limitation on his right to act is that he must be able to cite a federal law as the source of any decree which he issues.[40] Where a State of Siege has been declared, the National Assembly must remain in session throughout its duration. The measure was clearly designed to enable the President to move swiftly, and outside the ordinary constitutional apparatus, in dealing with the UPC insurrection and its aftermath. In this way, Ahidjo was, for instance, able to create a series of military courts in 1961, with powers to conduct trials arising from the rebellion, outside the framework of the ordinary courts and beyond the control of the federal judicial structure. Writing in 1967, Enonchong pointed out that these courts were still in existence, though he questioned their authority in the absence of a continued state of emergency.

A state of Special Emergency (*état d'exception*) may only be declared by the President when certain specified, though very broadly defined, situations are deemed to exist—where serious peril threatens the 'integrity of the national territory, or of the life, independence or institutions of the nation'. Before making the declaration, the President must consult (but need not have the consent of) the Prime Ministers of the federated states. Once a state of special emergency is declared, the President may take all such measures as he may deem necessary, without any limitation, except that he must inform 'the nation' by means of a 'message'. The constitution provides that in a state of special emergency the National Assembly automatically remains convened, but, in view of the wide powers conferred on the President, it is difficult to see what it could do to restrain him in the circumstances.

It is not surprising, therefore, that the constitution has been judged in terms of its contribution to 'presidentialism' rather more than for its efforts at federalism. An American lawyer undoubtedly exaggerated this tendency when he dismissed the constitution as adding just 'another irresponsible monocephalous executive to the ranks of African officialdom'.[41] But the phrase does focus attention on several significant characteristics of the Cameroun constitution; the President's claim to sovereignty on a basis which is at least equal to that of the National Assembly, his dominance over the Vice-President, and the fact that he cannot be called upon to account for a large measure of his acts to the legislature or any other authority, except the electorate every five years. A somewhat less severe, but equally pointed assessment of the Camerounian presidency is contained in

Gonidec's judgement that 'in reality, the constitution and legislation construct a constitutional regime characterised by a tendency to reinforce the position of the chief executive, that is to say the tendency towards a monocracy (*la monocratie*)'.[42]

It is, nevertheless, only fair to point out that the President is, in the last resort, theoretically subject to restraint and even removal in terms of the constitution, which provides a procedure for impeachment for acts of high treason done in the course of his duties. It goes without saying that the procedure has not been used—even in the case of alleged dereliction of duties on a lesser scale by the Vice-President or Ministers. It is, in any event, hedged by a requirement that a majority vote in the National Assembly must present the petition for impeachment to a Federal High Court especially set up to deal with these cases.[43]

The Federal Ministry

The actual administration of the day-to-day affairs of government is supervised by Ministers, who, together, constitute the federal government. In line with the decision to break with the constitutional tradition of both the Cameroun Republic and the Southern Cameroons by creating an executive presidency, parliamentary responsibility for or by the Ministers was discarded under the federal constitution.

The President is obliged to appoint Ministers and deputy-Ministers from each of the federated states. No mention is made of the number to be appointed, in absolute terms or from each of the states, and nothing is said about the ministries which they are to run. The President's complete discretion to appoint whomever he chooses is specifically stated, and in like manner it is made clear that Ministers are responsible to him alone and may be dismissed at his discretion.[44] No list of ministries is given in the constitution, and there is no indication of the sort of responsibilities which Ministers are to discharge. There was clearly a calculated decision, as well, to omit any reference to a cabinet, or to any degree of joint ministerial responsibility for government decisions— either in their relationship with the President or with the National Assembly.

In fact, references to the Ministers in the constitution are as cryptic as they are few. Apart from giving them a right of access to the National Assembly in order to take part in debates, and providing that 'the government' must furnish information to that body on request, Ministers are made liable to impeachment proceedings for 'conspiracy against the security of the state', and the constitution takes steps to ensure their independence from any outside allegiance. They are debarred from holding any elective office in a federated state, but not from being elected to the federal National Assembly itself. They are also debarred from occupying any 'post as national representative of a trade or professional association'. Furthermore, their position as Ministers is also declared to be 'incompatible with . . . any public employment or gainful activity' (a provision which must be very nearly completely unenforceable, but which is doubtless there to signal both the desirability of their being independent of any special interest groups and their dependence upon the President).[45]

The effect of these articles of the constitution is to reduce the ministry to an administrative apparatus and to limit its political significance. Gonidec takes the view that the Ministers are little more than clerks (*commis*), 'auxiliaries, administrative heads entirely dependent on the chief of state'. This is less than just in view of their very real administrative authority and their extensive activities in carrying out the detailed aspects of policy at a departmental level, as well as their prestige in the country as a whole; but it does accurately represent their subordinate place in the structure of government and the state, as well as their relative political impotence. These characteristics are emphasised from time to time by the President's use of his discretionary powers to change the composition of the ministry (by removing Ministers from office entirely, by shifting them from one department to another, or by promoting individuals from the post of deputy-Minister to a full ministerial appointment).

The use of presidential power in this way, and the patent control exercised by Ahidjo over participation in the government on a party basis (while a multiple party system existed) or from the different federated states was a source of dissatisfaction.[46] West Camerounians especially objected to both the political and constitutional dilution of the ministry's role, thus harking back to their Bamenda and Foumban proposals for a responsible government of the kind that existed before federation. Among other things, they demanded in 1964 that the constitution should be revised so as to provide that all government policy decisions be taken in a Council of Ministers.[47]

Although the President and his East Camerounian supporters rejected the specific request for the creation of a cabinet, and no constitutional revision took place, some concession was made to the notion of ministerial collegiality in a decree promulgated by the President in September 1964. This made provision for the convening of meetings of Ministers to look at and discuss bills and decrees of general interest; but its objects are the attainment of greater efficiency and of a measure of co-ordination between government departments, not the discussion of government policy or an enhancement of the Ministers' collective position in relation to the President or the legislature. In any event, it is the President's decision which results in a meeting of the Ministers, and he must convene the gathering. According to Johnson, such meetings occur infrequently.[48]

The number of Ministers has varied, and administrative responsibility for the direction of government departments is shared between them and the offices of the President and the Vice-President. Each ministry—and each department, if more than one is controlled by a single Minister—has a central administrative core of officials (sometimes referred to as its cabinet). As civil servants, these officials are responsible to the Minister for the work of a department and its servants throughout the country.

In 1970, there were ten Ministers in the government, each with responsibility for one of the following departments or group of departments: Justice; Foreign Affairs; Finance; Transport; Postal and Telecommunications; Planning and Development; Education, Youth and Culture; the Armed Forces; Labour and Social Welfare; Commerce and Industry; and Information and Tourism. In addition, there was one Minister of State (a designation which normally indicates a lower rank than that of a Minister) in charge of Federal Territorial Administration, and three deputy-Ministers: one each attached to the Ministries of Justice and Education, Youth and Culture, and a third whose function as deputy-Minister Delegate to the Federal Public Service meant that his responsibility was within the departmental apparatus controlled by the presidency. Two Ministers and two deputy-Ministers came from West Cameroun.

In addition to their purely administrative duties—in respect of which they may issue subordinate legislation known as *ordinances*, *arrêtés* and *décisions*—Ministers must liaise with the legislature, and account for the proper expenditure of the budgetary allocations for their departments. Decrees are, however, only promulgated by the President, and, even where they relate to an area within the competence of a ministry, they do not need to bear the signature of the appropriate Minister.[49] In other words, the President may act within the area nominally under the direction of a Minister without the latter's approval or assistance.

No description of the executive in Cameroun would be complete without further emphasis on the role of the presidency in the administration of government departments. An examination of the way in which the government functions reveals that in this sphere too the President is pre-eminent. In addition to his control over the appointment and dismissal of Ministers, the president directs an administrative apparatus of his own, which is composed of a large number of departments and services, whose total weight probably equals that of all the ministries combined. What is more, several of the operations controlled directly from the presidency operate on parallel lines to those which come under the aegis of particular ministries. The effect is to reinforce the predominance of the President in the executive sphere. At the same time, it ensures that no substantial accumulation of power accrues to any one Minister. More important still, it means that in respect of certain important ministries—which deal with security services, the army, the economy and the civil service—power is diffused, and responsibility shared with (if not often in practice subordinated to) the presidency.

Authority radiates from the presidency outwards, and it is certainly not possible for any Minister to challenge the power of the President in any of these essential fields. In addition to the departments he controls through the Minister of State for Federal Territorial Administration (the apex of the administrative system which operates in the federated states as well) and the deputy-Minister Delegate for the Federal Public Service, the presidency controls officials responsible for the following: (1) a Secretariat-General, which contains a Chancellery and personnel concerned with legislation and regulations; (2) a Civil Cabinet (or directorate), with technical advisers who deal with administrative and legislative matters, judicial affairs and economic affairs respectively;

130

(3) the Directorate of the National Archives; (4) a Military Cabinet (or directorate). Services attached to the presidency include: (5) a general directorate for the Control of the State; (6) the directorate of the Federal Security Police; and (7) a Treasury and economic complex, which includes supervision of statistical services relating to economics and finance, production, transport, social statistics as well as accounting and the analysis and synthesis of economic data.

The Vice-President was, in the same way, given additional responsibility for the services connected with the federal Ministry of Health until 1970, though this seems rather to be a means of providing him with some measure of real participation in the administration than an instance of the further accumulation of powers by the chief of state at the expense of the federal ministry.

The Federal Judiciary

The constitution describes the federal President as the 'guardian (*garant*) of the independence of the judicial authority' and gives him the power to appoint judges in the federated states.[50] It makes no direct reference to federal judges, but, since the Federal Court of Justice is composed of judges from the courts of the states, who are appointed by the President, his responsibility for the composition of the federal court is ensured in this way. In making judicial appointments, the President is to be assisted by the Federal Judicial Council (*Conseil Fédérale pour la Magistrature*), which is composed of representatives of the National Assembly, the Ministry of Justice, judges and expert nominees. Representation from both federated states in the council is guaranteed. In theory, there is no obligation on the President to follow the advice of the council, but in practice he has done so.

The original conception of the role of the federal court was restricted to dealing with constitutional matters and to those which involved federal-state conflicts or the breach of federal law. Caution was obviously needed, even at a technical legal level, in defining the scope of the court's powers since the letter and the spirit of the constitution were designed to preserve the existing systems of law in the two federated states. East Cameroun inherited the French system of courts and codes, while West Cameroun retained the system based on the English common law as it had been received and applied in Nigeria. The limits of

131

federal judicial authority have, however, been extended gradually, as attempts have been made to construct a single legal system, and as the relationship of state to federal law has become clearer. Nevertheless, a substantial and important body of law still falls outside the jurisdiction of the federal courts and remains the responsibility of the courts operating at state level. In addition, there are military tribunals which are charged with trying many crimes involving violence[51] and these, it has already been pointed out, come directly under the control of the President.

In terms of the constitution, the President must refer to the federal court any federal or state law which he considers to be in conflict with the constitution and, in the case of state laws, any law which appears to him to violate a federal law. The federal court may, in addition, be called upon to decide whether the National Assembly has correctly assumed power to deal with a particular topic. It may do so either at the request of the president of the National Assembly or of the President of the Republic.[52]

Since one of its principal functions is to resolve potential conflicts between the federal authorities and the states, and between the federated states themselves, the federal court is specifically empowered by the constitution to deal with cases which involve conflicts of jurisdiction between the highest courts in the states, or those which entail suits between governments of the two states, or between a state government and the federal government. In other words, it can deal with disputes between any two of the three governments in the federation, and it can exercise a measure of control over the legislatures at the federal or state level, where it is called upon to do so by the federal authorities.

None of these provisions gives much scope to the court to entertain suits brought by individual citizens, though it has been argued that the 'conflict-resolving' rule, which was intended to deal with states and their governments, could be invoked in order to 'avoid a possible denial of justice which is potential in the built-in conflicts within the Cameroon dual system'.[53]

As a result of changes in the jurisdiction of the courts which were introduced in 1965, however, the federal court acts as an appeal court for an important category of cases which arise at the state level. These relate to any complaint against the government of a federated state or against the federal government, as well as against any local authority or public corporation. Cases of this kind involve not only allegations that a particular act is illegal because it was not passed or undertaken in the correct manner or with the proper authority, but also *any* case relating to a claim for damages or in terms of a contract against an official of any of the governments or authorities mentioned, or which involve state land. In the first place, these cases are heard by local benches of the federal court in a federated state, and an appeal lies from their decision to the federal court.[54]

The federal court also has the right to hear appeals on matters relating to the constitution or to federal law. Here, it acts as a court of appeal from the Supreme Court of either federated state— the highest courts in the judicial hierarchy of the states—but it is empowered only to settle points of law which may have arisen there.[55] The fact that there has, since 1967, been a single federal criminal code for the entire country means that the authority of the federal court on appeal has automatically been extended to cover a wide range of matters which were formerly mainly within the jurisdiction of the separate legal systems of the states.

The Federal Court of Justice has a full bench, which sits at the federal level, and local benches which operate at state level. The full bench comprises five members, and an attempt is made to ensure that the judiciary from both the federated states is represented. The President of the court is the President of the East Cameroun Supreme Court, and two other (puisne) judges must also come from that court. The West Cameroun participation includes the Chief Justice of West Cameroun and one judge of the Supreme Court of the western state. Each of the two Supreme Courts also provides a list of three alternates, who may sit when any of the judges from its state is incapacitated. Where the President is unable to sit, his place is automatically taken by the Chief Justice of West Cameroun, and not by one of the other judges from East Cameroun.

The local bench of the federal court for each state is presided over by one of the actual or alternate members of the full bench from the state concerned, and may also consist of additional judges appointed specially to staff these courts.

One problem surrounds the operation of the Federal Court of Justice which is perhaps endemic in the nature of the Cameroun federal system. Despite the growth of a substantial body of federal law, there is still a good deal of uncertainty about what legal system the court will use when it gives judgement in any case before it. There is no federal law on this subject to prescribe the basis, or even the legal system in general terms, on which the court can (or should) reach its conclusions. Apparently, the problem of specifying a single, all-embracing set of principles which can govern judicial decisions in a mixed legal system has been left in abeyance. It is within the powers of the National Assembly to lay these down, just as it has dealt with the question of the composition of the court and its rules of procedure. But it has not done so yet, and, until it does, it will not be possible to say definitely what law will govern the decisions of the federal court.

Two possibilities have been suggested. The first—which approximates the system in the Sudan—would leave it entirely to the court to choose its own legal basis, that is, to select any set of legal principles which would provide justice in a given case. While this would involve an admirable prospect of judicial flexibility, it is less than realistic to expect it to work in the Cameroun context. The second alternative is far more likely to operate in the light of the country's special legal and historical circumstances: namely, that the court will apply the law prevailing in the federated state from which the case arose. This would enable the court to choose between applying the principles of the English common law in cases coming from West Cameroun and being guided by the principles of French Law in cases which originate from East Cameroun.[56] It still does not solve the problem of cases arising from federal law itself, but it would be surprising if these, too, were not judged according to the principles of French-derived law. The court owes much of its power to regulate constitutional matters and to deal with cases on appeal to the French judicial tradition; legislation emanating from the federal authorities is nearer in format to French than to any other legal pattern, and the majority of the court's members are familiar with that system and largely unacquainted with the English principles.

Other Federal Organs

The constitution provides for the creation of two other federal institutions: the Federal Judicial Council, and the Economic and Social Council.

The Federal Judicial Council (whose composition has already been described) is not only charged with 'assisting' the President in regard to the appointment of all judges (including those of the inferior or magistrates' courts) at the federal and state levels; it is also responsible for recommending to the President who should be appointed to other offices in the legal service, including that of the *Procureur-Général* and the prosecuting officials. It also has a right to be consulted on the exercise of the presidential prerogative of clemency. The Council contains representatives of both federated states, who are appointed for five years, and is presided over by the President.

A similar consultative body, the Federal Economic and Social Council, is referred to in Article 37 of the constitution, and is regulated by presidential decree. It is composed of 38 members (30 from East Cameroun and 8 from West Cameroun). It is purely advisory in nature, and may receive requests from the President, the Prime Ministers of the federated states or any of the legislative assemblies for advice on economic and social matters. It must be consulted on bills relating to these matters and to economic planning, and may be called upon to examine them 'within the limits of its technical competence'. Finance measures are specifically excluded from its jurisdiction. The Council reports to the National Assembly on the deliberations at its sessions, which take place twice a year, and together may not exceed a month in duration.[57]

In general, the purpose of the Council is to permit the expression of opinion by representatives of specialised interests within the fields of agriculture, commerce and industry, banking, salaried workers, co-operatives and the like on economic affairs.

THE FEDERATED STATES

The powers of the federated states are limited by the combined effect of the constitutional provisions which specify the very broad scope of authority given to the federal President and the federal National Assembly. Their Prime Ministers and their ministries are appointed by the President, and their legislatures may be dissolved by him. (It is only fair to point out that no attempt has been made to dissolve the legislatures, and that, at least in respect of West Cameroun, the President has taken great care to consult the legislature before making government appointments.) Their electoral systems, their courts and legal systems, their economic and financial arrangements, even the salaries of the members of their governments and legislatures, are subject to federal control and direction; so are their transportation and communication systems and a good deal of their administrative apparatus. Even within the areas over which they have been allotted jurisdiction by the federal constitution, they are subject to federal supervision; and their power to impose penalties when enacting legislation is both limited by federal law and derived from it.[58]

It seems reasonable, then, to argue that 'the provision of Article 38 which ostensibly purported to grant residual but undefined powers . . . was intended, in metaphorical terms, to serve as a mirage designed to condition psychologically the minds of the timorous souls that existed at the time of formulating the constitution, while at the same time succeeding in the primary objective of securing a strong united Cameroon'.[59] The legal language used here by Enonchong does not obscure his conclusion which is that the federated states have almost no power.

None the less, each federated state is provided with a separate constitution, which outlines the character of its institutions. Both states have a parliamentary form of government, with governments collectively responsible to their legislatures, though neither the Prime Minister nor any other Ministers (more correctly, Secretaries of State) need be members.

The federal constitution specifically retained the bi-cameral character of the West Cameroun state legislature by preserving the House of Chiefs, but East Cameroun has a single legislative chamber. The number of members in the East Cameroun Legislative Assembly is fixed by the federal constitution at one hundred, and that of the Western House of Assembly at thirty-seven. The West's House of Chiefs has twenty-two members. Although the consent of this house is not required for legislation—it has no veto, and can only delay finance measures by a month or other bills for up to six months—it does deliberate on bills and is more than merely an advisory body. It cannot initiate legislation.

Such power as is exercised legislatively at the state level rests in the Assemblies, although in real terms it is easier to establish the authority of the states by reference to the departments supervised by their governments than by looking at the constitutional provisions enacted in respect of the legislatures themselves in the constitutions of 1961. The Prime Minister's responsibilities in East Cameroun cover the general supervision of the state's government, while the Vice-Premier has responsibility for local government, police and lands. There are Secretaries of State for the Public Service, Finance, and for Public Works, whose portfolios are self-explanatory. The three remaining ministries are for Education, Rural Development (including agriculture and agricultural research; conservation of forests, water, wildlife and natural resources; and co-operatives), and Animal Husbandry.

Apart from his general duties as head of the state executive, the Prime Minister of West Cameroun controls the legal and judicial departments and the state police. A Secretary of State in his office is responsible for state development (which includes the activities of the Cameroon Development Corporation). Other Secretaries of State are concerned with the Public Service, Finance, Public Works and Transport, Natural Resources (including forestry and veterinary services), Lands and Surveys, Primary Education, and the Interior (which embraces Co-operatives, Community Development, Prisons, Lotteries and Customary Courts, as well as local government).

FEDERAL CONTROL AND STATE ADMINISTRATION

No description of Cameroun's administrative machinery would be adequate without some attempt to indicate the degree of federal control that is exercised over governmental operations, at all levels, within the federated states. This occurs in several ways.

Some government services are directly subject to the overall supervision of federal ministries. Those principally involved are the armed services and the *gendarmerie*, ports, customs, posts and telecommunications, health, information services (including the radio), and courts (including the federal legal service).

Administrative—as distinct from policy—authority over these departments is also in the hands of officials known as Federal Inspectors of Administration. In all, there are six of these for the country as a whole, five for regions in East Cameroun and one for West Cameroun as a separate region. They are responsible directly to the federal Minister of State for Territorial Administration (in the office of the federal President). Their duties include not only the supervision and co-ordination of federal services in their regions, but also liaison with state and federal government. They are responsible for the application of federal laws and for control

137

over federal civil servants within the areas of their jurisdiction. In addition, they have been given wide powers for the enforcement and maintenance of order, if necessary by the use of armed forces, gendarmes and police.[60]

Clearly, the federal inspectorate represents a major incursion of federal authority at state level, and a principal agency for the centralisation of government in Cameroun. This facet of their activities is the more evident in West Cameroun because it constitutes a separate region and its Federal Inspector wields great power. He controls operations whose extent approximates, if it does not actually exceed, that of the state government. What is more, he is not only beyond the control of that government, but also exercises authority over local officials, some of whose duties fall within the state's jurisdiction.

The federal control over local administration is, in fact, probably the most far-reaching of its state activities. Each region is divided into *départements*, under the control of a federal official known as a *préfet* and (in East Cameroun) these are further subdivided into *sous-départements* or *sous-préfectures*.[61] For their areas of jurisdiction, the officials in charge of these divisions are empowered to enforce laws and regulations, issue subordinate regulations and decisions of their own, and to take measures for security and the maintenance of public order.[62] In West Cameroun, the *préfets* replaced the District Officers who were the principal local officials before federation, but they continued to be responsible to the Secretary of State for the Interior and to the Prime Minister of the state government for some matters, while being subject to federal control in respect of many others. Johnson concludes that the 'effect was to progressively deprive West Cameroon of an autonomous administrative structure at the district or local level'.[63]

THE COURT SYSTEM[64]

Apart from superimposing the Federal Court of Justice as the highest court (in some matters) for the entire federation, the federal constitution has left the judicial systems in the two federated states much as they were prior to reunification in 1961.

Federal control over the judiciary is exercised through the Ministry of Justice and the Federal Judicial Council. But control is perhaps too strong a word to use in this context: federal effort has been directed principally towards the matter of appointments to the judicial and legal services, and to providing the initiative for the measure of unification which has been achieved of the laws applying in the two states. For the rest, the judiciary in each state maintains an existence separate from that of the other, and each applies different law.[65]

In East Cameroun, the highest court is the Supreme Court, which only has appellate jurisdiction on points of law (and not of fact) from inferior courts, courts of labour relations and special tribunals. It comprises a President and two judges, who preside over each of its sections—one concerned with general matters, the other with fiscal ones—as well as four puisne judges. Beneath the Supreme Court in the hierarchy are the Courts of Appeal, which are staffed by a President and three puisne judges. They hear appeals in civil or criminal matters from lower courts, but at first instance only have the right to hear criminal cases (when doing so, they are called Criminal Courts). They alone may pass a sentence of imprisonment exceeding ten years in length. There are four Courts of Appeal, one of which sits in Yaoundé and has a quorum of three judges; the others only have a single judge presiding. All Courts of Appeal go on circuit.

District courts of inferior jurisdiction are supposed to exist in each subdivision of a *département* (which corresponds roughly to a *sous-préfecture*), but in fact shortage of trained personnel has meant that fewer of these courts have been created. There are no limits on their capacity to hear civil matters, except that these must have arisen within the area of the court's jurisdiction. In criminal cases, they may not deal with felonies (i.e. serious crimes), but they may conduct preliminary investigations in respect of these. The district courts comprise at least one judge, and the intention is that there should be a bench of three for each of them. Appeal lies from a decision of a District Court to the Court of Appeal for the area in which the district is situated.

At the lowest level of the East Cameroun judiciary, there are the Grade I and Customary Courts, the former under a *sous-préfet* and the latter comprising a President and two elders appointed by the Minister of Justice on the recommendation of the *préfet* for the area. These courts have no criminal jurisdiction, and their civil authority is restricted to matters arising in the area for which they are established. But they deal with the bulk of civil cases in the state. An appeal may be made from their decisions to the appropriate Court of Appeal, and the *Procureur-Général* may refer a decision to the latter court of his own accord where he thinks an appeal is warranted.

The apex of the West Cameroun judicial system is the Supreme Court, which is composed of a Chief Justice and three puisne judges, any three of whom may sit in respect of civil or criminal appeals (whether on a question of fact, or law, or both). The High Court consists of the same judges, any one of whom may sit alone, either on appeal from the decision—criminal or civil—of a magistrate's court, or in the exercise of original jurisdiction in a matter over which a magistrates' court has no authority. In principle, the High Court may not deal with a matter involving customary law on most topics unless it does so on appeal or when a case is transferred to it from a customary court. An appeal lies from the High Court to the Supreme Court on any of its decisions (though the prosecution may appeal against an acquittal on a point of law alone).

Magistrates' Courts are presided over by officers of the rank of Magistrate or Chief Magistrate. The latter have the right to deal with civil cases involving no more than £500*; and in relation to crimes, they may only pass sentences of a maximum of £500 in fines or five years imprisonment. (Magistrates have a lower limit on their powers in monetary terms, in relation to civil and criminal matters.) Where they do not have authority to try a case, magistrates' courts may conduct preliminary enquiries. No magistrate has jurisdiction in respect of customary law unless a case is transferred to him from a customary court. An appeal lies from any decision of a magistrate's court to the High Court, which also has an automatic right to review any of their decisions.

There are both ordinary and appeal customary courts in West Cameroun. These are presided over by persons appointed by the Secretary of State for the Interior, who also defines the area and substantive extent of their jurisdiction. Normally, customary courts are composed of elders, who are confined to dealing with the inhabitants of a particular district or the members of a particular

* The sums are given in sterling since the operative statute is one passed in 1955, when this was the state's currency. The CFA franc equivalent would be roughly 330,000 francs.

tribe. Their powers vary, but, in respect of criminal matters they will normally have a maximum limit on their jurisdiction of a fine of £50 or twelve months imprisonment (with lesser grades being confined to £30 and six months). In civil matters, they may not normally make awards greater than £200 (sometimes only £100), and limits are also placed on their powers in respect of land and marriage cases. An appeal lies from the customary courts to the Customary Court of Appeal, which is established in the same way as the customary courts; and, from there, to the Supreme Court.[66]

HUMAN RIGHTS

Despite the elaborate provision for the court system and considerable discussion of the subject at Bamenda and Foumban before federation, neither the federal constitution nor either of the state constitutions provides for the enforcement of fundamental rights or civil liberties. Both the 1960 constitution of the Cameroun Republic and the Southern Cameroons (Constitution) Order in Council of the same year had detailed provisions on the subject, which contained elaborate lists of the rights guaranteed to individual citizens.

In the federal constitution of 1961, the main reference to the subject is contained in the first Article, one sentence of which reads: 'It [the Federal Republic of Cameroun] affirms its adherence to the fundamental freedoms set out in the Universal Declaration of Human Rights and the United Nations.' According to Johnson, this was inserted as a substitute for any substantive provision on the subject.[67] The only other references to the matter in any of the three constitutions—federal or state—are those in Article 6 of the federal constitution, which makes 'human rights' a federal matter, and Article 24 of the same constitution, which entitled the federal National Assembly to legislate on the 'protection of the freedom of the individual' and 'public liberties'.

What, then, is the position today? In the first place, it is necessary to point out that the affirmation in Article 1 of the constitution is of very little effect. It is very similar in practice to a device used in the 1960 Republican constitution of Ghana,[68] in terms of which the President swore to uphold a variety of fundamental principles. When put to the test, the Ghanaian courts found that provision to be little more than the expression of an intent, which conferred no right on anyone.[69] The Cameroun variant is of even less force in all probability, since the affirmation is made in terms of the Republic as a whole, and could thus hardly be enforceable against the President or any official. If Johnson is correct, no more than a wish was intended.

Methods of fulfilling that wish were left to be determined outside of the constitution itself. Dr Enonchong has argued at length—and with considerable force, not to say ingenuity—that, in the absence of any provision for civil rights in the federal constitution, the pre-existing laws governing the subject are still operative.[70] In the process of developing his argument, he asserts that parts of the constitutions which were in force in the last year before federation should still be applied.

The argument does much to point to the vacuum in this field in the law enacted since unification. It also offers an opportunity to the courts to fill the vacuum by taking advantage of ambiguities in the present constitution's reference to the continuation in force of laws which previously prevailed in the states before federation. But it must remain doubtful whether the courts will do this. Enonchong himself points out that the matter was avoided on the one occasion when it did arise before the West Cameroun Supreme Court. Even if the courts were bold enough to attempt the enforcement of constitutional rights taken over from a very different set of social and political circumstances in this way—and the legal arguments are by no means clear-cut—they would have to take account of the fact that the federal constitution does specify the subject as one of federal and not state competence.

In the circumstances of the federal constitution and its history, it would seem, then, that no protection is given by the constitution or any other federal law to human rights in Cameroun. Even if this is not what was intended, the fact remains that, since 1961, the federal legislature has had the power to enact the necessary legislation. It has not done so.

7. The Realities of Reunification

THE FORMAL STATE STRUCTURE created by the federal constitution established the main institutions of unified Cameroun, and provided unmistakable guidelines for the way in which they were to work. It was no loose framework, superimposed on existing patterns of social, political and economic organisation, but a solid foundation for their amalgamation into a single unit. Nevertheless, the constitution could not create the nation, nor eradicate instantly the substantial difficulties that stood in the way of nation-building within either federated state, or the inherited differences—in political tradition, language, culture, law and economic ties— between them. The growth of national consciousness and a national identity had to take place organically, along with the integration of the two states into a single entity.

Ahidjo was well aware of the problems, and made no attempt to disguise them. 'The independence of a people, of a country, is one thing,' he said somewhat more than two years after federation, 'the existence of a government, of an administration, town halls and chiefdoms is another. But a nation, a real nation, is something altogether different . . . It is the responsibility of we who govern, at all levels, to forge that nation, to forge that national unity.'[1]

The impetus to unity was provided by the constitution and stimulated from the federal capital in Yaoundé. But the pace was not forced. The process was slow and deliberate, but inexorable. It involved the dismantling of existing loyalties and apparatus in the course of constructing new ones; and it inevitably entailed greater changes in the west than it did in the east, given the overall framework of the new state and the political and numerical preponderance of the francophone eastern state within it.

The possibly traumatic effect which could have resulted if there had been too rapid a move towards greater uniformity was, however, avoided by the transitional measures allowed for in the constitution, and by the cautious rate at which innovations were introduced in the economic and administrative fields. The direct impact of unification was also softened, so far as the population as a whole was concerned, by the early emphasis on the creation

143

of political unity in the country through the formation of a single political party.

POLITICAL UNIFICATION

The circumstances which led to the establishment of a unified party structure were the result of different kinds of political developments in each state. The principal factor they had in common was the prevailing influence of the federal President, armed with the power invested in him by the federal constitution. It was undoubtedly Ahidjo who set in motion the major and decisive moves towards the establishment of the single party, and who determined the timing of its formation at each stage of its growth.

The decision to bring about a single dominant political party was no doubt reached as a result of ideological considerations. Ahidjo's early pronouncements on the subject do not differ greatly in this respect from those of a large number of other African leaders in the early sixties, who justified the emergence of one-party states on the basis of African 'tradition' or on the allegedly wasteful and disruptive effects of having too many parties within the body politic of a nascent state.[2] But the single party came about in Cameroun at least as much because of what Ahidjo later called a 'cold and rigorous analysis' of the political realities of the federation.[3] The process of unification itself reflected the pragmatic approach adopted in nearly all matters of state by the President, combined with a degree of ruthlessness on his part in dealing with opponents and a considerable amount of skill in seizing opportunities for advancing his policies at every available moment.

Ahidjo was always careful to stress that he aimed at the unification of the existing political parties, not at the creation of a one-party state. Thus he denied any intention of instituting 'a monolithic and even totalitarian party', while making it clear what he himself thought the prospective single party should look like:

> it would be dangerous, if only for the future, to adopt such a totalitarian party system, in which all the citizens of the country are forced, against their will, to join the party. I will state right now that it would be for the good of Cameroun if it had one big

unified party . . . which would be created when the parties
now in existence have come to an agreement. A great unified
national party, which convinced Camerounians would join
freely, a party within which democracy, freedom of speech and
debate would prevail, and in which several different tendencies
could co-exist, it being agreed that the minority would follow
the lead of the majority.[4]

In general, this distinction—between the *parti unifié* and the *parti
unique*—was always maintained; and, whatever its theoretical basis
in terms of ideals, this enabled Ahidjo to set about absorbing the
other parties, first in East Cameroun and later in the West as well.

East Cameroun

At the declaration of federation in October 1961, Ahidjo's
Union Camérounaise was already the majority party in East
Cameroun. Its tenuous control over the legislature there had been
increased by the decision of two other parties to join it. The first
had been Charles Assalé's *Mouvement d'Action Nationale* (MANC),
and Assalé was appointed Prime Minister of the state. Patronage
had also secured the adherence of the Bamiléké deputies of the
Front pour l'Unité et la Paix (FPUP) : no fewer than five—including
the former rebel leader Pierre Ninyim Kandem—were given
office in the new state government, and one of these (Victor Kanga)
was later to receive a place in the federal government as Minister
of National Economy. Even before reunification, these moves
towards a coalition had resulted in Ahidjo's receiving the support
of many more than the fifty-one UC deputies elected in 1960 to the
Cameroun Republic's National Assembly. But opposition parties
still existed. They expressed vigorous disapproval of Ahidjo's
policies when the federation came into being, particularly through
the *Parti des Démocrates* (PDC) led by Mbida, the recently-
legalised UPC under Matip and even by some of Okala's Socialists.
Though Okala himself accepted office, the members of his party
who opposed the government were joined by a new party—the
Parti Travailliste, under Dr Marcel Beybey-Eyidi.

By this time, however, Ahidjo, aided by a measure of success
in by-elections, was prepared to assert a claim by the UC to be the
only 'national party' in East Cameroun. From then on he was to
use much tougher methods to secure the disappearance of the

others. To a certain extent, he was able to benefit from the gradual running-down of PDC parliamentary support, through further resignations by members who joined the UC majority in the house, early in 1962.[5] An emphatic indication of the changed atmosphere however, came with the breaking up of the UPC party congress in January by armed soldiers.

But even this did not signal the end of the UPC or the demise of the rest of the opposition. The opposition leaders were, if anything, united by the growing fear that Ahidjo was determined to eliminate them politically. As a result, they joined together in April to form their own *Front National Unifié*, and in June issued an open letter vigorously attacking Ahidjo and alleging that he was intent on creating a dictatorship through the establishment of a one-party state. This was reinforced on June 23 by a manifesto published by the *Front* in pamphlet form, which repeated the charges against Ahidjo. It went on to reject specifically the concept of the *parti unifié*, as advocated by the UC, on the grounds that this was no more than a disguised attempt to accomplish political uniformity in Cameroun, that it would be achieved only by reducing 'the other Camerounians to the rank of slaves' and would lead to a 'fascist-type dictatorship'.[6] Within a matter of weeks there were drastic retaliatory measures which virtually extinguished the *Front* and silenced its leaders. They were arrested, after their homes had been searched, and were tried on charges which resulted, in part, from allegations that arms and ammunition had been found in their possession. On July 11, they were convicted of 'inciting hatred against the government and public authority, inciting conflict between ethnic and religious communities and disseminating news prejudicial to public authorities'. They were sentenced to the loss of their political rights, fined and imprisoned for three years.[7] The indictment and the sentences are a clear indication of the powers the government had assumed to deal with political recalcitrants as well as insurrectionaries. The immediate effect was to produce further defections by eleven more UPC, Socialist and PDC deputies.

East Cameroun was still not a one-party state, however.[8] Seven deputies remained in opposition (six *Démocrates* and one UPC) throughout the remainder of the existence of the first Legislative Assembly, but they were rendered ineffective by their small numbers and the parliamentary procedure which denied them representation on any of the Assembly's commissions. The PDC survived to field a list of ten candidates in the first elections held after reunification, those for the federal National Assembly in 1964. They were not successful in securing any seats because, they claimed, the government used a number of administrative devices —including delays and refusal to accept nominations, the banning of candidates' meetings, irregularities in the polling arrangements, and even ballot-rigging—to frustrate any chance of success they might have had.[9] The effect of these and earlier measures was to be seen in 1965, when neither the PDC nor any other party thought it worthwhile to make the effort once again in the elections for the East Cameroun Legislative Assembly.

Thus in less than four years the single party was achieved for East Cameroun, by a process of erosion and elimination. The stage was set for Ahidjo to pursue his goal of a unified national party for the entire federation.

But before looking at the parallel developments which had taken place in West Cameroun it is necessary to complete the picture in the east, where political activity in the party arena had been accompanied by the active suppression of the rebellion, or what remained of it.

By the time of the Cameroun Republic's independence, most of the rebel leaders were either in exile (first in Cairo, then in Guinea or Ghana), or dead. The exiled leaders continued a propaganda campaign against the new state with the publication of newspapers like *La Voix du Kamerun* and regular broadcasts in French and Arabic. Both media stressed not only the harshness and brutality of the armed forces in suppressing opposition, but also the occasional successes of small bands of insurgents with their attacks on villages, churches, schools and encampments. A good deal of attention was devoted to the role of the French government in supplying funds, military equipment and personnel to the Ahidjo regime and its army. The campaign was also aimed at preventing the recognition of the new government by African states, and was effective at least in respect of those states associated with the more radical pan-African policies of the 'Casablanca bloc' (Ghana, Guinea, Mali, the UAR, Algeria, Morocco and Tunisia).

Within the country itself, the rebel activity was at best sporadic and confined to a few areas in the Bamiléké country and those parts of the south which had substantial numbers of Bamiléké

147

settlers. With the return of many Bamiléké leaders to the UC, and the participation of one faction of the UPC in legal political activity from 1960, they were shorn of overt support and limited to underground campaigns.

Nevertheless, their impact was felt. In the political field, they spearheaded the opposition to Ahidjo, and the strenuousness of their campaign reinforced the determination of opposition political leaders like Matip and Beybey-Eyidi. Whether these leaders were in touch with them—as alleged by the government—or not, both of them declined to have anything to do with Ahidjo, refused offers of government positions, and, as has already been seen, maintained their opposition until they were imprisoned.

By 1963 most of the UPC's external support had fallen away, and the governments of Ghana and Mali had established relations with Ahidjo. There is little doubt that the rebellion had been effectively crushed. Ahidjo had, characteristically, applied a combination of political skill, social reform and military might to divide, undermine and ultimately overcome it although underground *maquisards* continued to operate in small groups for more than seven years afterwards. Customary land tenure had been regulated and changed to mitigate gross inequities and reduce landlessness in Bamiléké areas; and dissatisfaction among urban civil servants had been stifled by pay increases and the granting of generous family allowances. But the armed forces had also grown in size and effectiveness; and the methods they and the government used were far from gentle. Johnson reports the widespread belief that they employed brutal force, and were not above mass killings where this was considered necessary.[10] In one widely reported incident in 1962, some twenty or more political prisoners were alleged to have suffocated to death in a hermetically sealed goods wagon while being transported by train from one prison to another.[11]

It is difficult to assess the full extent of the insurrection, since no comprehensive account has been given of it to date by the government or by the UPC. There is no doubt, however, that it was widespread, and that during the eight or so years of its duration, it resulted in substantial damage. Total deaths have been estimated at between 10,000 and 20,000 civilians, and 1,000 military. Nearly 100 schools were destroyed, and a good number of hospitals, dispensaries, bridges and agricultural stations were put out of action. Hundreds of miles of roads and telegraph wires were rendered unusable. Total damage to *public* property in the Bamiléké region alone, was of the order of seven million dollars.[12]

Initial military aid from France of about five million dollars in terms of the accords of 1960[13] had produced an efficient armed force, under Camerounian command (though with French officers, *aides*, and technical personnel who played a substantial role in the earlier period of military activity). It was well-equipped, with mobile units and enough men and arms for eight infantry battalions and four platoons of armoured cars. Once the rebellion had been put down, Ahidjo was left with a considerable instrument of force under his control, shaped by the insurrection but available, after it had been quelled, to underpin the government. In 1966, the army still had four battalions in service, with two more planned. It also had an armoured squadron and a company of parachute troops. In all, the army numbered somewhat more than 2,000 officers and men, and it had some 500 vehicles at its disposal. In addition, the federal forces consisted of between two and three times that number of volunteer 'Civil Guard' regiments in the various regions. There were also rather more than 3,000 gendarmes (including 15 companies and 137 brigades in the *Gendarmerie Territoriale* and a *Mobile Gendarmerie* of 5 squadrons and 21 platoons).[14] Little attempt was made to obscure the size or the importance of the armed forces; they were in evidence in camps outside most major cities, and were often to be seen on manoeuvres in the country. Their presence at parades and on guard was no doubt intended as a reminder that they were at the disposal of the government, and could be used whenever necessary.

Le Vine concluded in 1963 that the *Union Camérounaise* had been the principal political beneficiary of the insurrection, as a result of the opportunities provided by the rebellion and its repression for Ahidjo to create a one-party state;[15] the President was greatly aided in keeping and consolidating his political gains afterwards by his acquisition of a sizeable and effective military apparatus.

West Cameroun

Neither the complete political control nor the military power which Ahidjo had obtained since independence were in themselves of direct significance in securing West Cameroun's acceptance of a unified political party. The former was undoubtedly a factor

149

which counted in the President's favour when he was engaged in discussions with Foncha and other leaders in the western state. But internal political developments in West Cameroun made any real intervention from the East unnecessary, if indeed it had ever been intended. More important in the long run was Ahidjo's skilful use of his federal constitutional powers and patronage to ensure the final outcome of political unification which he desired. The West Cameroun party system disintegrated of its own accord, as the dynamics of the federal system began to operate and political power came more and more clearly to be located at the centre.

At independence, Foncha and his KNDP enjoyed a narrow majority in the western legislature over the CPNC opposition. The provisional arrangements which came into force after reunification enabled continuity to be maintained through Foncha's retention of the office of Prime Minister of West Cameroun while assuming the federal vice-presidency. The KNDP's position was further reinforced in the elections at the end of 1961, which gave it twenty-four out of thirty-seven seats. An agreement between Foncha and Ahidjo, made in 1962, ensured that neither the UC nor the KNDP would be active in the other's territory, and created a formal alliance between the parties at the federal level. Three KNDP members were included in the federal ministry (S. T. Muna as a full Minister, E. T. Egbe and N. Ekhah-Nghaky as deputy-Ministers).

To a certain extent, this agreement represented tactical changes on the part of both parties. From Ahidjo's point of view, it meant a temporary abandonment of his emphasis on the need for a single national party; for Foncha, it involved a move towards unity and away from the kind of opposition he had previously expressed to a one-party state. Positively, each side gained as well: Ahidjo, by pre-empting any likelihood of a southern-based alliance against the UC, and Foncha by forestalling the possibility of co-operation (or even merger) between the UC and the CPNC, which had become the principal advocate in West Cameroun of the idea of a single party for the nation. (Given the steady decline in its support, and the powerlessness of its position as an opposition in a minority state, this policy made good sense for the CPNC, though it had limited appeal in West Cameroun at the time.)

Foncha had little difficulty in keeping the CPNC at bay. He

successfully side-stepped proposals for uniting the two parties, claiming that the only possible basis for such a merger was the adhesion of the CPNC members to the KNDP. But he was gradually becoming more definitely committed to the objective of a unified national party. The demise of the CPNC seemed in any event to be increasingly likely. It lost further ground through the defection of some of its members in the House of Assembly, and the KNDP gained an overwhelming majority, and secured all the seats, in the election for the ten federal National Assembly seats which was held in the first months of 1964.[16]

This victory represented the summit of Foncha's achievements in Cameroun politics. From then on, the basis of his own power became more and more precarious, and simultaneously the KNDP went into decline. The factor which precipitated both—and started the process which ended in the disappearance of separate parties in West Cameroun—was the need to find a successor for Foncha as Prime Minister of the western state when his constitutional right to hold both federal and state office ceased in 1965.

Foncha had apparently decided by 1963 that his future lay in the federal government, despite the relative lack of power entailed in the vice-presidency and the fact that he would be cut off from his base in the state through being located in Yaoundé. In the KNDP his decision produced a major contest for the vice-presidency of the party (Foncha remained life president) between Muna, the federal Minister, and Augustine Jua, the West Cameroun Secretary of State for Finance.[17] With personal and, to a limited extent, ethnic factors involved, but no ideological question apparently at issue,[18] Foncha supported Muna. He also supported Egbe for the other vacant post, secretary-general, against Nghaky. But Jua and Nghaky won at the party congress in 1963 by substantial majorities, after an intensive campaign at grass-roots level.

Foncha's prestige was already damaged by this result, but it was to suffer once more. Muna claimed that the appointment of the Premier was the constitutional prerogative of the federal President (with whom he obviously had closer contact as a federal Minister, though whether Ahidjo gave him any direct encouragement to continue his quest for the state office is not known). Jua's supporters, on the other hand, asserted the right of KNDP members in the state House of Assembly to be heard on this matter. When these were consulted at a party caucus meeting in 1965, the vote went in Jua's favour. Accordingly, Foncha declined to submit Muna's name to the President, and called on him to accept the party's decision. When Muna refused to do so, Foncha accused him of trying to split the party, and ultimately suspended him and seven of his supporters from membership. Thus Foncha fell out with both factions of the party in turn.

Ahidjo, meanwhile, gained from the dispute. His right to appoint the Prime Minister was unquestioned, and he exercised it, after proper consultation with the KNDP, in favour of Jua. At the same time, he was able to display a degree of aloofness from the dispute, and retained the allegiance of the Muna faction, even after they had been expelled from the KNDP and had formed their own party, by keeping Muna and Egbe on in the federal government.

Another consequence of these developments was the diminution of the KNDP support in the legislature, which led to the formation of a coalition between the KNDP and the CPNC. Dr Endeley, the CPNC leader, and the state's leading advocate of party unification, became Leader of Government Business from 1966 onwards. With the Muna faction (now the official opposition in the state legislature as the Cameroon United Congress) closely associated with Ahidjo and Yaoundé, there had never been a greater measure of agreement in West Cameroun on the question of national unity.

It was not long before Ahidjo moved to settle the issue once and for all. Earlier attempts to formulate proposals for a single party had been made by the Committee of Co-ordination which had been set up in terms of the KNDP-UC agreement of 1962, but these had not been very successful. Little more than agreement in principle had been established, and even this modest advance had received a setback with the defeat of Muna and Egbe (who had both been involved in trying to work out details as members of the committee). But in 1966 Ahidjo was able to take the initiative himself. He did so by summoning the leaders of the three West Cameroun parties to a meeting with the Prime Minister of East Cameroun and himself at Yaoundé in June. With considerable adroitness, he secured their agreement within two days to the dissolution of all existing political parties in both states, and the creation of a new one to be known as the *Union Nationale Camérounaise*/Cameroon National Union (UNC/CNU).

Once agreement on this point had been reached, Ahidjo was

quick to set August as the deadline for the birth of the new party. Details of its framework were left to a steering committee, whose composition reflected not only the dominant position of the eastern state and its single party (22 members), but also stressed the weakness of the west in absolute as well as relative terms: they were given eight members, four from the KNDP and two each from the other two parties.

Thus the UNC emerged in mid-August, after the UC had made the gesture of dissolving itself first, and the others had followed suit. Ahidjo was President, Foncha and the East Cameroun Prime Minister, Dr Tchoungi, were Vice-Presidents, and an executive committee was formed which included members representing all the former West Cameroun groupings as well as a large majority from the former UC.

The UNC has most of the formal attributes of a major national party, with a structure that includes cells or branches at local level, sub-sections in districts and sections in the larger adminis-trative units of the country. It also has a central bureaucratic apparatus (a central committee and an executive). By March 1969, nearly three years after its formation, however, it had held only one national party congress. The history of the party reflects its character as one which united the leadership in the nation rather than the memberships of its various constituents. Though Ahidjo has from time to time stressed the role of the party in bringing political education to the mass of the population, and as an agent of national unification, it is still better described as a party of the Camerounian élites than as a mass party.[19]

Most of the political initiative in Cameroun still emanates from the state, not the party. Though there is some degree of identity between the positions held by leaders in the party and those they are given in the various governments of the federation, the general impression is that the decisions are made at the centre and com-municated to the branches and the nation: the stimulus seldom comes from below, except on matters of purely local interest. Politics in Cameroun have a distinctly impersonal quality, which is the consequence of the predominance of the state over the party, and the President over the state.

Developments in the years since the creation of the UNC, particularly in West Cameroun, show how this has worked in practice. Jua, after his success in 1965, lost ground when it came

153

to the selection of candidates for the single party's list in the 1967 West Cameroun House of Assembly elections. He himself was replaced as Prime Minister in 1968, when the President appointed Muna to that office. Other members of the former Cameroon United Congress gained office as the speaker of the western House and in the federal government. Later, in 1970, Foncha was dropped as Vice-President and replaced by Muna, who was allowed to continue to hold his western office—despite the constitutional provision which prohibited this, and which had led Foncha to retire in the first place as Prime Minister, thus precipitating the break-up of the KNDP. The wheel had turned full circle.

In relation to East Cameroun affairs, there has been no such clear change in the power structure, although alterations have been made at frequent, if irregular, intervals in its government and in the state's representatives at the federal level. These have represented promotions or demotions for individuals on grounds of competence or popularity (or the lack of them). There has been little suggestion of nepotism—on ethnic or personal grounds—in relation to governmental reorganisation. The initiative has, nevertheless, always clearly come from Ahidjo rather than as a result of popular demand. While there has been a continuous attempt to see that an ethnic balance is maintained, key federal ministries—particularly those concerned with the presidency and the army—have for the most part remained in the hands of northern leaders, since their loyalty to Ahidjo is likely to be greater.

Despite the relative calm which the country enjoys politically, there is still more than a suggestion that the army is needed to maintain security. The only major trial which occurred up to 1970 was that of Victor Kanga in 1967. After being demoted to the post of Minister of Information and Tourism, Kanga was alleged to have been responsible for circulating a pamphlet which claimed that his removal was caused by the need to protect influential people who would have been subject to scrutiny over their financial dealings. He was tried by a military court and sentenced to five years imprisonment, a fine of 1 million francs CFA, and confiscation of his property. The fact that Kanga and two other officials who were dismissed at the same time are Bamiléké led to widespread speculation that the moves were directed against that tribe. Evidence for this is scant. Bamiléké are—and always have been—in important positions, both in the federal and eastern state governments. Since the Bamiléké are prominent urban migrants (in numbers and in commerce), there is a degree of resentment of them in the larger cities, which leads to some rumours about their political ambitions and trustworthiness. It is never possible to judge the accuracy of this type of allegation.

UPC activity declined considerably after the death of its Secretary-General, Ostende Ofana, who was killed by the army in March 1966. Nevertheless, two years later Ahidjo was still apparently convinced that a guerrilla campaign was being mounted against him.[20] In 1970 it was reported that the President found it necessary to take strict precautions over his own safety, both in Yaoundé and while on tour. The military was still noticeable in some areas.[21] In July two nurses were killed and substantial quantities of medical supplies stolen in an attack on a dispensary at Loum in the south. But the UPC may have received its *coup de grâce* the following month, when the last of the old leaders, Ernest Ouandié, was captured at Mbanga. Ouandié was tried and sentenced to death in January 1971 along with six others, including the Bishop of Nkongsamba. The sentence aroused considerable international protest and there was a plea for clemency from the Pope. As a result, the death sentences on the bishop and two others were commuted to life imprisonment. Ouandié was, however, executed. According to one report, this left only one known UPC leader at large, Woungli Massaga, who had been in exile for some time and was thought to be living in Cuba.[22]

The federal government has increased its powers over the information media and now controls not only the French and English transmissions of the radio, but also the press. Although a number of newspapers are still published in both states, they are dependent on the government news agency for nearly all national and international news, and are subject to constant surveillance by security authorities. Indiscretions may result in their suppression, either permanently or temporarily.

In much the same way as with the political parties, central control by the state has come to be exerted over the trade unions as part of the process of political unification. By 1963, mergers had reduced the number of union groups in the eastern state to two: the *Fédération Syndicale du Cameroun* and the *Union des Syndicats Croyants du Cameroun*. The existence of secular and religious trade unions reflected long-standing divisions in the labour movement of Cameroun (as of other francophone countries). The old left-wing *Union des Syndicats Confédérés du Cameroun* (USCC) had disappeared, and its members had been absorbed by the other two.

Nevertheless, the existence of the two bodies and the nature of the division enabled Ahidjo to point to 'foreign influences', internal factions, ideological splits and personal disputes in the labour movement, and to call for unity between the confederations. The matter was referred to several times by the President, but no direct attempt was made to intervene in union affairs until late in the 1960s. The most emphatic demand for unity came in 1969 at the first party conference, and the West Cameroon Trade Union Congress was included with the two from East Cameroon, though it was not notably deficient in any of the respects criticised by the President.

Within six months of the party conference, unity was a reality—and again took place by a joinder of the existing organisations under the new name of the *Union des Travailleurs du Cameroun* (Workers Union of Cameroun), whose formation was announced early in October.

Ahidjo's suggestion that unification would help to overcome the 'powerlessness' of the trade unions has yet to be tested. The high rate of unemployment in the country must contribute considerably to their impotence, and must be at least as much its cause as any organisational or ideological problems they have experienced in the past.

It is clear, however, that Ahidjo sees the role of the trade unions as being an arm of government policy rather than an independent source of pressure on behalf of their members. His attitude to labour relations in general is well represented by his description of the new Labour Code of 1967 as one which would 'eliminate demagogy, sterile opposition, subterranean action, in a word the subversion in labour [matters] which is the enemy of production just as subversion in the state is the enemy of independence, peace and prosperity'.[23]

The task of the trade unions as outlined in Ahidjo's address to the party in 1969 is to:

ensure the application of labour legislation within the undertaking (? works), but also to ensure the discipline of workers and their output; to assist in the vocational training and general education of their members so that they become efficient workers and citizens conscious of development problems; associate themselves with the mobilisation of the masses for national construction; collaborate with the government to ensure the improvement of workers' conditions, within the framework of an overall policy of economic and social progress.[24]

In other words, they must not hinder the course of national economic development as conceived by the government and implemented through its economic policies.

FORGING NATIONAL UNITY

The unification of the political life of the country was an important corollary of the efficient functioning of the institutions of the new state. A scarcely less significant aspect of the federation's development since independence has been the government's deep commitment to overcoming the differences between the two states making up the nation.

For the population of West Cameroun as a whole—as distinct from the élite—political unification was less important than the efforts made in other fields. Integration of their patterns of living has involved a series of adjustments to the requirements of unity. Sometimes, the simple need to standardise services throughout the country meant the abandonment of aspects of their daily lives which had become ingrained during more than forty years of British administration and now had to be uprooted.

It was not always the substitution of the East's French-derived system for the West's English-style arrangements that made changes necessary. Sometimes, the alterations were less drastic, and resulted from the search for a new, common Camerounian pattern which would embrace the established orders and values without necessarily extinguishing them. Some of the changes were the inevitable result of the creation of a new state, and could be justified even more easily in the context of a developing nation unable to afford the luxury of duplicate arrangements. Others sprang from a genuine attempt to give content to a new nationalism, one of whose sources had been the yearning for a single Camerounian culture.

The real nature of the challenge created by the existence of

157

distinguishable cultures in East and West Cameroun did not lie in deciding which of the two systems would predominate in the new framework. With the numerical and economic superiority of the francophone area in the political sphere, this was a foregone conclusion. What had to be decided was whether integration could take place without subordination, predominance without domination—and, if the first of each of these alternatives, how this was to be achieved.

The success of the government in this regard is something which cannot be established without resort to guesswork because there has been decreasing opportunity for registering dissent. But even if West Cameroun has had very little choice as integration has proceeded, it is still possible to measure the headway made by looking at the extent to which West Camerounians have acquiesced in the changes, the degree to which they have managed to adapt to them, and in turn suit them to their own purposes; the ways in which westerners have played a part in formulating some of the new policies, and resisting others.

All these factors—acquiescence, adaptation, participation and resistance—have been present, in varying degrees, at one time or another and in different combinations. They have been responsible for the fact that integration has proceeded, if not always smoothly at least continuously since the federation was established. And they have been aided by the subtle pressures which Yaoundé has exerted, often obliquely, rather than try to dictate solutions; and by the relatively relaxed pace at which change has been allowed to take place in the ten years since reunification.

Physically, relations between the two states during the forty-six years which preceded unification were thwarted not so much by natural frontiers as by the totally different lines along which patterns of communication had been developed by France and Britain within each area. Thus each maintained a port with considerable facilities (at Douala and Victoria-Tiko respectively), but since trade was with the metropolis in each case there was little, if any, traffic between them. This was even more true of overland transport. Roads had been constructed along parallel lines both at the coast and northwards; access from one side to the other was never easy, and frequently non-existent. Rail facilities had been extended only northwards in the francophone area, not westwards; and in West Cameroun nothing at all had been built except a small gauge-track in the south during the German period for the benefit of the palm-oil (and later rubber) plantations. Telephone and telegraph communication was stifled by the fact that the Southern Cameroons' grids were linked to Nigeria, and traffic eastwards had to be treated as an international operation, which meant routing via London and Paris. Seldom can there have been a clearer example of the combination of neglect and shortsightedness on the part of two colonial powers administering adjacent territories.

The physical isolation was compounded by the currency and trading allegiances of the two states, which in turn required the existence of customs barriers between them; and by the need for passports to travel across the international frontiers created by divided rule—and sustained, first by the colonial powers, then by the Cameroun and Nigerian governments as the spread of rebellion threatened political stability. On top of all this, there remained the very real obstacles to communication which resulted from the use of different languages in government, administration and economic life.

The combined effect of all these factors—together with the existence of distinctive educational systems and different patterns of religious affiliation—was to ensure the effective separation of the two Camerouns before 1961. They also created one of the main paradoxes of the reunification period. For, as isolation came to be broken down, so friction between the disparate patterns in the two sections of the country had to be contemplated. The prospect of this friction, and the need to avoid it, was in many ways responsible for the measured pace at which integration was made to proceed. Along with a paucity of economic resources and the need to rely on foreign—and often French—aid for the major projects, this was a more significant factor than any actual resistance or substantial opposition encountered in West Cameroun.

The first steps in the integration process were relatively minor efforts at standardisation in the economic and transportation spheres, as a prelude to more far-reaching changes. Thus, in 1962 there came the introduction of the CFA franc as the federation's currency, to replace the Nigerian pound in the west; and, in the same year, traffic was made to travel on the right-hand side of the road throughout the country. Despite some initial difficulty with the currency and exchange rates, neither move caused any major dislocation.[25] Other early changes were principally concerned with the establishment of statistics on economic and demographic matters, as a basis for future planning.[26]

Real advances in transport networks were planned as early as 1963, when a start was made on a survey for the extension of the railway system to link Kumba to Douala (as part of an overall development of rail facilities throughout the country). Work was begun on the project some years later, and was completed in 1969. While this was being done, an effort was made, with American aid funds, to improve the internal road system of West Cameroun by resurfacing and virtually remaking large portions of the Kumba-Mamfe route, while French funds contributed to restoring the surface of the abysmal road from Kumba southwards to Victoria and Tiko, as well as that from Kumba via Tombel to the main Douala-Bafoussam road in East Cameroun. The total sums involved did not much exceed four million dollars, but the effect was to overcome years of neglect which had added to the isolation of the west and emphasised the inferiority of its facilities. Improvements were also made by the development of internal air transport, through the establishment of the state-financed Cameroon Air Transport corporation. As a result, contact became possible not only with areas of the interior (such as Mamfe and Bamenda), hitherto only regularly accessible in good weather during the dry season, but also with Douala by means of a fifteen-minute flight from Tiko in a light aircraft.

As late as 1969, however, really extensive communication between East and West was still restricted. There was no direct road, rail or air travel from Yaoundé to anywhere in West Cameroun; and the journey from Douala to Tiko by road—not much more than twenty miles as the crow flies—was a long and hazardous affair, involving a 125-mile detour via Kumba or the crossing of a stretch of water by a ramshackle ferry capable of handling only one or two cars (or a single truck) at a time. The great breakthrough came in April 1969, with the opening of a new stretch of road which crossed a short bridge over the Moungo river and reduced the journey to less than an hour. This had been planned since 1965 and was financed by French aid. It undoubtedly produced the first genuine feeling among East as well as West Camerounians in the south that they were at last within easy reach of one another.

Economically, the effect of the new road was felt as well. The movement of goods and produce between Douala, the country's main commercial centre, and Victoria and Tiko became a simple matter. Customs barriers had already been lifted between the two federated states in 1966—a necessity once Cameroun entered the UDEAC customs union. Discriminatory tariffs had been abandoned, with a resultant shift from the reliance in West Cameroun on British and Commonwealth imports to those from France and the countries of the European Common Market. But, until the new road was opened, supplies were irregular and more costly, and price increases had caused a measure of dissatisfaction. Victoria with its beaches and Buea with its mountain coolness benefited from a significant increase in tourist traffic from Douala and abroad, though a question mark hung over the future of the ports at Tiko and Victoria as access to the bigger and more advanced facilities at Douala for the export of plantation crops now became possible.[27]

The integration of the administrative system in West Cameroun has already been described in general terms, and there is no doubt that the influence of the federal inspectorate and the federal government came to be felt increasingly after unification. Yet, as Ardener points out, the impact of the changes was mitigated by the fact that, for the most part, federal services—such as transport, posts and telegraphs, and justice—were controlled by West Camerounian Ministers.[28] Again, supervision of local government by federal officials took place side by side with the retention of the old pattern of local authorities, based on ethnic units and chiefdoms or their equivalents, rather than the imposition of new ones modelled on the eastern pattern. The difficulties which surrounded the introduction of federal control were felt to a far greater extent by the members of the West Cameroun government and the civil service than at the local level, although District Officers did experience a degree of tension in sorting their respective relationships with the state and federal governments in their dual capacities as DOS and *préfets*. Local authorities were also directly affected when their funds (and their tax-collecting functions) were placed under federal rather than under state control in 1965. But the retention of Chiefly prestige, both individually and collectively in the House of Chiefs, did much to mollify them and compensate for the loss of real power and influence.

In the legal fields, unification has proceeded very slowly. The structural integration of the judicial system scarcely masks the profound differences that continue to exist between the courts in the two states, the laws they enforce, the procedures they follow and the legal professions which serve them. At a purely visual level, there remains the attachment of the West Cameroun bar and bench to the wigs and gowns they took over from Britain. But more important is the fact that the entire civil law of West Cameroun—including not only contracts and company law, but also procedure, marriage and inheritance as well as land law—are still founded on English principles. Even where substantial gaps exist (for instance, the almost total absence of any law on insolvency) they have not been filled.

Reform and unification have occurred, under the direction of a federal commission established in 1966 by the Ministry of Justice and staffed by representatives of both legal systems in the federation. But so far it has produced only a uniform marriage registration system, a federal labour code, and a single penal code. The last of these represents a considerable achievement, not only because it successfully reconciled important differences between the French and the English criminal law, but also because it was seized upon as an opportunity for innovations concerning sentencing (for example, rehabilitation and minimum sentences), derived from some contemporary thinking on criminology as well as from customary law.[29] Nevertheless, it must be recognised that even in the criminal law sphere, a great area of difference remains between the two states. Criminal procedure, in particular, has yet to be standardised. And it is here that the ordinary West Camerounian would be most threatened by the adoption of the eastern system. Procedural differences between the two systems include the West's emphasis on the innocence of an accused until he is proved guilty; and the English rules of evidence differ from the French in the elaborate provision they make to protect an accused person from having confessions extracted from him unwillingly, among numerous other liberal rules which favour the individual against the state. Even the new criminal law itself may not survive intact after it has been interpreted in the light of these rules, particularly since Supreme Court decisions form part of the body of the law in West Cameroun by creating precedents binding on lower courts, while in East Cameroun they do not necessarily have this effect.

The national jurisdiction of the *gendarmerie* meant that its impact was felt (and feared) in the period shortly after independence, since armed quasi-military police were not part of the West Cameroun tradition. But the continued presence of a separate police force in West Cameroun, under state control, has meant that no widespread drastic change has taken place in police methods. In 1970, however, the police were due to be 'federalised', and the consequences here—in terms of the way in which they interpret their powers, the different methods of the East Cameroun police, and the degree to which they would be prepared to submit to control by the courts—could well produce a more extensive reaction.

The staffing of the courts themselves, and of the legal profession, has reflected the differences in the law, and reinforced them. Judges in West Cameroun have either been British or British-trained,* with an equivalent reliance on France in the case of East Cameroun. Although the Federal University had been training lawyers since 1962, most West Camerounian lawyers were still being educated in Nigeria until 1968. That year saw the creation of the first full-time training course for magistrates and legal officers for West Cameroun at the *Ecole Nationale pour l'Administration et la Magistrature* in Yaoundé. The first graduates from the course—all of whom had law degrees, from either the Federal University or universities in Britain and Nigeria—went into the West Cameroun legal service in the middle of 1969. Attendance at the course is now a compulsory requirement for the practice of law. In addition, in order to ensure that lawyers are in future educated in Cameroun and trained in Cameroun law, the federal government has terminated the scholarships of students studying abroad.

It is too early to judge the efficacy of these measures, but the combined effect of the University degree and the compulsory course from Yaoundé is likely to be an increasing number of lawyers whose main grounding is in the dominant East Camerounian legal system, and who have a rather less extensive

* The Chief Justice is Jordanian (with experience in Palestine, the Sudan and Northern Nigeria); and the other three judges are Irish, Cypriot and Camerounian. In the past, the judiciary has included West Indians. Mr Justice Endeley, the Camerounian judge, was trained in Nigeria and the UK.

knowledge of the West's laws. The long-term result may well be the harmonisation of the legal systems in the direction of assimilating the French-based system in West Cameroun; an immediate consequence may be that lawyers and magistrates from that state will be able to move freely between the two systems.

A real barrier to any such movement would, however, be that of language. Despite the formal recognition of the fact that Cameroun is a bilingual country, there is still only a very small part of the population for whom this is a reality. French is the language of the federal administration, except in West Cameroun where English has to be used. Even in this case, it is not unusual to discover senior francophone officials in federal departments (for instance the customs officials in Victoria) who experience considerable difficulty in communicating with their juniors, with resulting confusion and tension.

Thus the deep attachment to the colonial languages and cultures which was built up (particularly by the French, but also by the British) during the period of alien rule has persisted. The fact that most people in West Cameroun have a less perfect knowledge of English* than their eastern counterparts have of French has not made this any the less so. Early fears that West Cameroun would lose its cultural identity by being submerged under the more pervasive and less tolerant francophone influence undoubtedly limited the enthusiasm for bilingualism there, and have slowed its growth. But many of these inhibitions have been overcome. It has increasingly come to be realised—very largely as a result of Dr Fonlon's urging, even before he became a federal Minister[30]—that a wider knowledge of both the official languages, French and English, especially in West Cameroun, could safeguard the future of English and provide the foundation upon which a common Camerounian culture might be built.

At the administrative level, a degree of encouragement was provided by permitting civil servants to take courses in a second language, and facilities for bilingual teaching were provided by UNESCO in Yaoundé and in Buea. At the same time, salary bonuses were offered by the government for proficiency in the two languages. Some improvement did result from these moves, but the

* Creole (or pidgin English) is much more widely spoken than English in the West, though it is not of course taught in schools or used for official business.

level of bilingualism is still not high, and although it is now slightly less rare to encounter a bilingual official, bilingualism is far more in evidence among officials of the Western state than those of the East Cameroun or federal governments.

Education is a federal responsibility. As a result, reform has been stimulated and enforced from the centre, though it has often been left to state authorities to administer the changes. Even though the federated states have charge of primary education this too has been the subject of reforms introduced by the federal government along with changes in secondary, technical and higher education. In West Cameroun, the official principally concerned with the reform was the Federal Cultural Delegate, who supervised the move from an eight-year primary curriculum to a six-year course on a par with that of East Cameroun. The fact that the official, though in the federal service, was a West Camerounian was of considerable use in enabling the changes to proceed smoothly, and in making western concern over them known to the federal authorities.

Changes were also made in the examinations for entry into secondary schools, but the most extensive reorganisation took place at the secondary level itself. Here, the emphasis was on the introduction of a two-stage system, with vocational training playing a major part in the first stage and the full course leading to a general qualification—the *license* or *baccalauréat*. Though an inter-mediate examination (usual in the French system) disappeared, the product was far more closely modelled on East Cameroun's existing diploma than on the English General Certificate of Educa-tion, which fell away completely. The reforms were also directed to the content of the subjects taught; and, especially in the case of history and geography, these were given an African, and a Camerounian, flavour which they had not previously had.

It was at the secondary level that the learning of both official languages became compulsory, as early as 1963. This created few problems in East Cameroun, where large numbers of secondary schools run by the state had always taught English, though on a fairly rudimentary basis. In West Cameroun, however, the plan met with some resistance. Despite the very small number of secondary schools there (none of which was at that time run by the government), concern was expressed over the ability of the teachers to meet the demands of teaching the double language programme

165

properly. Even more worrying than the availability of adequate teaching staff, was the adverse effect on proficiency in English that was thought would result if French were taught fully as well. Whether or not these fears were justified, a decision was taken at the beginning to teach French only to those students who had a solid grounding in English. By 1967, however, it was officially laid down that the syllabuses and the timetables in all secondary schools in the federation would be identical. The problems had, to a certain extent, been overcome by the development of excellent facilities at the Federal Bilingual Grammar School (*Lycée*) at Man-O-War bay, which was later rehoused in impressive new buildings near Buea. It remains the main state secondary school in West Cameroun, as well as the only one in the country which is formally designated 'bilingual'.

The difference in educational tradition between the states was also reflected in the greater role played by private (i.e. mission) education in the West, where 85 per cent of the pupils attend mission schools. The main effects of this have been a greater emphasis on religious instruction in all schools there, and a less rigorous system of supervision by the state than is the case in East Cameroun. While a greater measure of government control and inspection has already been introduced in West Cameroun, no attempt has been made to do away with the religious content of education, and the disparity between the two systems remains at both primary and secondary levels.

The harmonisation of the educational system has always been accompanied by the suspicion in West Cameroun that a process of assimilation of the eastern system was involved which would ultimately lead to the disappearance of the West's distinctive cultural features. This fear alone does not justify Johnson's conclusion that 'perhaps disappointment among at least West Cameroonians was more profound in the field of education than in any other'.[31] But the development of education has favoured East Cameroun, particularly as regards secondary schooling. This can be seen from the enrolment statistics for 1968 :[32]

	Primary	Secondary
East	567,000	37,237
West	162,000	4,531

Thus, the number of pupils in primary schools in West Cameroun actually exceeds the proportion of West Camerounians in the population as a whole (20 per cent), but they have only one-ninth of the secondary school places. At both school levels, it is true, there has been a substantial increase in the figures over those for the pre-unification period[33] (though comparison is made more difficult in respect of secondary education, since many students from West Cameroun then attended schools in Nigeria). But the absolute number in secondary schools remains depressingly low for a population of more than 1,000,000, and the disproportion between the two states is a justifiable cause for disquiet.

A similar imbalance exists in higher education. Where there are several technical colleges in East Cameroun (six were listed in 1969),[34] West Cameroun is served by one, though it also has the pre-university level College of Arts, Science and Technology at Bambui.[35]

At the Federal University in Yaoundé, fewer than 7 per cent of the two thousand students are from the West. The University has, in several other ways, reflected some of the general trends in educational development. Established in 1962 with funds from France, it was envisaged as a bilingual institution which would bring together, and promote, not only the English and the French but also the African traditions in Cameroun culture. In fact it has made little headway in this direction, and has remained substantially monocultural. The language of instruction and the members of staff are mostly French. With the exception of the English Department in the Faculty of Letters, and a few courses on the West Cameroun legal system in the Law Faculty,[36] virtually no attempt is made to teach in English; and no attempt is made to teach any African language. The staff includes fewer than half a dozen West Camerounians in all faculties (though there are, of course, somewhat more from East Cameroun).[37] Examinations are almost entirely in French.

The result is that the small number of West Camerounian students alone have become bilingual, of necessity, while neither students nor staff members from East Cameroun or France make any major concession to the need to know or use English.

The University itself has been modelled on the French pattern, with an unduly large concentration on the Faculty of Law (which includes Economics and Politics). Of the 2,000 students enrolled in 1968, more than 60 per cent were in this faculty alone, with agriculture taking only 4 per cent and the remainder divided roughly evenly between Arts, Sciences and Education. African studies are taught in the Faculty of Letters, but as part of the general courses on history and sociology. An Institute of African Studies was established in 1970, but it is purely administrative in character and neither admits students nor conducts courses.

In part, the failure of the University to live up to the hopes of those who, like Fonlon, saw in it a major agency for the development of bilingualism and the creation of a new cultural synthesis for Cameroun is due to its heavy dependence on foreign, and particularly French, aid. The situation may change as the federal government comes to assume a greater proportion of its budget and makes more staff appointments on its payroll. But there is little evidence of this happening yet. Indeed some qualified West Camerounians have been unable to obtain jobs in the University because France will not provide the funds and the federal government cannot.

Ahidjo has shown an awareness of the problems, but has counselled patience. He has correctly pointed out that bilingualism must, to a large extent, depend for its success on the desire of the students to become bilingual and not on any compulsory measures. But no such trend has emerged spontaneously so far, and it is doubtful whether it will do so while French- and English-based cultures, as well as the languages themselves, remain so greatly in disequilibrium in the country.

Two general conclusions may be drawn about the process of unification in Cameroun during the ten years since independence. The first is that there has been a steady but continuous growth in the influence of East Cameroun and its values in most spheres in the federation. And the second is that West Cameroun, however much its influence on and significance within the Federal Republic have diminished, retains a separate identity, which has neither merged with nor been submerged in a single national character. The gap between the two cultures has been bridged, but it has by no means disappeared. The success of political integration has yet to be matched in other areas, and until it is, Cameroun will continue to present a challenge to those who, like Fonlon, see it as having an historic mission to provide the basis for a wider African unity.

8. Unification and Economic Development

WHILE ECONOMIC DEVELOPMENT in Cameroun since independence has not attained the measure of advance achieved by some of the fastest-growing African states (like the Ivory Coast), its growth has nevertheless been impressive. This is no small achievement in a country which faced not only the endemic obstacles of poverty and underdevelopment, but also had to cope with reconstruction after a damaging period of rebellion, as well as with the extra burdens imposed by unification.

Ahidjo's characteristic pragmatism extended to the economic field. His firm commitments to the pursuit of political stability and steady economic growth have gone together, and he has for the most part eschewed an ideological approach to economic questions. The hallmark of his policies has been the acceptance of a coldly realistic view of the opportunities for economic expansion and the basis on which it is to be accomplished. This has entailed a determined effort to secure the participation of foreign capital, both public and private, through policies of internal fiscal restraint and the provision of investment incentives and guarantees aimed at external support. Again, he has to a very large extent succeeded, although at the cost of a heavy dependence on France.

Ahidjo has described his economic policy as one of 'planned liberalism'. An early affirmation of his belief in 'African socialism' has in practice been translated into a measure of economic planning. Two five-year plans were formulated, and contained the framework in which overall economic objectives were set; and a Ministry of Economic Planning exists to supervise their implementation. But the government does not dominate the economy, or indeed seek to do so. Where the state has contributed capital to industry, it has done so for the most part by way of co-operation in joint enterprises with private (and mostly foreign) investors. Nationalisation has not, apparently, been contemplated; it certainly has not been threatened.

169

Ahidjo's pragmatic policy is nowhere better described than in the outline he gave of 'planned liberalism' in a speech in New York:

We have, in fact, deliberately chosen planned liberalism as our method of development. If planning expresses our concern, however legitimate, to make an efficient use of the resources available, to limit the role of chance in economic undertaking and consciously orientate development towards measured and predetermined targets, we are, on the other hand, convinced that liberalism remains a decisive factor of progress . . . because, finally, it alone can reconcile harmoniously the demands of rationalisation with the necessity of private (international) co-operation in a country where saving is still in an elementary stage of growth, and the State, even though it may be called upon, by force of circumstance, to play a determining role of impulsion and control, is far from possessing the means of assuming the whole 'burden' of development.[1]

If planning has not been conspicuously successful in accomplishing all that was envisaged for the country,[2] the policy as a whole has resulted in the continuous growth in the level of economic activity (as reflected in the Gross Domestic Product) and has produced a higher standard of living in the rural as well as the urban areas. Government estimates in 1970 put the rate of growth of the GDP as high as 6·5 per cent in real terms for the previous four years. The object is the doubling of the national income by 1980.

Like most African countries, Cameroun still remains substantially dependent on agriculture. Despite the efforts at industrialisation, the contribution of agriculture to the Gross Domestic Product is still around 40 per cent. About 85 per cent of the population are employed in the agricultural sector alone. Most of the production —of cash crops as well as for subsistence—takes place in small holdings. In West Cameroun there has continued to be a measure of emphasis on plantations for the production of export commodities, and a small proportion of the population is employed in this way as wage-earners (about 20,000). But this is not the pattern in the rest of the country. Outside the timber industry, agricultural production is essentially in the hands of small-scale farmers.

For the vast majority of the population, incomes have remained low. The percentage of the population involved in agriculture has not fallen noticeably although the percentage contribution of agriculture to the Gross Domestic Product has dropped. The effect of this continued pressure on individual incomes in the agricultural sector might have been felt less if there had been any significant increase in the price of agricultural goods; but there has in fact been no dramatic rise in the market prices of agricultural commodities, and where prices have risen they have often risen more slowly than those of the manufactured and imported goods needed by people whose earnings come from agriculture. Despite a consistent increase in the production of nearly all crops, the estimated annual average earnings per capita for the agricultural sector as a whole were 30,000 francs CFA in 1965.[3] This is a global figure, however, and more detailed investigation in the same year revealed that cocoa farmers in the south and centre of the country (who constitute some two-thirds of the population of those areas and about 13 per cent of the entire population) had an annual income of just over 44,000 francs CFA for a family of four.[4] While cattle farmers in the north did a little better on a per capita basis— with 68,000 francs CFA for a family of five—non-cocoa farmers were estimated by Hugon to have an average income per family of around 19,000 francs CFA.[5]

Cameroun is also severely dependent on agriculture for the bulk of its exports, and thus for its foreign earnings. Despite an increase in industrial production at the impressive annual rate of 12 per cent in the four years preceding 1967, two-thirds of the total exports of around 39 billion francs CFA in that year were still agricultural in origin, and the figure had been as high as 75 per cent in earlier years. This has meant that the country has been very much the victim of fluctuations in the world prices of commodities like cocoa, which dropped by as much as 28 per cent in 1965-6.

The potentially disastrous effects of price variations have been offset by the improvement of farming techniques, which has led to greatly increased production, and by crop diversification. This has meant that the impact of individual commodity price decreases has been mitigated. Still, it was possible for Ahidjo to point out in 1968 that, while cocoa output had increased by a third between 1959 and 1966, the value of the crop had only risen from 20 to 21 billion francs CFA over the same period.[6] When seen against the consistent annual increase in the cost of imported manufactured goods over the same period, the effect has been even more severe.

171

Ahidjo pointed out some years earlier than a ton of cocoa, which had purchased 880 metres of cloth in 1960, could only buy 300 metres in 1965; and there were similar, if not greater, reductions in the ability to obtain imported goods such as cement and corrugated tin roofing.[7] But cocoa still remains the biggest single export commodity. It represented 27 per cent of the value of all exports in 1968. The two varieties of coffee—arabica and robusta—are, for all practical purposes, produced for export alone. Coffee and cocoa together still account for more than half the value of exports (52 per cent in 1968), with cotton a long way behind at 5 per cent (and bananas, rubber, groundnuts, tobacco and palm oil between them amounting to less than 9 per cent).[8]

Minerals have not played an important part in the Cameroun economy. Several expatriate companies have been granted licences to explore for off-shore oil, but none has yet been found in commercially exploitable quantities. The country does have one of the largest known deposits of bauxite in Africa, at Martap in the north, and the production of alumina from bauxite has been technically possible since the harnessing of hydro-electric power at Edea. But the absence of adequate transportation facilities has prevented exploitation of the deposits. The transportation problem will be overcome when the Transcameroun railway, designed to link Yaoundé with Ngaoundéré in the north, has been extended the full 630 kilometres. Substantial aid from the European Development Fund (17·3 million dollars), United States AID (9·2 million dollars) and France (8·2 million dollars) has made extension of the line possible for nearly half the overall distance already, and plans for the remainder of its construction are well under way. Nevertheless, it is a startling fact that aluminium is produced in Cameroun, but from foreign bauxite. The giant French-financed *Compagnie Camérounaise de l'Aluminium Pechiney-Ugine* (Alucam) started production at Edea on the basis of a long-term contract for the utilisation of bauxite imported from Guinea, and this may well have been an important factor in holding up the construction of the railroad to the north.

Alucam's production of aluminium from imported Guinean bauxite represents a substantial contribution to Cameroun's export total. As the mainstay of the only metallurgical industry in the whole of francophone Africa, the company has played

172

an important part in securing Cameroun's role in that entire economic context. It is the country's principal consumer of electricity (which it obtains at a remarkably favourable price, rather less than a twentieth of the charge to the least preferred customers), and it employs some 2,000 people at high rates of pay. It is also responsible for a quarter of the total tonnage exported through Douala, as well as for a substantial proportion of the goods traffic carried by the railways.

Important as these contributions are, they mean that three valuable services—ports, railways and electricity supplies—are dependent on the operations of a single, giant, expatriate corporation. The value of the company's contribution to the Cameroun domestic economy is diminished considerably by the fact that it uses foreign raw materials, and by the freedom it enjoys from taxation and import duties. Only 5 per cent of its total turnover goes on salaries. Its management is entirely expatriate, its entire production is exported (two local manufacturers of aluminium products, Socatral and Alubassam, were, until 1968, dependent on imported aluminium for their activities), and nearly all of its earnings and profits are sent abroad.[9]

To a lesser extent the defects noticed in relation to Alucam are also present in many of the other industrial activities which were begun in the early 1960s. Although domestic savings have started to grow in the last few years and foreign investment only accounted for about a seventh of total investment in 1967, most of the capital for industrial development—particularly in the formative years up to 1965—came from private foreign sources. Encouraged by a liberal investment code, which provided considerable benefits including freedom from local taxation and duties for anything up to twenty-five years, some 34 billion francs CFA are estimated to have entered the country up to 1965. (Tax advantages in the private sector for foreign companies were abolished in 1969, and a 1 per cent minimum turnover tax was imposed on all companies. The effect was an increase in taxation of foreign businessmen of between 43 and 60 per cent.) The availability of cheap electrical power and the improvement of transport facilities, no doubt also played a part in developing industry, both for domestic consumer goods and for export in the UDEAC area.

As a result, a large number of enterprises of varying sizes came into existence, principally in or around Douala, for the manufacture of domestic consumer products (breweries and food processing factories, some of which use only local agricultural produce such as coffee, sugar and cocoa). There are also factories for making plastic household goods and aluminium utensils. Elsewhere, there are impregnation plants for the timber industry, and a dozen or more establishments for the manufacture of furniture. Factories in Yaoundé and Douala produce various chemical products, including soap, insecticides, detergents and paints. Bastos has a large cigarette factory in Yaoundé, and matches are made in Douala. There are cycle and car assembly plants on a small scale, and batteries and spark plugs are also manufactured. Several firms supply the building trade by producing cement and bricks.

Many of these concerns have been started with imported capital. Some have, however, been aided by government agencies, through the *Banque Camérounaise de Développement* or the *Société Nationale de l'Investissement*. On the whole, the government has not participated in the larger projects, or has only taken minority holdings in the bigger ventures. Of twenty-one projects which had received government investment capital by 1968, only five involved majority holdings by the state. The largest project in which it has participated is the *Société des Grands Hotels*, whose principal endeavour was the construction of a magnificent luxury hotel on the slopes of Mont Febe, overlooking Yaoundé, which was opened in 1969. The government's investment amounted to 212 million francs CFA, which was 70 per cent of the company's capital. More significantly perhaps, this sum represented just over a fifth of the total government investment in industry and commerce.[10]

The textile industry has grown significantly, and is important for its use of local products, most of which come from the north (leather for shoes and cotton for cloth). A major breakthrough was made in 1970, with the opening of two new factories by Cicam. One of these, in Garoua, was the first major industrial undertaking in the north of the country. Together, the two plants will constitute the largest textile complex in francophone Africa, with a production capacity of 13 million metres of cloth annually, and a projected total turnover of around 1 billion francs CFA a year. Capital for the project was met partly from private sources and partly by the participation of a consortium of European and African-based banks, as well as from funds contributed by France and the EEC.[11]

Despite the real growth in the industrial sphere, industry still plays a subsidiary role when compared not only to agriculture, but also to commerce. The combined contribution of manufacturing and the construction industry to the GDP has increased by nearly 50 per cent since 1964, but it still only amounts to 10 per cent of the total. Industrial growth has also tended to be capital-rather than labour-intensive, and there are only about 80,000 people employed in both industry and commerce throughout the country. A new brewery set up in 1970 by Guinness in Douala involved capital investment of around 1,000 million francs CFA, but was only expected to employ 250 people (not all of whom, of course, will be Camerounian).[12] In general, this tendency to capital-intensive investment has contributed to an estimated unemployment figure for urban areas alone of 150,000. (With another 400,000 said to be in 'disguised unemployment' in rural areas,[13] the total unemployed represents somewhat more than 11 per cent of the population.)

There is no doubt that industry has meant increased wages for those who are employed. The government has, particularly since the enactment of the labour code, established minimum wages for industry as well as for agriculture. These are around 37 francs CFA per hour in the major industrial areas (Douala, Yaoundé, Edea and Buea), and about 20 francs CFA in the lowest-paid regions.[14] Thus a manual labourer in Douala could expect to earn not less than 90,000 francs CFA a year, a semi-skilled worker 120,000 francs CFA and a skilled artisan between 200,000 and 300,000 francs CFA, depending on his qualifications.[15] The establishment of minimum wage levels was no doubt as well-intentioned as it was politically necessary, but it may well have contributed to the high unemployment figure and to the capital-intensive nature of industrial undertakings, by increasing labour costs in industry.

The government has tried to guard against the dangers of inflation, however, and wages have remained virtually unchanged in the urban areas since 1963. Agricultural wages have also remained virtually static. Thus the government's policy may prove to have been short-sighted. It has stimulated investment, but has also created a source of difficulty by increasing unemployment

175

relatively as well as absolutely (the total number of persons employed in the civil service and in industry and commerce is 200,000; the unemployment figure in urban areas is 150,000). Another effect of government policy has been to create a distinctly privileged class of highly-paid employees in the towns, who are vastly better off than their counterparts in agriculture. Their position is also a constant reminder to the urban unemployed of their under-privileged position. There is, in other words, an increasingly sharp social stratification, and the beginnings of a class structure which was not previously noticeable in Cameroun.

Industry has also meant a significant rise in the number of expatriates. Their number has more than doubled in fifteen years, and is now around 15,000 (including employees *and* their dependants). While the largest increase—in Douala, from 6,500 to 11,000 —has kept pace roughly with the growth of the town, expatriates still appear to occupy most of the top positions in manufacturing, trade, banking and transportation. Hugon's estimate is that, between them, Europeans earn some 20 billion francs CFA a year (as compared with 24 billion for more than 80,000 Camerounians in the private sector of commerce and industry).[16] Expatriates' earnings comprise something like one-sixth of the total national income: they constitute roughly one-third of one per cent of the population.

The impact of expatriates is also felt in other ways. Foreign companies are responsible for about 17 per cent of the country's national product. Foreigners are also the principal reason for the importation of a substantial quantity of luxury foods and drink: food and beverages imported in 1967 cost 5·3 billion francs CFA, a quarter of which was spent on luxuries. Expatriates are wont to live at a high standard,[17] and the cost of living for foreigners is the third highest in Africa and is almost on a par with the larger cities of North America.

More important still is the extent to which Europeans repatriate their earnings directly, and not just by buying foreign goods. It is not known how much money is sent out of the country by expatriates, but one estimate suggests that the total amount is equal to the amount of capital which enters the country from abroad.[18] In other words, the economic benefit of foreign private investment to Cameroun is almost completely offset by repatriated earnings and profits.

The larger foreign companies—like the United Africa Company and its subsidiaries in East and West Cameroun, SCOA and UTC, as well as several others—exercise an immense influence on the trading and transport (road haulage) areas of the economy. They also dominate importing and exporting, though some attempt has been made by the government to regulate these aspects of their near-monopoly position by a system of import licensing.[19]

The role of the government in the country's economy, though not particularly noticeable as a direct participant in industry, is not to be underestimated. In the first five years of the federation's existence, Cameroun was receiving direct budgetary support from France (to the tune of 1·75 billion francs CFA in 1962–3, but an average of 1·1 billion francs CFA annually until 1965). It has balanced, and progressively increased, its budget since then, though it was only able to operate a budgetary surplus for the first time in 1969.[20] The general policy has been one of restraint, with a growth rate of 15 per cent annually at the beginning of the decade being reduced to between 7 per cent and 9 per cent for the rest of the period. Increases in expenditure have been matched by rises in revenue (the result of economic expansion rather than any substantial increases in taxation). A striking feature of the budget is the high expenditure on salaries and the relatively low provision for capital projects. While the latter have been financed by aid from abroad, the former have grown steadily both in number and in cost. Capital expenditure has, in fact, remained roughly constant at about 10 per cent of the budget.[21]

The high administrative expenditure is, in part, the result of the existence of three governments, since federal officers are required in the federated state as well as at the centre. The federal government has also had to provide subventions for the West Cameroun budget continuously in each year since reunification. By 1965, this accounted for three-quarters of that state's revenue and was of the order of 2 billion francs CFA; it has, if anything, increased since that date.[22]

The principal item of expenditure is, however, salaries. They account for nearly two-thirds of the total, or some 26 billion francs CFA in 1969. A good deal of this is absorbed by the army; though no figures are available for the total number of persons employed by the federal government, the global figure for the country (including employees of the federated states) was somewhere in the region of 60,000.[23] Salaries have not increased greatly—the policy of restraint has been applied especially stringently to the public services—nor have the total numbers in government employ risen sharply, though a projected salary increase in 1970 (on top of a modest rise in 1969) was given as the main reason for a 12 per cent increase in the cost of running the government.[24]

Although wage rates have kept relatively steady, individual earnings in government services have risen considerably, mainly because Africanisation policies have meant that Camerounians now occupy most of the jobs in the middle and upper ranks of the civil service. This has meant rapid promotion along the existing salary scales. Another source of the increase in individual earnings has been the provision of generous family allowances and lodgings for most senior officials. (In 1968 lodgings alone—for higher civil service and expatriate technical staff—accounted for 600 million francs CFA.) In general, the replacement of expatriate personnel in the administration has not meant a diminution in the government wage bill. It has, if anything, led to an increase. Expatriates' wages were often met from aid funds; Camerounians are paid by the government. The level of salaries goes with the job rather than with the nationality of its occupant.

The high total expenditure on wages is reflected in the following average earnings of employees in government service: daily paid workers (*journaliers*) received about 160,000 francs CFA per year, senior officers around 1,170,000 francs CFA and the highest level, *cadres supérieurs* (equivalent to permanent secretaries and the like), nearly 1,400,000 francs CFA in 1965,[25] apart from allowances and perks. A glance at the average earning figures already given for the agricultural, and even the private industry sectors, shows that government employees form perhaps the most privileged group in the Cameroun population. As a class, they are only less prosperous than the expatriates.

When considered in relation to the total number of persons employed in the non-traditional sectors of the economy—government employees comprise 30 per cent of the 200,000 persons in employment—it is clear that the government's policies are not only creating a privileged class, but also play a major part in increasing the population of the larger towns such as Yaoundé, Douala, Edea and Victoria-Buea. This swelling of the urban population takes place at a cost to the economy as a whole, and to the rural areas in particular; but it is also detrimental to the towns themselves. The economy suffers from the inflationary effects of high wages and the heavy emphasis on the south; the rural areas enjoy a lower relative prosperity because of the concentration of wealth in the towns and the loss of productive man-power; and the towns, in turn, are over-populated and have to bear the burden of very high unemployment.

Hugon has pointed out the dangers of the budgetary emphasis on wages and administration generally. After drawing attention to the fact that expenditure on any new project in the public sector necessarily involves an increase in recurrent expenditure and must lead to a more rapid increase in the budget than in the national income, he continues: 'the growth of government services encourages the rural exodus, sets in motion an inflationary process, and reduces the flow of public investment in the productive sector.' [26]

Despite the relatively low level of expenditure on capital projects, the government has been instrumental in bringing about substantial development in the social as well as the purely economic infrastructure. Progress in both fields has, however, been the result of considerable amounts of foreign aid, principally from France and the EEC, and also to a lesser extent from the United States and West Germany.

In the social services—education and health—advance has tended to consolidate the superior position of the southern portions of the country. While progress in these areas has made the government increasingly aware of the need to promote more even development throughout the country, it has also created further pressures on the government for continued expenditure in the developed areas through the more rapid rise in population in the south and greater migration to the towns located there.

Reference has already been made to the overall figures for education and it is worth noting that illiteracy has been overcome to the extent that for the entire country more than 65 per cent of children of school age are being educated. While this figure tends to disguise the differences between the regions (the percentage is as high as 90 per cent for parts of the south like the areas surrounding Yaoundé, and only 24 per cent in parts of the north) the government has made an effort to see that the rate of growth in the north is greater than that in the south. In 1969, it was possible to report a growth rate in education of 8 per cent a year in the north, while it was only 4 per cent for East Cameroun as a whole.

Medical facilities have also been extended, and by the end of the second five-year plan the federation expected to have some 71 hospitals, 38 leprosaria and 731 dispensaries. Still, the country as a whole could only count one doctor for every 26,000 inhabitants in 1969 (1 : 40,000 if the public health services alone were used in the calculation); and it must be remembered that medical services are much more highly developed in urban than in rural areas. Thus, government statistics claim only one hospital bed for every 1,750 inhabitants in the north, while there is one for every 370 of the population in the centre-south of the country.[27] As a result, the expectation of life is still very low: 51 years in the southern areas, 41 in West Cameroun, but only 33 in the north as a whole and as low as 24 in some of the Kirdi areas;[28] and, although infant mortality is decreasing, it remains high.

The economy continues to grow at more than twice the rate of population increase (5 per cent as against 2·1 per cent); but the south is growing more rapidly than the north. So, with the economy itself not subject to strain as a result of population growth, the government may still find itself in the unenviable position of being forced by demographic pressure to favour the south even more than it has done so far, thus exacerbating the differences between the two areas.

There have been very real efforts to develop the north, through the construction of roads and the extension of the railway, as well as by stimulating greater production of cotton and groundnuts, and the establishment of processing plants for both commodities. But the north is—and seems likely to remain—the least developed part of the country. Recent figures are not available, but in 1964 southern areas of East Cameroun produced six times as much as the north, and personal incomes were on average more than three times as great there as in the north. Since then, developments of the kind already mentioned may have altered the position in absolute terms, but the general trend has been to perpetuate the imbalance, if not actually to increase it as a result of the industrial concentration around Douala, Yaoundé and Edea.

Foreign aid has played an important part in the Cameroun

economy. France has always been the biggest contributor, and in the first five years was responsible for as much as two-thirds of all aid, which was distributed roughly equally between capital projects, technical assistance and direct budgetary assistance to the government.[29] Since the budgetary assistance ceased, at the end of 1965, French aid has been divided between the first two categories.

In recent years, France has supplied just less than half the total aid received by Cameroun. Aid from the European Economic Community has increased correspondingly, principally through the European Development Fund (FED). In terms of the first agreement with the Associated states of the common market, 10·1 billion francs CFA was allocated to Cameroun, and this was followed by the allocation of a further 7·1 billion francs CFA for the five years up to 1969. German aid contributed a total of around 2·2 billion francs CFA during the five years to 1965 (excluding technical assistance), as compared with 26 billion by France, 14·1 billion by the FED, 5 billion by US AID, and 3 billion by all of the others.[30] Russian aid has been small, but includes the building of a radio transmitter. Loans and credits from the World Bank and its subsidiaries have amounted to 18 million dollars (approximately 4·5 billion francs CFA).

Cameroun's heavy reliance on foreign aid for capital projects has already been noted. In general, it has been responsible for at least half of all public investment, and, to a considerable extent, funds for this purpose have come from sources other than France. Thus the FED and US AID have contributed substantially to major projects such as road construction, the Transcameroun railway and educational programmes (other than the university).

French aid (mainly from the *Fonds d'Aide et de Co-opération* (FAC)) is not unduly burdensome. Most of it has consisted of grants, which are not repayable, and Cameroun has not been saddled with any large measure of debts to repay. But the fact that funds from France are distributed between capital and recurrent expenditure has meant that their impact has been rather less than that of private French capital. The high proportion of aid which goes to technical assistance is also significant. This has meant that a great deal of French aid money has been paid to French personnel —working on capital projects, as well as within the social services, the civil service (as advisers), and the army. Though the number

181

of French nationals employed in this way will no doubt decline as more and more qualified Camerounians become available to replace them, the effect has also been to underscore the French 'presence' in Cameroun so far, and to swell the number of expatriates working within the Cameroun economy, with the consequences described earlier.

The patterns of external trade in Cameroun also reflect a high degree of dependence on France and the EEC. The country has, for the most part, paid its way internationally, and has had a favourable balance of trade for nearly all of the years since independence, despite disadvantageous fluctuations in world commodity prices. Nevertheless, it still relies on imports for most of the raw materials needed for manufacturing, all of its capital goods, and even some of its staple food supplies. Thus, imports of rice flour and sugar have all increased in recent years, some by as much as 90 per cent between 1964–7.[31] As a result of increased manufacturing locally, a smaller proportion of consumer goods has been imported in recent years: the ratio dropped from 41 per cent to 31 per cent of the total imports between 1962 and 1967, but this still represented over 11 billion francs CFA.[32] Recently, French markets have accounted for less than 40 per cent of the total exports (37 per cent in 1967), as against well over 50 at the beginning of the decade (52 per cent in 1962).

There has been no corresponding decrease, however, in the reliance on France as a source of imports. On the contrary, goods imported from France have increased from 50 per cent to 54 per cent of the total over the same period. A continuation of this trend would benefit both parties: Cameroun would gain by diversifying its export markets; and France would gain by reducing its need to support Camerounian products while allowing its own exports to play an increasing part in the Cameroun economy.[33] (This favourable result for the French balance of payments leaves out of account the general advantage of the trade pattern to France through its contribution to the franc zone as a whole. Cameroun is, of course, tied to this zone through the *Communauté Financière Africaine* (CFA): devaluation of its currency followed almost automatically on the French devaluation of 1969.) It is already clear that French imports dominate the consumer sector of the economy; and it looks as though they might do so to an even greater extent in the future.

Cameroun has also benefited from its membership of the *Union Douanière et Economique de l'Afrique Centrale* (UDEAC), a customs union formed in 1965 with four neighbouring states (Chad, Congo-Brazzaville, the Central African Republic and Gabon). Its principal aim was the harmonisation of their economies. The community has established a single external tariff on imported goods: it was this which compelled Cameroun to end internal differences and customs duties between East and West Cameroun in 1966, since these involved preferential treatment for British and Commonwealth products in the western state. UDEAC has brought increased trade for the port of Douala, which serves other member states, particularly the land-locked Chad and the CAR. There has also been an increase in the use of Cameroun's overland transportation facilities, which has heightened the need for improved roads and railways, and has provided an added incentive for the grant of foreign aid for this purpose.

The treaty's benefits have been as important for Cameroun's manufacturing industry, since its immediate effect was to double the available market (to a total of more than 11·6 million), though this is of potential rather than immediate value. A common investment code has also been to Cameroun's advantage: the freedom from import duties, direct and indirect taxes available under Cameroun's own legislation are duplicated in respect of enterprises which undertake to export to other UDEAC members, and some forty-three firms have been established in Cameroun as a result. More than half of these sold 90 per cent of their products in Cameroun itself, and only one had sales of more than 40 per cent to other UDEAC countries, although four companies in the textile and shoe industry depend on Chad and the CAR for a fifth of their turnover.

The economic effects of reunification on West Cameroun have been mixed. In the first four years of the new regime, the state had to reorientate its monetary system, its trade, and its reliance on external British support for trade and aid. Metrication was the least of its problems, though at a personal level this did cause some measure of hardship. Internal trade was affected by the need to shift away from a reliance on Nigeria for manufactured products, and on Britain and the Commonwealth for exports and imports. While Commonwealth preference continued to operate until six months after the UDEAC agreement came into force (i.e. until mid-1966), the immediate effect of having to import goods from and through East Cameroun was inflationary. Johnson estimates that the difference in prices between the two states may have been as high as 100 per cent, which severely affected the West Cameroun population.[34] The higher prices also had the effect of making local produce more costly, since the prices paid in East Cameroun for West Camerounian products were a good deal higher than they were in the west.[35] But trade between the two states benefited West Cameroun at least as much as East Cameroun. More serious, perhaps, was the decline in revenue for West Cameroun. With the loss of excise duties on Nigerian goods (beer and cigarettes for the most part), and the absence of the support which had been received from the Nigerian federal treasury, it came to need a budgetary subvention from Yaoundé to an increasing extent, and still does. An important export market was lost as Commonwealth preference was phased out. Banana production in particular was severely affected; production never recovered from the blow, especially since disease struck shortly afterwards and ruined the crop. As a result, total exports declined, despite the switch by plantations to a greater emphasis on rubber and palm oil. More-over, the support previously given to the large plantations by the Commonwealth Development Corporation disappeared. The loss, which amounted to some £2–3 million (1·2–2 billion francs CFA) was not compensated for despite an outright grant from the UK to the West Cameroun government of £575,000. Private investment also declined in the period immediately after reunification;[36] this was not offset by the expansion in trading activity in West Cameroun which followed opportunities created within the new federal framework.[37]

It is necessary to offset against these losses the gains that followed from federation. The most noticeable gain was in the substantial foreign aid from France, the FED and US AID, none of which countries had previously made any contribution to the Southern Cameroons. This aid contributed considerably to the improvement of the infrastructure of the federated state—its roads and communications, as well as education and health services. No doubt the main reason for these developments was the federal government's desire to consolidate West Cameroun's attachment to the federation by overcoming its physical isolation, but the result was to help overcome the state's backwardness as well. West Cameroun not only has the fastest growth rate in primary education, it also shares the high rate of population increase in the south of the country because of its improved medical facilities. Incomes have risen as a result of the establishment of minimum wages by the federal government; if they are not as high as those in East Cameroun, this only reflects the comparatively underdeveloped state of the western economy.

Federal assistance has resulted in the diversification of crops. Coffee plays a much more important part than it did before, though it is of the less lucrative robusta variety; experimental attempts to grow tea on plantations in the south have been complemented by a large-scale agricultural development project for the Ndop plain in the north of the region. However, industrial growth has not been a consequence of unification: Douala and other parts of East Cameroun will inevitably continue to dominate in this respect, as well as to attract urban migrants from the west who in the past made for the CDC plantations as a major source of employment. Similarly, development of the port facilities at Victoria will be determined by its ability to complement rather than to compete with Douala's facilities. Off-shore oil prospects near Victoria represent West Cameroun's major hope for development in terms of natural resources, and for industrial growth. But until this proves to be viable, progress will be an adjunct rather than a major contributor to the growth in the remainder of the federation. West Cameroun, like the north of the country, only produces a fraction of the south-east's contribution to the economy. The benefits already gained from reunification—in the form of increased wages, lower direct taxation, and better facilities for transport and health—can only be consolidated by closer integration with East Cameroun even at the cost of psychological and cultural strain, as the move into francophone Africa becomes total.

The general conclusion to be drawn from this description of the Cameroun economy is that 'like most African countries, two fundamental traits characterise [it]: dualism and dependence'. Gonidec's terse judgement[38] points not only to the country's underlying economic problems, but also to the difficulties confronting the government as a result of its policies in the economic field some ten years after independence.

The essential dualism of the economy derives from the fact that 85 per cent of the population still depend on agriculture for a livelihood while most development has been concentrated on the urban-industrial sector. This is a problem partly inherited from the colonial period, but government policies have so far only reduced the emphasis on agriculture at the cost of increasing the disparity between urban and rural incomes. Similarly, the divide between the north and the south of the country, and that between East and West Cameroun, are the product of Cameroun's very special experience during the period of alien rule. While government policies have succeeded in avoiding complete concentration on the south-east, they have not as yet arrested the growing disparities between these parts of the country. On the contrary, they have probably added to problems of regional disequilibrium by creating an urban-based class structure in the south; and if this were not in itself a source of prospective political difficulties, government industrial policies have resulted in high unemployment and overcrowding in the towns, which appear to have been accepted as the unfortunate but inevitable corollary of rapid urban development.

Overall, the economy has remained dependent: the reliance on the colonial power for economic well-being in the years before independence has been translated in the contemporary context into a dependence on several foreign nations but still principally on France. The monetary system, the great bulk of capital and consumer goods, public and private investment, and—most important of all—the sale of its agricultural products are dependent upon foreign support. Improvements have certainly been made. Budgetary support is no longer necessary; domestic savings have increased so as to reduce the need for foreign capital; agreements, like UDEAC, have brought about a diversification of clients, just as the EEC has made it possible to distribute external dependence on trade and aid over a wider range of countries.

Ahidjo, as a realist, has not attempted to disguise the extent of his need for support from abroad. When talking of industrialisation as a 'safeguard of our economic independence', he was careful to add: 'I say a certain [kind of] independence, for no country

186

in the world, even if it be among the most powerful, can validly claim that it is economically independent.'[39]

The problems which face Cameroun now are, to some extent, the result of growth and are much less harmful than those which would have followed stagnation. But the danger is that their solution may not lie in more growth alone, since this may merely entrench, or even increase, existing imperfections. The real test of the country's economy—and of Ahidjo's realism—will come as economic advance increasingly involves the need to translate growth based on external dependence into more widely dispersed prosperity based on internal harmony.

9. Cameroun, Africa and the World

THE HISTORY of federal Cameroun's political and economic development since independence reflects a gradual and continuous process of adjustment to the less pleasant facts of life, and a measure of success in dealing with them, based on a hardheaded and almost phlegmatic realism. Its progress in the field of international relations against even greater odds, particularly within Africa, must be counted among its substantial achievements; this was accomplished with the restrained determination and perseverance which are the hallmarks of Ahidjo's *realpolitik*.

The international position in which reunified Cameroun found itself at the outset was not encouraging. France's benevolent attitude and the friendship of most francophone African states at independence were important assets and have continued to be the basis of Cameroun's international support. But the internal rebellion, which had been going for nearly five years before independence, continued after federation to colour the attitude of the external world to the new state.[1]

More important were the activities of the UPC abroad. By 1961 it had established close contacts with a number of African governments and was accepted by several pan-Africanist political parties as a political ally in the last stages of the anti-colonial campaign. It had conducted operations in exile from the Sudan, the United Arab Republic, Ghana and Guinea. If the campaigns started abroad did not amount to much internally, the propaganda broadcast from Cairo, Conakry and Accra certainly prejudiced the chances of the Ahidjo regime being easily accepted within the African framework. Organisations supporting the UPC in London and Paris—where its material was also published extensively—influenced the still significant numbers of the African intelligentsia and their sympathisers who were studying and working in these capitals.[2] The party had also apparently established cordial relations with the USSR and China; although the Soviet Union had recognised Cameroun from the outset, its attitude to the new state was equivocal,[3] while the Peking government continued to receive visits from UPC leaders in exile, and to support them with money and material.[4] Nor had Cameroun got off to a good start at the United Nations. The vote against federation in the northern part of the British Cameroons had come as something of a shock to Ahidjo, who had launched a bitter attack against the United Kingdom at the General Assembly in 1961. Although his complaint that Britain had conducted the plebiscite unfairly and improperly was rejected after an investigation, it had the immediate effect of causing a rift with Nigeria, and was to be the subject of legal action at the International Court of Justice. Pending the outcome of this case, Cameroun was lukewarm in its support for the UN, though it co-operated closely with its agencies.[5]

Nevertheless, relations with Britain and Nigeria did not remain strained for long. In February 1963, a treaty of co-operation was signed with Nigeria at Lagos which recognised the importance of relations between the neighbouring states, and provided in detail for measures concerning trade and the movement of persons between the two states. In May Ahidjo visited Britain with full official honours, and various forms of aid were agreed upon. In December, the International Court declined to decide the dispute over the Northern Cameroons[6] and although the issue still caused some rancour in Yaoundé, this removed the last barrier to effective co-operation. Relations continued to be friendly, with Britain supplying a small amount of aid and technical assistance, mainly in the form of English language teachers in the West Cameroun schools and the Federal University. Trade with Britain, never extensive, dropped considerably after the ending of Commonwealth preference in West Cameroun in 1966. With Britain contemplating entry into the EEC this situation could change, though it has made little attempt to take advantage of what could be considered an easy point of entry into francophone Africa.

Relations with the UN have also undergone change. Cameroun now participates fully in the major organs in New York, and receives assistance through UNESCO and the UN Development Programme. In the case of the USSR, there have been no major changes, though official visits have been exchanged and the Soviet Union maintains a fairly substantial embassy staff in Yaoundé. Despite a small aid programme, the USSR does not seem to be extensively involved with Cameroun.

China only established relations with the Ahidjo government in 1971. Cameroun did not recognise Peking, and exchanged diplomatic representatives with the Formosa (Taiwan) Nationalist government, which also conducted a small—and very largely token—aid programme, principally in relation to experimental agricultural techniques, outside Yaoundé and near Bafut in the West Cameroun grasslands. Cameroun also recognised South Korea and South Vietnam. Outside of Africa, France, the USA and West Germany have all made major contributions of aid and are important in respect of trade.

Despite the substantial contributions of the European Development Fund to Cameroun and its infrastructure, as well as the growing importance of trade with the Common Market countries, relations with the EEC underwent some strain after 1968 as difficulties were experienced over the negotiation of a second agreement between the members and the associated states.[7] However, Cameroun is unlikely to be in any worse position than the other African states in this regard. The falling away of price supports for primary products from tropical countries could affect Cameroun severely; this caused Ahidjo to register his disappointment and concern at the end of the 1969 negotiations on the second agreement. The delay in ratifying the convention also proved worrying—based as it was on the apparent reluctance of France's partners to increase their contributions to the FED, which some of them see as a hidden subsidy which they are being called upon to make to the former French possessions.

It was, however, within the African continent that Cameroun made its most extensive advances in the field of foreign relations. In the early years after reunification, it successfully established relations with Liberia—then a leading state among the more 'moderate' African countries; through President Tubman, Ahidjo was able to achieve some measure of accommodation with Ghana. Although Ahidjo remained cautious in his attitude to Ghana throughout Nkrumah's rule because of the support that had been given to the UPC, the two countries did, in fact, exchange diplomats in 1962. A similar distance was observed in relation to the UAR, even though Ahidjo made official visits to Cairo. The establishment of diplomatic relations between the two countries did not stop Ahidjo from retaining close contact with Israel, which has given a small amount of aid to Cameroun besides providing a number of technical advisers for the government. Israel has also engaged in a number of commercial ventures in collaboration with the government. The UAR has no aid programme in spite of some efforts which have been made in this direction. (In conversation with the UAR Ambassador in 1968, it emerged that the Cameroun government had not responded especially favourably to overtures or even done anything to implement an offer by the UAR to supply a professor of Arabic studies to the Federal University.)

Ahidjo has expanded relations elsewhere in Africa, both bilaterally and through regional organisations of a restricted as well as a pan-African character. Building upon the base of support within the former French colonies, Cameroun has always been an active participant in its groupings: first as the 'Brazzaville' group, and later as the Union of African and Malagasy States, as well as the organ for economic co-operation between these states, the Common Organisation of African and Malagasy States (the UAM and OCAM respectively).[8] The headquarters of the latter were based in Yaoundé and Cameroun played an important part in its meetings. Ahidjo gained prestige from his position as host to heads of state by presiding over OCAM gatherings from time to time.

On a somewhat more restricted scale geographically, UDEAC was of rather more practical significance to Cameroun in the economic field. Difficulties were experienced with some of the other member states which, on occasion, felt that the Union unduly favoured Cameroun and Gabon to their own disadvantage. The Central African Republic and Chad both withdrew from the organisation on these grounds in 1968; but they reverted to it shortly afterwards and no permanent rift exists between them and Cameroun. Ahidjo has also been able to mediate in disputes involving the CAR, Chad and Congo-Brazzaville, although Cameroun does not appear to have been directly involved in internal developments in any of these countries, some of which, like the Congo, have had successive changes in government, or in the Chad revolt.

Cameroun also succeeded in avoiding possible embarrassment with others of its neighbouring states. The Nigerian civil war of 1967–70 undoubtedly produced difficulties for Cameroun. It was widely assumed in the early stages of the war that Cameroun, which has substantial numbers of Ibo residents and border tribes with close ethnic ties to those in secessionist Biafra, would be seriously affected by the hostilities. Refugees did cross the border in considerable numbers after war broke out, and aircraft from Enugu and Port Harcourt in the enclave continued to land in Douala and Tiko, despite complaints from the Federal Military Government. Cameroun, however, took effective measures to seal its border with Nigeria, and a mobile wing of its *gendarmerie* was moved up to Mamfe to secure the frontier. Ahidjo was allegedly able to fend off criticism concerning the aircraft landings by pointing out that a ban placed on Biafran planes would involve recognition of the breakaway state. Internally the police were used to restrain Ibo residents,[9] while a small armed force stationed at Mamfe was expanded somewhat.

Later, the situation became more complicated, because of the evident support which Biafra was receiving from France. It is possible that the Ahidjo government came under pressure from General de Gaulle to allow military and relief supplies to enter Biafra from Cameroun but Ahidjo did not permit his territory to be used for either purpose—though planes may well have had to overfly Cameroun to reach Gabon. Throughout the period, Ahidjo maintained an attitude of strict neutrality. He was careful to confine his activities to participation within the committees and delegations established by the Organisation of African Unity to mediate between the disputing parties. He was, throughout, a staunch supporter of the OAU policy of not permitting existing borders to be altered without the consent of their governments.

The other neighbouring state within which developments could have involved Cameroun is Equatorial Guinea, which became independent in October 1968. This state is composed of two non-contiguous parts, the island of Fernando Po (some twenty miles from Douala and Victoria) and a mainland area, formerly Rio Muni, on the south-eastern border of Cameroun. Although only a very small proportion of the population of Fernando Po is ethnically related to the peoples of Cameroun,[10] the island is of obvious strategic importance to Cameroun. Nevertheless, Cameroun has made no attempt to annex either Fernando Po or any part of Rio Muni, despite suggestions that it might be interested in acquiring the former.[11] It has exchanged diplomats with the new state, and avoided any involvement during a period of disturbance which led to a *coup d'état* in 1969.

In the case of Equatorial Guinea, Ahidjo may have been influenced by a desire to avoid any conflict with Nigeria over the territory, but there can be little doubt that his attitude was also the result of his very close identification with the Organisation of African Unity and its policies of non-interference by member states in each other's internal affairs. His rise to prominence within this organisation—he was the OAU's chairman in 1969–70—was perhaps the most striking indication of the success of his foreign policy, representing the most complete triumph he achieved over the early hostility to Cameroun and its President expressed by Nkrumah and other radical pan-Africanist leaders. Cameroun was among the OAU's founder members, and Ahidjo had attended the conference in Addis Ababa in 1963 at which its charter was drafted. As a member of the 'Monrovia bloc' of less radical governments, Cameroun formed part of the majority within the OAU. Although it did not play an especially prominent part in the organisation's activities, it has studiously applied OAU policies and has not qualified its support for them, either orally or in practice. Both at the UN and in its own trade and immigration policies it has, for instance, supported efforts to carry out the boycott of South Africa and sanctions against Rhodesia. On occasion, this involved Ahidjo in strong criticism of France and the UK.[12] Similarly—and in direct contrast to both Gabon and the Ivory Coast—it specifically prohibits the entry of persons and goods from South Africa and Portuguese territories.*

Cameroun's potential as an important living example of the functioning of African unity has long been recognised, both inside the country and abroad; this was part of the inspiration to re-unification among the intellectual élite of the federation.[13] Cameroun successfully withstood many of the strains imposed by the problems of national integration, and it has done a good deal better than most other attempts at unity between states on the African continent.[14] Johnson nevertheless claims that:

> Most Cameroon leaders even failed to emphasise the one truly distinctive mission the country could embark on—an effort to project the Cameroon experiment with political union and political integration of disparate cultural legacies on a broader scale.[15]

* Visitors to Cameroun are left in no doubt that their entry visas for the country are only issued on condition that they are not used for travel to any of these areas.

He attributes this to a tendency on Ahidjo's part to play down this facet of Cameroun's character.

There is little doubt that African Unity is not a subject on which Ahidjo has chosen to dwell at length, either at home or abroad. He has on occasion made references to the need for unity in general terms, and to African Unity as 'that objective which is dear to all Africans'.[16] But the language in which he has done so has either made it clear that his enthusiasm is rhetorical, or it has been guarded and limited to an endorsement of specific organisations like the UAM, OCAM or UDEAC. A combination of cautiousness and pragmatism has led him to avoid anything which might sound more ambitious.

Ahidjo was not anxious, in the context of Cameroun politics, to stress unduly the divergent cultural and political backgrounds of the two parts of the country. In the first years after reunification he was, in any event, intent upon making sure that the institutions of the new state worked properly themselves before any wider claim could be made for them as a model for other countries, or for the continent as a whole. There was also the task of internal political unity which had to be completed.

Political pre-occupation at home was also accompanied by a distinct lack of ideological sympathy with the kind of unity that had been advocated by Nkrumah and the radical pan-Afri-canists. Johnson says that Ahidjo 'stated explicitly during the elaboration of the new constitution that he considered the union not to create a new political or moral organisation but to fulfil an old one'.[17] This statement accorded well with his disposition towards a gradualist approach to unity within the OAU.

The early advocates of total African Unity, both before and at the founding of the Organisation, had always been opposed by those who saw regional bodies, or co-operation between smaller numbers of more homogeneous states as a necessary first stage in the process. This was certainly the view of most members of the UAM and the Monrovia bloc, of which Cameroun was a member and Ahidjo an articulate spokesman. Thus, even at the Addis Ababa meeting to found the OAU, Ahidjo is said to have rejected 'every rigid constitutional form' of political union as being prema-ture, and to have added that, for the moment, he wanted neither federation nor confederation for the African continent.[18] He was even more emphatic in a speech to the *Union Camérounaise* at Bafoussam some two years later:

> For Cameroun, the matter is clear. A continental government at the present hour appears to raise anew a pure political utopia. This would be a snare for all African peoples, the construction of a false façade and a parade [for the benefit of] the exterior, an instrument without any real effectiveness for true evolution, [or] improvement in the life of the African, a source of confusion, indeed of difficulties in the way of inter-African co-operation.[19]

The passage of time has seen this cautious view echoed by other African leaders. But Ahidjo's speech was made in 1965. Cameroun has, since then, solved a number of her own internal problems, and may well be able to provide the solution to those which remain. In the meanwhile, the country has enjoyed political stability, and Ahidjo's own position of influence in Africa has grown. It is just possible that, if federal Cameroun can make its own unity even more real and substantial, Ahidjo the pragamatist may be able to point to his own national experience as the concrete foundation for the continental structure.

Appendixes

I. THE FRENCH MANDATE FOR CAMEROUN

MANDATE for the Administration of Part of the former German Territory of the Cameroons conferred upon the Government of the French Republic, confirmed and defined by the Council of the League of Nations.—London, July 20, 1922.

The Council of the League of Nations:

Whereas by Article 119 of the Treaty of Peace with Germany, signed at Versailles on the 28th June, 1919, Germany renounced in favour of the Principal Allied and Associated Powers all her rights over her oversea possessions, including therein the Cameroons; and

Whereas the Principal Allied and Associated Powers agreed that the Governments of France and Great Britain should make a joint recommendation to the League of Nations as to the future of the said territory; and

Whereas the Governments of France and Great Britain have made a joint recommendation to the Council of the League of Nations that a mandate to administer, in accordance with Article 22 of the Covenant of the League of Nations, that part of the Cameroons lying to the east of the line agreed upon in the Declaration of the 10th July, 1919, of which mention is made in Article 1 below, should be conferred upon the French Republic; and

Whereas the Governments of France and Great Britain have proposed that the mandate should be formulated in the following terms; and

Whereas the French Republic has agreed to accept the mandate in respect of the said territory, and has undertaken to exercise it on behalf of the League of Nations:

Confirming the said mandate, defines its terms as follows:

Art. 1. The territory for which a mandate is conferred upon France comprises that part of the Cameroons which lies to the east of the line laid down in the Declaration signed on the 10th July, 1919, of which a copy is annexed hereto.

This line may, however, be slightly modified by mutual agreement between His Britannic Majesty's Government and the Government of the French Republic where an examination of the localities shows that it is undesirable, either in the interests of the inhabitants or by

196

reason of any inaccuracies in the map, Moisel 1 : 300,000, annexed to the Declaration, to adhere strictly to the line laid down therein.

The delimitation on the spot of this line shall be carried out in accordance with the provisions of the said Declaration.

The final report of the Mixed Commission shall give the exact description of the boundary line as traced on the spot; maps signed by the Commissioners shall be annexed to the report. This report, with its annexes, shall be drawn up in triplicate; one of these shall be deposited in the archives of the League of Nations, one shall be kept by the Government of the Republic and one by His Britannic Majesty's Government.

2. The Mandatory shall be responsible for the peace, order and good government of the territory and for the promotion to the utmost of the material and moral well-being and the social progress of its inhabitants.

3. The Mandatory shall not establish in the territory any military or naval bases, nor erect any fortifications, nor organise any native military force except for local police purposes and for the defence of the territory.

It is understood, however, that the troops thus raised may, in the event of general war, be utilised to repel an attack or for defence of the territory outside that subject to the mandate.

4. The Mandatory:

(1) Shall provide for the eventual emancipation of all slaves, and for as speedy an elimination of domestic and other slavery as social conditions will allow;

(2) Shall suppress all forms of slave trade;

(3) Shall prohibit all forms of forced or compulsory labour, except for essential public works and services, and then only in return for adequate remuneration;

(4) Shall protect the natives from measures of fraud and force by the careful supervision of labour contracts and the recruiting of labour;

(5) Shall exercise a strict control over the trade in arms and ammunition and the sale of spirituous liquors.

5. In the framing of laws relating to the holding or transference of land, the Mandatory shall take into consideration native laws and customs, and shall respect the rights and safeguard the interests of the native population.

No native land may be transferred, except between natives, without the previous consent of the public authorities, and no real rights over native land in favour of non-natives may be created except with the same consent.

The Mandatory shall promulgate strict regulations against usury.

6. The Mandatory shall secure to all nationals of States members

of the League of Nations the same rights as are enjoyed in the territory by his own nationals in respect of entry into and residence in the territory, the protection afforded to their person and property, movable and immovable, and the exercise of their profession or trade, subject only to the requirements of public order, and on condition of compliance with the local law.

Further, the Mandatory shall ensure to all nationals of States members of the League of Nations, on the same footing as his own nationals, freedom of transit and navigation, and complete economic, commercial and industrial equality; provided that the Mandatory shall be free to organise essential public works and services on such terms and condition as he thinks just.

Concessions for the development of the natural resources of the territory shall be granted by the Mandatory without distinction on grounds of nationality between the nationals of all States members of the League of Nations, but on such conditions as will maintain intact the authority of the local Government.

Concessions having the character of a general monopoly shall not be granted. This provision does not affect the right of the Mandatory to create monopolies of a purely fiscal character in the interest of the territory under mandate and in order to provide the territory with fiscal resources which seem best suited to the local requirements; or, in certain cases, to carry out the development of natural resources, either directly by the State or by a controlled agency, provided that there shall result therefrom no monopoly of the natural resources for the benefit of the Mandatory or his nationals, directly or indirectly, nor any preferential advantage which shall be inconsistent with the economic, commercial and industrial equality hereinbefore guaranteed.

The rights conferred by this Article extend equally to companies and associations organised in accordance with the law of any of the members of the League of Nations, subject only to the requirements of public order, and on condition of compliance with the local law.

7. The Mandatory shall ensure in the territory complete freedom of conscience and the free exercise of all forms of worship which are consonant with public order and morality; missionaries who are nationals of States members of the League of Nations shall be free to enter the territory and to travel and reside therein, to acquire and possess property, to erect religious buildings and to open schools throughout the territory; it being understood, however, that the Mandatory shall have the right to exercise such control as may be necessary for the maintenance of public order and good government, and to take all measures required for such control.

8. The Mandatory shall apply to the territory any general international Conventions applicable to his contiguous territory.

9. The Mandatory shall have full powers of administration and legislation in the area subject to the mandate. This area shall be administered in accordance with the laws of the Mandatory as an integral part of his territory and subject to the above provisions.

The Mandatory shall therefore be at liberty to apply his laws to the territory subject to the mandate, with such modifications as may be required by local conditions, and to constitute the territory into a customs, fiscal or administrative union or federation with the adjacent territories under his sovereignty or control; provided always that the measures adopted to that end do not infringe the provisions of this mandate.

10. The Mandatory shall make to the Council of the League of Nations an annual report to the satisfaction of the Council. This report shall contain full information concerning the measures taken to apply the provisions of this mandate.

11. The consent of the Council of the League of Nations is required for any modification of the terms of the present mandate.

12. The Mandatory agrees that, if any dispute whatever should arise between the Mandatory and another member of the League of Nations relating to the interpretation or the application of the provisions of the mandate, such dispute, if it cannot be settled by negotiation, shall be submitted to the Permanent Court of International Justice provided for by Article 14 of the Covenant of the League of Nations.

The present instrument shall be deposited in original in the archives of the League of Nations. Certified copies shall be forwarded by the Secretary-General of the League of Nations to all members of the League.

Done at London, the 20th day of July, 1922.

II. The British Mandate for the Cameroons

The Council of the League of Nations:

Whereas by Article 119 of the Treaty of Peace with Germany signed at Versailles on June 28th, 1919, Germany renounced in favour of the Principal Allied and Associated Powers all her rights over her oversea possessions, including therein the Cameroons; and

Whereas the Principal Allied and Associated Powers agreed that the Governments of France and Great Britain should make a joint recommendation to the League of Nations as to the future of the said territory; and

Whereas the Governments of France and Great Britain have made

Cameroun

a joint recommendation to the Council of the League of Nations that a mandate to administer in accordance with Article 22 of the Covenant of the League of Nations that part of the Cameroons lying to the west of the line agreed upon in the Declaration of July 10th, 1919, referred to in Article 1, should be conferred upon His Britannic Majesty; and

Whereas the Governments of France and Great Britain have proposed that the mandate should be formulated in the following terms; and

Whereas His Britannic Majesty has agreed to accept the mandate in respect of the said territory, and has undertaken to exercise it on behalf of the League of Nations in accordance with the following provisions;

Confirming the said mandate, defines its terms as follows:

Article 1

The territory for which a mandate is conferred upon His Britannic Majesty comprises that part of the Cameroons which lies to the west of the line laid down in the Declaration signed on July 10th, 1919, of which a copy is annexed hereto.

This line may, therefore, be slightly modified by mutual agreement between His Britannic Majesty's Government and the Government of the French Republic where an examination of the localities shows that it is undesirable, either in the interests of the inhabitants or by reason of any inaccuracies in the map, Moisel 1 : 300,000, annexed to the Declaration, to adhere strictly to the line laid down therein.

The delimitation on the spot of this line shall be carried out in accordance with the provisions of the said Declaration.

The final report of the Mixed Commission shall give the exact description of the boundary line as traced on the spot; maps signed by the Commissioners shall be annexed to the report. This report with its annexes shall be drawn up in triplicate: one of these shall be deposited in the archives of the League of Nations, one shall be kept by His Britannic Majesty's Government, and one by the Government of the French Republic.

Article 2

The Mandatory shall be responsible for the peace, order and good government of the territory, and for the promotion to the utmost of the material and moral well-being and the social progress of its inhabitants.

Article 3

The Mandatory shall not establish in the territory any military or naval bases, nor erect any fortifications, nor organise any native military force except for local police purposes and for the defence of the territory.

Article 4

The Mandatory:

(1) shall provide for the eventual emancipation of all slaves, and for as speedy an elimination of domestic and other slavery as social conditions will allow;

(2) shall suppress all forms of slave trade;

(3) shall prohibit all forms of forced or compulsory labour, except for essential public works and services, and then only in return for adequate remuneration;

(4) shall protect the natives from abuse and measures of fraud and force by the careful supervision of labour contracts and the recruiting of labour;

(5) shall exercise a strict control over the traffic in arms and ammunition and the sale of spirituous liquors.

Article 5

In the framing of laws relating to the holding or transfer of land, the Mandatory shall take into consideration native laws and customs, and shall respect the rights and safeguard the interests of the native population.

No native land may be transferred, except between natives, without the previous consent of the public authorities, and no real rights over native land in favour of non-natives may be created except with the same consent.

The Mandatory shall promulgate strict regulations against usury.

Article 6

The Mandatory shall secure to all nationals of States Members of the League of Nations the same rights as are enjoyed in the territory by his own nationals in respect of entry into and residence in the territory, the protection afforded to their person and property, and acquisition of property, movable and immovable, and the exercise of their profession or trade, subject only to the requirements of public order, and on condition of compliance with the local law.

Further, the Mandatory shall ensure to all nationals of States Members of the League of Nations on the same footing as to his own nationals, freedom of transit and navigation, and complete economic, commercial and industrial equality; except that the Mandatory shall be free to organise essential public works and services on such terms and conditions as he thinks just.

Cameroun

Concessions for the development of the natural resources of the territory shall be granted by the Mandatory without distinction on grounds of nationality between the nationals of all States Members of the League of Nations, but on such conditions as will maintain intact the authority of the local Government.

Concessions having the character of a general monopoly shall not be granted. This provision does not affect the right of the Mandatory to create monopolies of a purely fiscal character in the interest of the territory under mandate and in order to provide the territory with fiscal resources which seem best suited to the local requirements; or, in certain cases, to carry out the development of natural resources, either directly by the State or by a controlled agency, provided that there shall result therefrom no monopoly of the natural resources for the benefit of the Mandatory or his nationals, directly or indirectly, nor any preferential advantage which shall be inconsistent with the economic, commercial and industrial equality hereinbefore guaranteed.

The rights conferred by this article extend equally to companies and associations organised in accordance with the law of any of the Members of the League of Nations, subject only to the requirements of public order, and on condition of compliance with the local law.

Article 7

The Mandatory shall ensure in the territory complete freedom of conscience and the free exercise of all forms of worship which are consonant with public order and morality; missionaries who are nationals of States Members of the League of Nations shall be free to enter the territory and to travel and reside therein, to acquire and possess property, to erect religious buildings and to open schools throughout the territory; it being understood, however, that the Mandatory shall have the right to exercise such control as may be necessary for the maintenance of public order and good government, and to take all measures required for such control.

Article 8

The Mandatory shall apply to the territory any general international conventions applicable to his contiguous territory.

Article 9

The Mandatory shall have full powers of administration and legislation in the area subject to the mandate. This area shall be administered in accordance with the laws of the Mandatory as an integral part of his territory and subject to the above provisions.

The Mandatory shall therefore be at liberty to apply his laws to the territory under the mandate subject to the modifications required by local conditions, and to constitute the territory into a customs, fiscal or administrative union or federation with the adjacent territories under his sovereignty or control, provided always that the measures adopted to that end do not infringe the provisions of this mandate.

Article 10

The Mandatory shall make to the Council of the League of Nations an annual report to the satisfaction of the Council, containing full information concerning the measures taken to apply the provisions of this mandate.

Article 11

The consent of the Council of the League of Nations is required for any modification of the terms of this mandate.

Article 12

The Mandatory agrees that, if any dispute whatever should arise between the Mandatory and another Member of the League of Nations relating to the interpretation or the application of the provisions of the mandate, such dispute, if it cannot be settled by negotiation, shall be submitted to the Permanent Court of International Justice provided for by Article 14 of the Covenant of the League of Nations.

The present instrument shall be deposited in original in the archives of the League of Nations. Certified copies shall be forwarded by the Secretary-General of the League of Nations to all Members of the League.

Done at London, the twentieth day of July one thousand nine hundred and twenty-two.

III. The Trusteeship Agreement for French Cameroun

Whereas the territory known as the Cameroons lying to the east of the line agreed upon in the Declaration signed on 10th July, 1919, has been under French administration in accordance with the mandate defined under the terms of the instrument of 20th July, 1922; and

Whereas, in accordance with Article 9 of that instrument, this part of the Cameroons has since then been "administered in accordance with the laws of the Mandatory as an integral part of his territory and subject to the provisions" of the mandate, and it is of importance, in the interests of the population of the Cameroons, to pursue the administrative and political development of the territories in question, in such a way as to promote the political, economic and social advancement of the

203

Cameroun

inhabitants in accordance with Article 76 of the Charter of the United Nations; and

Whereas France has indicated her desire to place under trusteeship in accordance with Articles 75 and 77 of the said Charter that part of the Cameroons which is at present administered by her; and

Whereas Article 85 of the said Charter provides that the terms of trusteeship are to be submitted for approval by the General Assembly;

Now, therefore, the General Assembly of the United Nations approves the following terms of trusteeship for the said Territory.

Article 1

The Territory to which the present Trusteeship Agreement applies comprises that part of the Cameroons lying to the east of the boundary defined by the Franco-British Declaration of 10th July, 1919.

Article 2

The French Government in its capacity of Administering Authority for this Territory under the terms of Article 81 of the Charter of the United Nations, undertakes to exercise therein the duties of trusteeship as defined in the said Charter, to promote the basic objectives of the trusteeship system laid down in Article 76 and to collaborate fully with the General Assembly and the Trusteeship Council in the discharge of their functions as defined in Articles 87 and 88.

Accordingly the French Government undertakes:

1. To make to the General Assembly of the United Nations the annual report provided for in Article 88 of the Charter, on the basis of the questionnaire drawn up by the Trusteeship Council in accordance with the said Article, and to attach to that report such memoranda as may be required by the General Assembly or the Trusteeship Council.

To include in that report information relating to the measures taken to give effect to the suggestions and recommendations of the General Assembly or of the Trusteeship Council.

To appoint a representative and, where necessary, qualified experts to attend the meetings of the Trusteeship Council or of the General Assembly at which the said reports and memoranda will be examined.

2. To appoint a representative and, where necessary, qualified experts to participate, in consultation with the General Assembly or the Trusteeship Council, in the examination of petitions received by those bodies.

3. To facilitate such periodic visits to the Territory as the General Assembly or the Trusteeship Council may decide to arrange, to decide jointly with these bodies the dates on which such visits shall take place,

and also to agree jointly with them on all questions concerned with the organisation and accomplishment of these visits.

4. To render general assistance to the General Assembly or the Trusteeship Council in the application of these arrangements, and of such other arrangements as these bodies may take in accordance with the terms of the present Agreement.

Article 3

The Administering Authority shall be responsible for the peace, order and good government of the Territory.

It shall also be responsible for the defence of the said Territory and ensure that it shall play its part in the maintenance of international peace and security.

Article 4

For the above-mentioned purposes and in order to fulfil its obligations under the Charter and the present Agreement, the Administering Authority:

Shall:

1. Have full powers of legislation, administration and jurisdiction in the Territory and shall administer it in accordance with French law as an integral part of the French territory, subject to the provisions of the Charter and of this Agreement.

2. Be entitled, in order to ensure better administration, with the consent of the territorial representative Assembly, to constitute this Territory into a customs, fiscal or administrative union or federation with adjacent territories under its sovereignty or control and to establish common services between such territories and the Trust Territory, provided that such measures should promote the objectives of the international trusteeship system.

May:

1. Establish on the Territory military, naval or air bases, station national forces and raise volunteer contingents therein.

2. Within the limits laid down in the Charter, take all measures of organisation and defence appropriate for ensuring:

(*a*) the participation of the Territory in the maintenance of international peace and security.

(*b*) the respect for obligations concerning the assistance and facilities to be given by the Administering Authority to the Security Council,

(*c*) the respect for internal law and order,

(*d*) the defence of the Territory within the framework of the special agreements for the maintenance of international peace and security.

Cameroun

Article 5

The Administering Authority shall take measures to ensure to the local inhabitants a share in the administration of the Territory by the development of representative democratic bodies, and, in due course, to arrange appropriate consultations to enable the inhabitants freely to express an opinion on their political régime and ensure the attainment of the objectives prescribed in Article 76 (*b*) of the Charter.

Article 6

The Administering Authority undertakes to maintain the application to the Territory of the international agreements and conventions which are at present in force there, and to apply therein any conventions and recommendations made by the United Nations or the specialised agencies referred to in Article 57 of the Charter, the application of which would be in the interests of the population and consistent with the basic objectives of the trusteeship system and the terms of the present Agreement.

Article 7

In framing laws relating to the holding or transfer of land, the Administering Authority shall, in order to promote the economic and social progress of the native population, take into consideration local laws and customs.

No land belonging to a native or to a group of natives may be transferred, except between natives, save with the previous consent of the competent public authority, who shall respect the rights and safeguard the interests, both present and future, of the natives. No real rights over native land in favour of non-natives may be created except with the same consent.

Article 8

Subject to the provisions of the following Article, the Administering Authority shall take all necessary steps to ensure equal treatment in social, economic, industrial and commercial matters for all States Members of the United Nations and their nationals and to this end:

1. Shall grant to all nationals of Members of the United Nations freedom of transit and navigation, including freedom of transit and navigation by air, and the protection of person and property, subject to the requirements of public order, and on condition of compliance with the local law.

2. Shall ensure the same rights to all nationals of Members of the United Nations as to his own nationals in respect of entry into and

residence in the Territory, acquisition of property, both movable and immovable, and the exercise of professions and trades.

3. Shall not discriminate on grounds of nationality against nationals of any Member of the United Nations in matters relating to the grant of concessions for the development of the natural resources of the Territory, and shall not grant concessions having the character of a general monopoly.

4. Shall ensure equal treatment in the administration of justice to the nationals of all Members of the United Nations.

The rights conferred by this Article on the nationals of Members of the United Nations apply equally to companies and associations controlled by such nationals and formed in accordance with the law of any Member of the United Nations.

Nevertheless, pursuant to Article 76 of the Charter, such equal treatment shall be without prejudice to the attainment of the trusteeship objectives as prescribed in the said Article 76 and particularly in paragraph (*b*) of that Article.

Should special advantages of any kind be granted by a Power enjoying the equality of treatment referred to above to another Power, or to a territory whether self-governing or not, the same advantages shall automatically apply reciprocally to the Trust Territory and to its inhabitants, especially in the economic and commercial field.

Article 9

Measures taken to give effect to the preceding article of this Agreement shall be subject to the overriding duty of the Administering Authority, in accordance with Article 76 of the Charter, to promote the political, economic, social and educational advancement of the inhabitants of the Territory, to carry out the other basic objectives of the international trusteeship system and to maintain peace, order and good government. The Administering Authority shall in particular be free, with the consent of the territorial representative Assembly:

1. To organise essential public services and works on such terms and such conditions as it thinks just.

2. To create monopolies of a purely fiscal character in the interest of the Territory and in order to provide the Territory with the fiscal resources which seem best suited to local requirements.

3. To establish or to permit to be established under conditions of proper public control, in conformity with Article 76, paragraph (*d*), of the Charter, such public enterprises or joint undertakings as appear to the Administering Authority to be in the interest of the economic advancement of the inhabitants of the Territory.

Cameroun

Article 10

The Administering Authority shall ensure in the Territory complete freedom of thought and the free exercise of all forms of worship and of religious teaching which are consistent with public order and morality. Missionaries who are nationals of States Members of the United Nations shall be free to enter the Territory and to reside therein, to acquire and possess property, to erect religious buildings and to open schools and hospitals throughout the Territory.

The provisions of this Article shall not, however, affect the right and duty of the Administering Authority to exercise such control as may be necessary for the maintenance of public order and morality, and for the educational advancement of the inhabitants of the Territory.

The Administering Authority shall continue to develop elementary, secondary and technical education for the benefit of both children and adults. To the full extent compatible with the interests of the population it shall afford to qualified students the opportunity of receiving higher general or professional education.

The Administering Authority shall guarantee to the inhabitants of the Territory freedom of speech, of the press, of assembly and of petition, subject only to the requirements of public order.

Article 11

Nothing in this Agreement shall affect the right of the Administering Authority to propose at any future date the designation of the whole or part of the Territory thus placed under its trusteeship as a strategic area in accordance with Articles 82 and 83 of the Charter.

Article 12

The terms of the present Trusteeship Agreement shall not be altered or amended except as provided in Articles 79, 82, 83 and 85, as the case may be, of the Charter.

Article 13

If any dispute whatever should arise between the Administering Authority and another Member of the United Nations, relating to the interpretation or the application of the provisions of the present Trusteeship Agreement, such dispute, if it cannot be settled by negotiation or other means, shall be submitted to the International Court of Justice provided for by Chapter XIV of the Charter of the United Nations.

Article 14

The Administering Authority may enter, on behalf of the Territory, any consultative regional commission, technical organ or voluntary association of States which may be constituted. It may also collaborate, on behalf of the Territory, with international public or private institutions or participate in any form of international co-operation in accordance with the spirit of the Charter.

Article 15

The present Agreement shall enter into force as soon as it has received the approval of the General Assembly of the United Nations.

IV. THE TRUSTEESHIP AGREEMENT FOR THE BRITISH CAMEROONS

Whereas the Territory known as Cameroons under British Mandate and hereinafter referred to as the Territory has been administered in accordance with Article 22 of the Covenant of the League of Nations under a Mandate conferred on His Britannic Majesty; and

Whereas Article 75 of the United Nations Charter signed at San Francisco on 26th June, 1945, provides for the establishment of an international trusteeship system for the administration and supervision of such territories as may be placed thereunder by subsequent individual agreements; and

Whereas under Article 77 of the said Charter the international trusteeship system may be applied to territories now held under Mandate; and

Whereas His Majesty has indicated his desire to place the Territory under the said international trusteeship system; and

Whereas, in accordance with Articles 75 and 77 of the said Charter the placing of a territory under the international trusteeship system is to be effected by means of a Trusteeship Agreement;

Now therefore the General Assembly of the United Nations hereby resolves to approve the following terms of trusteeship for the Territory.

Article 1

The Territory to which this Agreement applies comprises that part of the Cameroons lying to the west of the boundary defined by the Franco-British Declaration of 10th July, 1919, and more exactly defined in the declaration made by the Governor of the Colony and Protectorate of Nigeria and the Governor of the Cameroons under French Mandate which was confirmed by the exchange of notes between His Majesty's Government in the United Kingdom and the French Government of

Cameroun

9th January, 1931. This line may, however, be slightly modified by mutual agreement between His Majesty's Government in the United Kingdom and the Government of the French Republic where an examination of the localities shows that it is desirable in the interests of the inhabitants.

Article 2

His Majesty is hereby designated as Administering Authority for the Territory, the responsibility for the administration of which will be undertaken by His Majesty's Government in the United Kingdom of Great Britain and Northern Ireland.

Article 3

The Administering Authority undertakes to administer the Territory in such a manner as to achieve the basic objectives of the international trusteeship system laid down in Article 76 of the United Nations Charter. The Administering Authority further undertakes to collaborate fully with the General Assembly of the United Nations and the Trusteeship Council in the discharge of all their functions as defined in Article 87 of the United Nations Charter, and to facilitate any periodic visits to the Territory which they may deem necessary, at times to be agreed upon with the Administering Authority.

Article 4

The Administering Authority shall be responsible (*a*) for the peace, order, good government and defence of the Territory, and (*b*) for ensuring that it shall play its part in the maintenance of international peace and security.

Article 5

For the above-mentioned purposes and for all purposes of this Agreement, as may be necessary, the Administering Authority:

(*a*) shall have full powers of legislation, administration and jurisdiction in the Territory and shall administer it in accordance with his own laws as an integral part of his territory with such modification as may be required by local conditions and subject to the provisions of the United Nations Charter and of this Agreement;

(*b*) shall be entitled to constitute the Territory into a custom, fiscal or administrative union or federation with adjacent territories under his sovereignty or control, and to establish common services between such territories and the Territory where such measures are not inconsistent with the basic objectives of the international trusteeship system and with the terms of this Agreement;

(*c*) and shall be entitled to establish naval, military and air bases, to erect fortifications, to station and employ his own forces in the Territory and to take all such other measures as are in his opinion necessary for the defence of the Territory and for ensuring that it plays its part in the maintenance of international peace and security. To this end the Administering Authority may make use of volunteer forces, facilities and assistance from the Territory in carrying out the obligations towards the Security Council undertaken in this regard by the Administering Authority, as well as for local defence and the maintenance of law and order within the Territory.

Article 6

The Administering Authority shall promote the development of free political institutions suited to the Territory. To this end the Administering Authority shall assure to the inhabitants of the Territory a progressively increasing share in the administrative and other services of the Territory; shall develop the participation of the inhabitants of the Territory in advisory and legislative bodies and in the government of the Territory, both central and local, as may be appropriate to the particular circumstances of the Territory and its people; and shall take all other appropriate measures with a view to the political advancement of the inhabitants of the Territory in accordance with Article 76 (*b*) of the United Nations Charter. In considering the measures to be taken under this Article the Administering Authority shall, in the interests of the inhabitants, have special regard to the provisions of Article 5 (*a*) of this Agreement.

Article 7

The Administering Authority undertakes to apply in the Territory the provisions of any international conventions and recommendations already existing or hereafter drawn up by the United Nations or by the specialised agencies referred to in Article 57 of the Charter, which may be appropriate to the particular circumstances of the Territory, and which would conduce to the achievement of the basic objectives of the international trusteeship system.

Article 8

In framing laws relating to the holding or transfer of land and natural resources, the Administering Authority shall take into consideration native laws and customs, and shall respect the rights and safeguard the interests, both present and future, of the native population. No native land or natural resources may be transferred except between natives, save with the previous consent of the competent public authority. No real rights over native land or natural resources in favour of non-natives may be created except with the same consent.

Article 9

Subject to the provisions of Article 10 of this Agreement, the Administering Authority shall take all necessary steps to ensure equal treatment in social, economic, industrial and commercial matters for all Members of the United Nations and their nationals and to this end:

(*a*) shall ensure the same rights to all nationals of Members of the United Nations as to his own nationals in respect of entry into and residence in the Territory, freedom of transit and navigation, including freedom of transit and navigation by air, acquisition of property both movable and immovable, the protection of persons and property, and the exercise of professions and trades;

(*b*) shall not discriminate on grounds of nationality against nationals of any Member of the United Nations in matters relating to the grant of concessions for the development of the natural resources of the Territory, and shall not grant concessions having the character of a general monopoly;

(*c*) shall ensure equal treatment in the administration of justice to the nationals of all Members of the United Nations.

The rights conferred by this Article on nationals of Members of the United Nations apply equally to companies and associations controlled by such nationals and organised in accordance with the law of any Member of the United Nations.

Article 10

Measures taken to give effect to Article 9 of this Agreement shall be subject always to the over-riding duty of the Administering Authority in accordance with Article 76 of the United Nations Charter to promote the political, economic, social and educational advancement of the inhabitants of the Territory, to carry out the other basic objectives of the international trusteeship system, and to maintain peace, order and good government. The Administering Authority shall in particular be free:

(*a*) to organise essential public services and works on such terms and conditions as he thinks just;

(*b*) to create monopolies of a purely fiscal character in order to provide the Territory with the fiscal resources which seem best suited to local requirements, or otherwise to serve the interests of the inhabitants of the Territory;

(*c*) where the interests of the economic advancement of the inhabitants of the Territory may require it, to establish or permit to be established, for specific purposes, other monopolies or undertakings having in them an element of monopoly, under conditions of proper public control; provided that, in the selection of agencies to carry out the purposes of this paragraph, other than agencies controlled by the Government or those in which the Government participates, the Administering Authority shall not discriminate on grounds of nationality against Members of the United Nations or their nationals.

Article 11

Nothing in this Agreement shall entitle any Member of the United Nations to claim for itself or for its nationals, companies and associations, the benefits of Article 9 of this Agreement in any respect in which it does not give to the inhabitants, companies and associations of the Territory equality of treatment with the nationals, companies and associations of the State which it treats most favourably.

Article 12

The Administering Authority shall, as may be appropriate to the circumstances of the Territory, continue and extend a general system of elementary education designed to abolish illiteracy and to facilitate the vocational and cultural advancement of the population, child and adult, and shall similarly provide such facilities as may prove desirable and practicable in the interests of the inhabitants for qualified students to receive secondary and higher education, including professional training.

Article 13

The Administering Authority shall ensure in the Territory complete freedom of conscience, and, so far as is consistent with the requirements of public order and morality, freedom of religious teaching and the free exercise of all forms of worship. Subject to the provisions of Article 8 of this Agreement and the local law, missionaries who are nationals of Members of the United Nations shall be free to enter the Territory and to travel and reside therein, to acquire and possess property, to erect religious buildings and to open schools and hospitals in the Territory. The provisions of this Article shall not, however, affect the right and duty of the Administering Authority to exercise such control as he may consider necessary for the maintenance of peace, order and good government and for the educational advancement of the inhabitants of the Territory, and to take all measures required for such control.

8—C * *

Cameroun

Article 14

Subject only to the requirements of public order, the Administering Authority shall guarantee to the inhabitants of the Territory freedom of speech, of the press, of assembly, and of petition.

Article 15

The Administering Authority may arrange for the co-operation of the Territory in any regional advisory commission, regional technical organisation, or other voluntary association of States, any specialised international bodies, public or private, or other forms of international activity not inconsistent with the United Nations Charter.

Article 16

The Administering Authority shall make to the General Assembly of the United Nations an annual report on the basis of a questionnaire drawn up by the Trusteeship Council in accordance with Article 88 of the United Nations Charter. Such reports shall include information concerning the measures taken to give effect to suggestions and recommendations of the General Assembly and the Trusteeship Council. The Administering Authority shall designate an accredited representative to be present at the sessions of the Trusteeship Council at which the reports of the Administering Authority with regard to the Territory are considered.

Article 17

Nothing in this Agreement shall affect the right of the Administering Authority to propose, at any future date, the amendment of this Agreement for the purpose of designating the whole or part of the Territory as a strategic area or for any other purpose not inconsistent with the basic objectives of the international trusteeship system.

Article 18

The terms of this Agreement shall not be altered or amended except as provided in Article 79 and Articles 83 or 85, as the case may be, of the United Nations Charter.

Article 19

If any dispute whatever should arise between the Administering Authority and another Member of the United Nations relating to the interpretation or application of the provisions of this Agreement, such dispute, if it cannot be settled by negotiation or other means, shall be submitted to the International Court of Justice provided for in Chapter XIV of the United Nations Charter.

V. THE CONSTITUTION OF THE FEDERAL REPUBLIC OF CAMEROON

PART I

The Federal Republic of Cameroon

1. (1) With effect from the 1st October 1961, the Federal Republic of Cameroon shall be constituted from the territory of the Republic of Cameroon, hereafter to be styled East Cameroon, and the territory of the Southern Cameroons, formerly under British trusteeship, hereafter to be styled West Cameroon.

(2) The Federal Republic of Cameroon shall be democratic, secular and dedicated to social service;

it shall ensure the equality before the law of all its citizens;

and it proclaims its adherence to the fundamental freedoms written into the Universal Declaration of Human Rights and the Charter of the United Nations.

(3) The official languages of the Federal Republic of Cameroon shall be French and English.

(4) The motto shall be: "Peace, Work, Fatherland."

(5) The flag shall be of three equal vertical stripes of green, red and yellow, charged with two gold stars on the green stripe.

(6) The capital shall be Yaounde.

(7) The national anthem of the Federation shall be: "O Cameroon, cradle of our forefathers."

(8) The seal of the Federal Republic of Cameroon shall be a circular medallion in bas-relief, forty-six millimetres in diameter, bearing on the reverse and in the centre the head of a girl in profile turned to the dexter towards a coffee branch and flanked on the sinister by five cocoa pods, encircled beneath the upper edge by the words "Federal Republic of Cameroun" and above the lower edge by the national motto "Peace—Work—Fatherland."

(9) The subjects of the Federated States shall be citizens of the Federal Republic with Cameroonian Nationality.

2. (1) National sovereignty shall be vested in the people of Cameroon who shall exercise it either through the members returned by it to the Federal Assembly or by way of referendum;

nor may any section of the people or any individual arrogate to itself or to himself the exercise thereof.

(2) The vote shall be equal and secret, and every citizen aged twenty-one years or over shall be entitled to it.

(3) The authorities responsible for the direction of the State shall

hold their powers of the people by way of election by universal suffrage, direct or indirect.

3. (1) Political parties and groups may take part in elections; and within the limits laid down by law and regulation their formation and their activities shall be free.

(2) Such parties shall be bound to respect the principles of democracy and of the national sovereignty.

4. Federal authority shall be exercised by:
(*a*) the President of the Federal Republic, and
(*b*) The Federal National Assembly.

PART II
Federal Jurisdiction

5. The following subjects shall be of federal jurisdiction:
(1) Nationality;
(2) Status of Aliens;
(3) Rules governing the conflict of Laws;
(4) National Defence;
(5) Foreign Affairs;
(6) Internal and External Security of the Federal State, and Immigration and Emigration;
(7) Planning, Guidance of the Economy, Statistical Services, Supervision and Regulation of Credit, Foreign Economic Relations, in particular Trade Agreements;
(8) Currency, the Federal Budget, Taxation and other Revenue to meet federal expenditure;
(9) Higher Education and Scientific Research;
(10) Press and Broadcasting;
(11) Foreign Technical and Financial Assistance;
(12) Postal Services and Telecommunications;
(13) Aviation and Meteorology, Mines and Geological Research; Geographical Survey;
(14) Conditions of Service of Federal Civil Servants, Members of the Bench and Legal Officers;
(15) Regulation as to procedure and otherwise of the Federal Court of Justice;
(16) Border between the Federated States;
(17) Regulation of Services dealing with the above subjects.

6. (1) The following subjects shall also be of federal jurisdiction—
(*a*) Human Rights;

(*b*) Law of Persons and of Property;

(*c*) Law of Civil and Commercial Obligations and Contracts;

(*d*) Administration of Justice, including rules of Procedure in and Jurisdiction of all Courts (but not the Customary Courts of West Cameroon except for appeals from their decisions);

(*e*) Criminal Law;

(*f*) Means of Transport of federal concern (roads, railways, inland waterways, sea and air) and Ports;

(*g*) Prison Administration;

(*h*) Law of Public Property;

(*i*) Labour Law;

(*j*) Public Health;

(*k*) Secondary and Technical Education;

(*l*) Regulation of Territorial Administration;

(*m*) Weights and Measures.

(2) The Federated States may continue to legislate on the subjects listed in this article, and to run the corresponding administrative services until the Federal National Assembly or the President of the Federal Republic in its or his field shall have determined to exercise the jurisdiction by this Article conferred.

(3) The executive or legislative authorities as the case may be of the Federated States shall cease to have jurisdiction over any such subject of which the Federal authorities shall have taken charge.

7. (1) Wherever under the last preceding Article the authorities of the Federated States shall have been temporarily enabled to deal with a federal subject, they may legislate on such subject only after consultation with the Federal Co-ordination Committee.

(2) The chairman of the said Committee shall be a Federal Minister, and the members shall be nominated by the President of the Federal Republic in view of their special knowledge.

PART III

The President of the Federal Republic

8. (1) The President of the Federal Republic of Cameroon, as head of the Federal State and head of the Federal Government, shall ensure respect for the Federal Constitution and the integrity of the Federation, and shall be responsible for the conduct of the affairs of the Federal Republic.

(2) He shall be assisted in his task by the Vice-President of the Federal Republic.

9. (1) The President and Vice-President of the Federal Republic

shall be elected together on the same list, both candidates on which may not come from the same Federated State, by universal suffrage and direct and secret ballot.

(2) Candidates for the offices of President and Vice-President of the Federal Republic must be in possession of their civic and political rights, and have attained the age of thirty-five years by the date of the election, the nomination of candidates, the supervision of elections and the proclamation of the result being regulated by a federal law.

(3) The offices of President and Vice President of the Republic may not be held together with any other office.

10. (1) The President of the Federal Republic shall be elected for five years and may be re-elected.

(2) Election shall be by majority of votes cast, and shall be held not less than twenty or more than fifty days before the expiry of the term of the President in office.

(3) In the event of vacancy of the Presidency for whatever cause the powers of the President of the Federal Republic shall without more devolve upon the Vice-President until election of a new President.

(4) Voting to elect a new President shall take place not less than twenty or more than fifty days after the vacancy.

(5) The President shall take oath in manner to be laid down by federal law.

11. (1) Ministers and Deputy Ministers shall be appointed by tʜᴜ President of the Federal Republic from each Federated State at his choice, to be responsible to him and liable to be dismissed by him.

(2) The office of Minister or Deputy Minister may not be held together with elective office in either Federated State, office as member of a body representing nationally any occupation, or any public post or gainful activity.

12. The President of the Federal Republic shall—

(1) represent the Federal Republic in all public activity and be head of the armed forces;

(2) accredit ambassadors and envoys extraordinary to foreign powers;

(3) receive letters of credence of ambassadors and envoys extraordinary from foreign powers;

(4) negotiate agreements and treaties;

Provided that treaties dealing with the sphere reserved by Article 24 to the federal legislature shall be submitted before ratification for approval in the form of law by the Federal Assembly;

218

(5) exercise the prerogative of clemency after consultation with the Federal Judicial Council;

(6) confer the decorations of the Federal Republic;

(7) promulgate federal laws as provided by Article 31;

(8) be responsible for the enforcement of federal laws and also of such laws as may be passed by a Federated State under the last paragraph of Article 6;

(9) have the power to issue statutory rules and orders;

(10) appoint to federal civil and military posts;

(11) ensure the internal and external security of the Federal Republic;

(12) set up, regulate and direct all administrative services necessary for the fulfilment of his task;

Provided that where he considers it advisable he may after consultation with the heads of the Governments of the Federated States assume authority over such of their services as exercise federal jurisdiction as defined by Article 5 or 6—

and may by Decree delegate any part of his functions to the Vice-President of the Federal Republic.

13. The Governments of the Federated States shall be bound, before adopting any measure which may impinge upon the Federation as a whole, to consult the President of the Federal Republic who shall refer the matter to the Committee provided by Article 7 for its opinion.

14. The President of the Federal Republic shall refer to the Federal Court of Justice under Article 34 any federal law which he considers to be contrary to this Constitution, or any law passed by a Federated State which he considers to be in violation of the Constitution or of a federal law.

15. (1) The President of the Federal Republic may where circumstances require proclaim by Decree a State of Emergency, which will confer upon him such special powers as may be provided by federal law.

(2) In the event of grave peril threatening the nation's territorial integrity or its existence, independence or institutions, the President of the Federal Republic may after consultation with the Prime Ministers of the Federated States proclaim by Decree a State of Siege.

(3) He shall inform the nation by message of his decision.

(4) The Federal National Assembly shall without more be in session throughout the State of Siege.

PART IV

The Federal Legislature

16. The Federal National Assembly shall be renewed every five years, and shall be composed of members elected by universal suffrage and direct and secret ballot in each Federated State in the proportion of one member to every eighty thousand of the population.

17. Federal laws shall be passed by simple majority of the members.

18. Before promulgating any bill the President of the Federal Republic may of his own accord or on request by the Prime Minister of either State request a second reading, at which the law may not be passed unless the majority required by the last preceding Article shall include a majority of the votes of the members from each Federated State.

19. (1) The Federal National Assembly shall meet twice a year, the duration of each session being limited to thirty days, and the opening date of each session being fixed by the Assembly's steering committee after consultation with the President of the Federal Republic.

(2) In the course of one such session the Assembly shall approve the Federal Budget:

Provided that in the event of the Budget not being approved before the end of the current financial year the President of the Federal Republic shall have power to act according to the old Budget at the rate of one twelfth for each month until the new budget is approved.

(3) On request of the President of the Federal Republic or of two thirds of its membership the Assembly shall be recalled to an extraordinary session, limited to fifteen days, to consider a specific programme of business.

20. The Federal National Assembly shall adopt its own standing orders, and at the opening of the first session of each year shall elect its Speaker and steering committee.

The sittings of the Federal National Assembly shall be open to the public:

Provided that in exceptional circumstances and on the request of the Federal Government or of a majority of its members strangers may be excluded.

21. Federal elections shall be regulated by a federal law.

22. Parliamentary immunity, disqualification of candidates or of sitting members, and the allowances and privileges of members shall be governed by a federal law.

PART V
Relations Between the Federal Executive and Legislature
23. Bills may be introduced either by the President of the Federal Republic or by any member of the Federal Assembly.

24. Of the subjects of federal jurisdiction under Articles 5 and 6, the following shall be reserved to the legislature:
(1) the fundamental rights and duties of the citizen, including:
(*a*) protection of the liberty of the subject.
(*b*) human rights.
(*c*) labour and trade union law.
(*d*) duties and obligations of the citizens in face of the necessities of national defence.

(2) the law of persons and property, including:
(*a*) nationality and personal status.
(*b*) law of moveable and immoveable property.
(*c*) law of civil and commercial obligations.

(3) the political, administrative and judicial system in respect of:
(*a*) elections to the Federal Assembly.
(*b*) general regulation of national defence.
(*c*) the definition of criminal offences not triable summarily and the authorisation of penalties of any kind, criminal procedure, civil procedure, execution procedure, amnesty, the creation of new classes of Courts.

(4) the following matters of finance and public property:
(*a*) currency.
(*b*) federal budget.
(*c*) imposition, assessment and rate of all federal dues and taxes.
(*d*) legislation on public property.

(5) long-term commitments to economic and social policy, together with the general aims of such policy.
(6) The Educational System.

25. Bills laid on the table of the Assembly shall be considered in the appropriate committee before debate on the floor of the House.

26. The text laid before the House shall be that proposed by the President of the Federal Republic when the proposal comes from him, and otherwise the text as amended in committee; but in either case amendments may be moved in the course of the debate.

27. The President of the Federal Republic may at his request address the Assembly in person, and may send messages to it; but no such address or message may be debated in his presence.

28. Federal Ministers and Deputy Ministers shall have access to the Assembly and may take part in debates.

29. (1) The programme of business in the Assembly shall be appointed by the chairmen's conference, composed of party leaders, chairmen of committees and members of the steering committee of the Federal National Assembly, together with a Federal Minister or Deputy Minister.

(2) The programme of business may not include bills beyond the jurisdiction of the Assembly as defined by Articles 5, 6 and 24; nor may any bill introduced by a member or any amendment be included which if passed would result in a burden on public funds or an increase in public charges without a corresponding reduction in other expenditure or the grant of equivalent new supply.

(3) Any doubt or dispute on the admissibility of a bill or amendment shall be referred for decision by the Speaker or by the President of the Federal Republic to the Federal Court of Justice.

(4) The programme of business shall give priority, and in the order decided by the Government, to bills introduced or accepted by it.

(5) Any business shall on request by the Government be treated as urgent.

30. (1) The Government shall be bound to furnish to the Federal National Assembly any explanation and information on its activities in reply to written or oral questions by the Assembly or to any Committee of Inquiry set up by the Assembly to inquire into governmental activities.

(2) The procedure of all such inquiry and supervision shall be laid down by a federal law.

31. (1) The President of the Federal Republic shall promulgate laws passed by the Federal National Assembly within fifteen days of their being forwarded to him, unless he receive a request for a second reading; and at the expiry of such period the Speaker may record his failure to promulgate and do so himself.

(2) Laws shall be published in both official languages of the Federal Republic.

PART VI

The Judiciary

32. (1) Justice shall be administered in the Federation in the name of the people of Cameroon by the competent Courts of each State.

(2) The President of the Federal Republic shall ensure the independence of the judiciary, and shall appoint to the bench and to the legal service of the Federated States.

(3) He shall be assisted in his task by the Federal Judicial Council, which shall give him its opinion on all proposed appointments to the bench and shall have over members of the bench the powers of a Disciplinary Council; and which shall be regulated as to procedure and otherwise by a federal law.

33. (1) The Federal Court of Justice shall have jurisdiction—

(a) to decide conflicts of jurisdiction between the highest Courts of the Federated States;

(b) to give final judgment on such appeals as may be granted by federal law from the judgments of the superior Courts of the Federated States wherever the application of federal law is in issue;

(c) to decide complaints against administrative acts of the federal authorities, whether claiming damages or on grounds of ultra vires;

(d) to decide disputes between the Federated States, or between either of them and the Federal Republic.

(2) The composition of, the taking of cognizance by, and the procedure of the Federal Court of Justice shall be laid down by a federal law.

34. Where the Federal Court of Justice is called upon to give an opinion in the cases contemplated by Articles 14 or 29, its numbers shall be doubled by the addition of personalities nominated for one year by the President of the Federal Republic in view of their special knowledge or experience.

35. Warrants, orders and judgments of any Court of Justice in either Federated State shall be enforceable throughout the Federation.

PART VII

Impeachment

36. (1) There shall be a Federal Court of Impeachment which shall be regulated as to composition and taking of cognizance and in other respects by a federal law.

223

(2) The Federal Court of Impeachment shall have jurisdiction, in respect of acts performed in the exercise of their offices, to try the President of the Federal Republic for high treason, and the Vice-President of the Republic and Federal Ministers, and Prime Ministers and Secretaries of State of the Federated States for conspiracy against the security of the State.

PART VIII
Federal Economic and Social Council
37. There shall be a Federal Economic and Social Council which shall be regulated as to powers and in other respects by a federal law.

PART IX
The Federated States
38. (1) Any subject not listed in Articles 5 and 6, and whose regulation is not specifically entrusted by this Constitution to a federal law shall be of the exclusive jurisdiction of the Federated States, which within those limits, may adopt their own Constitutions.

(2) The House of Chiefs of the Southern Cameroons shall be preserved.

39. (1) The Prime Minister of each Federated State shall be nominated by the President of the Federal Republic and invested by a simple majority of the Legislature Assembly of that State.

(2) Secretaries of State shall be appointed to the Government by the President on the proposal of the Prime Minister after his investiture.

(3) The Secretaries of State may in like manner be dismissed.

40. (1) Legislative power shall be exercised in the Federated States by a Legislative Assembly, elected for five years by universal suffrage and direct and secret ballot in such manner as to ensure to each administrative unit representation in proportion to its population:

Provided that in West Cameroon the House of Chiefs may exercise specified legislative powers, to be defined, together with the manner of their exercise, by a law of the Federated State in conformity with this Constitution.

(2) There shall be one hundred representatives in the Legislative Assembly of East Cameroon, and thirty-seven representatives in the Legislative Assembly of West Cameroon.

(3) The electoral system, qualifications for candidates and disqualification of sitting members, parliamentary immunity and the allowances of representatives shall be regulated by a federal law.

41. (1) Each Legislative Assembly shall adopt its own standing orders and shall annually elect its steering committee.

(2) It shall meet twice a year, the duration for each session being limited to thirty days, on dates to be fixed by the steering committee after consultation with the Prime Minister of the Federated State, and so that the opening date of the budgetary session shall be later than the approval of the federal budget.

(3) On request of the Prime Minister, of the President of the Federal Republic or of two thirds of its membership, it shall be recalled to an extraordinary session limited to fifteen days, to consider a specific programme of business.

42. The sittings of each Legislative Assembly shall be open to the public:

Provided that in exceptional circumstances on the request of the Government or of a majority of its members strangers may be excluded.

43. Bills may be introduced either by the Government of each Federated State or by any representative in the Legislative Assembly, and shall be passed by a simple majority.

44. (1) A motion of no-confidence passed by a simple majority, or a vote of censure passed by an absolute majority shall oblige the Prime Minister to place his resignation in the hands of the President of the Federal Republic or be declared to have forfeited his office; and the President may then dissolve the Legislative Assembly.

(2) Persistent discord between the Government and the Legislative Assembly shall enable the President of the Federal Republic to dissolve. the latter of his own accord or on the proposal of the Prime Minister

(3) New elections shall be held within two months of dissolution.

(4) Until investiture of a new Prime Minister the outgoing Government shall be responsible for the despatch of current business.

45. (1) The Speaker of each Federated State shall within twenty-one days forward bills passed to the President of the Federal Republic, who shall within a further fifteen days promulgate them.

(2) Within the said period the President of the Federal Republic may either request a second reading by the Legislative Assembly or act under Article 14.

(3) At the expiry of such period the Speaker of the Legislative Assembly in question may record the President's failure to promulgate and do so himself.

46. In so far as they do not conflict with the provisions of this Constitution the existing laws of the Federated States shall remain in force.

PART X
Amendment of the Constitution

47. (1) No bill to amend the Constitution may be introduced if it tend to impair the unity and integrity of the Federation.

(2) Bills to amend the Constitution may be introduced either by the President of the Federal Republic after consultation with the Prime Ministers of the Federated States, or by any member of the Federal Assembly:

Provided that any bill introduced by a member of the Assembly shall bear the signatures of at least one third of its membership.

(3) The amendment may be passed by a simple majority of the membership of the Federal Assembly:

Provided that such majority include a majority of the membership elected from each Federated State.

(4) The President of the Federal Republic may request a second reading of a bill to amend the Constitution as of any other federal bill, and in like manner.

PART XI
Transition and Special

48. The jurisdiction defined in Article 5 shall pass without more to the federal authorities as soon as they are set up.

49. The Government of each Federated State shall forward to the Federal Government all papers and records necessary for the performance of its task, and shall place at the disposal of the Federal Government the services destined to exercise federal jurisdiction under the authority of the latter.

50. Notwithstanding anything in this Constitution, the President of the Federal Republic shall have power, within the six months beginning from the 1st October 1961, to legislate by way of Ordinance having the force of law for the setting up of constitutional organs, and, pending their setting up, for governmental procedure and the carrying on of the federal government.

51. The President of the Republic of Cameroon shall be for the duration of his existing term the President of the Federal Republic.

52. For the duration of the term of the first President of the Federal Republic the Prime Minister of West Cameroon shall be Vice-President of the Federal Republic; and the disqualifications prescribed by Article 9 for the Vice-President of the Federal Republic shall during that period be inapplicable.

53. With effect from the 1st October, 1961 the National Assembly of the Republic of Cameroon and the House of Assembly of the Southern Cameroons shall become the first Legislative Assembly of East Cameroon and of West Cameroon respectively.

54. Until the 1st April, 1964 the Federal Assembly shall be composed of members elected from among themselves by the Legislative Assemblies of the Federated States according to the population of each State in the proportion of one member to every eighty thousand of the population.

55. Notwithstanding the provisions of Article 11, and until the election of a Federal Assembly under Article 16, the offices of Federal Minister and Deputy Minister may be held together with parliamentary office in either Federated State.

56. The Government of the Republic of Cameroon and the Government of the Southern Cameroons under British trusteeship respectively shall become on the 1st October, 1961 the Governments of the two Federated States.

57. Pending the setting up of the Federal Economic and Social Council, the Economic and Social Council of the Republic of Cameroon shall be preserved.

58. Pending approval of a definitive federal budget a provisional federal budget shall be drawn up and shall be financed by contributions from each Federated State to be settled after agreement with the Government of each such State.

59. This Constitution shall replace the Constitution of the Republic approved on the 21st February, 1960 by the people of Cameroon; shall come into force on the 1st October, 1961; and shall be published in its new form in French and in English, the French text being authentic.

60. (1) For the purposes of this Constitution the population of each Federated State shall on the faith of the statistics of the United Nations Organisation, be taken to be as follows:

East Cameroon	3,200,000
West Cameroon	800,000

(2) Such figures may be amended by a federal law in the light of significant variation established by census.

Yaounde, the 1st September, 1961   Ahmadou Ahidjo

Notes and References

1. CAMEROUN AND ITS PEOPLE—THE BACKGROUND

1. Much of the factual information on the geography of Cameroun on which this section is based is derived from P. Billard, *Le Cameroun Fédéral*, Vol. 1, and J. A. Ngwa, *An Outline Geography of the Fédéral Republic of Cameroun*

2. Disputed areas at the coast and in the interior were the subject of negotiations between Nigeria and Cameroun to demarcate the frontier between the two states as late as July 1970. See *Africa Research Bulletin* (Political, Social and Cultural Series), p. 1805

3. This was to be a source of considerable rancour in the early relations between Cameroun and both Nigeria and Britain. Even after reunification, President Ahidjo described the resulting division as 'the amputation from Cameroun of an important part of its territory and its population under the United Kingdom, which in contempt of the obligations imposed on it by the trusteeship agreements in effect not only placed Western Cameroun under Nigerian authority but also divided into two parts the country over which it had to assume trusteeship'. Communication to the Nation, December 4, 1963 (Author's translation)

4. UDEAC. See below, Chapters 8 and 9

5. The traffic along the Benoué was interrupted for some years in the late 1960s as a result of the closure of the boundary between Nigeria and Cameroun following the attempted secession of Nigeria's eastern region. It was only opened again in 1970. See *Africa Research Bulletin* (Political, Social and Cultural Series), p. 1837

6. See G. M. D. Guillaume, *Notes on the Cameroun Mountain*, Buea 1966, which provides a list of eruptions reported between 1800 and 1959 on p. 4

7. The term is used here to designate one of the six administrative divisions into which the Federal Republic is divided, i.e. the West Cameroun Region, and the Coastal, Central, Eastern, Western and Northern regions

8. See E. Ardener, 'The Nature of the Reunification of Cameroon' in A. Hazlewood (ed.), *African Integration and Disintegration*, pp. 296–6, for a critique of some of the ways in which ethnic groups have been classified, and comments on the significance of 'ethnicity'

9. *The Cameroons From Mandate to Independence*, pp. 6–11; in this

228

he follows Murdock, *Africa: its Peoples and their Culture*, 1959, who in turn based his categories on J. H. Greenberg, *Studies in African Linguistic Classification*, 1955. But see the doubts expressed by E. Ardener, loc. cit

10. Johnson, *The Cameroon Federation*, 1970, p. 67, suggests that 'as these groups become more exposed to modern communications and economic activity, it is expected that the dangers of open political conflict between the[m and the Fulani will] be heightened'

11. The Bornu empire had in turn been preceded by the more ancient empire of Kanem, which dated from the ninth century. See Mveng, *Histoire du Cameroun*, Ch. 5, who describes it in some detail. See also M. Crowder, *The Story of Nigeria* and Thomas Ketchoua, *Contribution à l'Histoire du Cameroun*

12. Mveng, op. cit., p. 225; M. McCulloch 'The Tikar' in McCulloch, Littlewood and Dugast, *Peoples of the Central Cameroons*, p. 20

13. Johnson, op. cit., p. 47, gives an instance of fighting as recently as 1951

14. See Littlewood, 'The Bamum' in *Peoples of the Central Cameroons*, pp. 53-4

15. This was first reported in 1907, and was described by I. Dugast and M. D. W. Jeffreys in *L'Ecriture Bamoun*. See Littlewood, op. cit., p. 38

16. Johnson, op. cit., p. 55, says that they were armed by the government and retaliated against Bamiléké attacks in 1960, inter alia by despatching 1,000 warriors to raise the *chefferie* at Bamendjin

17. The term Mfon had been relinquished in favour of Sultan by Njoya

18. Johnson, op. cit., p. 45

19. C. Tardits, *Les Bamilékés de l'Ouest Cameroun*, 1960. The title of this work refers to the western part of East Cameroun not to the federated state of West Cameroun. On pp. 111-13, the author lists 107 chiefdoms

20. Thirty-seven had fewer than 1,000 people in 1957, and three were less than 100 strong. Ibid.

21. They are often referred to as belonging to the Semi-Bantu linguistic group, but this has been disputed, with some authorities suggesting that they are *sui generis* and others that they form a Bantu sub-group of the central branch of the Niger Congo family of languages. See Littlewood, 'The Bamiléké' in *Peoples of the Central Cameroons*, p. 95

22. Ibid.

23. Ibid., pp. 102-14

24. Johnson, op. cit., p. 53

25. Tardits, op. cit., Tables pp. 61–2
26. Mveng, op. cit., p. 247–8
27. Johnson, op. cit., p. 59; Welch, *Dream of Unity*, p. 181 n. 73
28. E. Ardener, *Coastal Bantu of the Cameroons*, p. 33. This useful volume in the Ethnographic Survey of Africa also provides a good deal of valuable information on the history of contact with Europeans at the coast
29. The French spelling is used here. Ardener uses the English form Duala, and other authors have used it to distinguish the people from the town or port to which they lent their name and which is given the French form. There does not seem to be any point in sustaining this distinction
30. E. Ardener, op. cit., pp. 14–15 provides the demographic data on which these rough estimates are based; his figures were published in 1956 and are somewhat lower, but allowance has been made for natural increase
31. Mveng, op. cit., pp. 52–8 discusses this in detail. See also R. Cornevin, *Histoire de l'Afrique des origines à nos jours*, pp. 66 ff.
32. Evidence that the slave trade was in existence as early as 1500 comes from P. Pereira's *Esmeraldo do Situ Orbis*, 1505; See Ardener, op. cit., p. 17
33. H. Rudin, *The Germans in the Cameroons*, p. 19, points out that the mere fact that the officials responsible were termed consuls suggests that Britain regarded the areas as foreign territory.

2. Conquest and Division: German Rule and its Aftermath

1. See S. Ardener, *Eye-Witnesses to the Annexation of Cameroon, 1883–1887*, pp. 63–83, for the texts of many of these treaties
2. See Rudin, *The Germans in the Cameroons*, pp. 29 ff., and H. A. Turner, 'Bismarck's Imperialist Venture: Anti-British in Origin' in Gifford and Lewis (eds.), *Britain and Germany in Africa*, pp. 47–82
3. See K. O. Dike, *Trade and Politics in the Niger Delta*, pp. 216–7, and Robinson, Gallagher and Denny, *Africa and The Victorians*. p. 165
4. Letter signed by King Acqua (Akwa), Prince Dido Acqua, Prince Black, Prince Joe Garner and Prince Lawton on August 7, 1879; S. Ardener op. cit., pp. 19–20, Le Vine, *The Cameroons from Mandate to Independence*, p. 20
5. S. Ardener, loc. cit.
6. Ibid., pp. 20–1
7. Le Vine, op. cit., p. 21
8. S. Ardener, op. cit., p. 22

9. Rudin, loc cit.
10. E. Mveng, *Histoire du Cameroun*, pp. 291–2, using the text given in J-R Brutsch, 'Les Traités Camérounais', *Etudes Camérounaises*, Nos. 47–8, March-June, 1955. Neither Rudin nor Ardener give the full text, which they suggest has been lost. The Brutsch text appears to have been discovered among the German archives relating to the Manga Bell case of 1914. The original of the treaty was in English; that used by Brutsch a German translation, which he in turn rendered into French. The version quoted is the present author's translation of the latter
11. S. Ardener, op. cit., p. 22; the text of Woermann's letter to Schmidt is given as an appendix to Ardener on pp. 84–5
12. Ibid., p. 24
13. Rudin, op. cit., pp. 55 ff.; S. Ardener, op. cit., pp. 31–40
14. Rudin, op. cit., pp. 60–1
15. Le Vine, op. cit., p. 25
16. Mveng, op. cit., pp. 297–8; E. Ardener, *Coastal Bantu of the Cameroons*, pp. 24–5
17. I. Dugast, *Inventaire Ethnique du Sud Cameroun*, p. 59
18. See E. M. Chilver, *Zintgraff's Explorations in Bamenda, 1889–1892*, *passim*; Mveng, op. cit., pp. 300–2
19. Rudin, op. cit., p. 207
20. Ibid., p. 195
21. Rudin, op. cit., p. 200
22. Ibid., p. 202
23. Ibid., pp. 204–5
24. Ibid., p. 203
25. Ibid., pp. 288 ff.
26. S. H. Bederman, *The Cameroons Development Corporation*, p. 14; Rudin, pp. 248–9
27. Rudin, p. 341
28. Ibid., pp. 236, 331–4
29. Ibid., p. 326
30. Ibid., p. 335
31. Ibid., p. 328
32. Le Vine, op. cit., p. 51
33. Rudin, op. cit., pp. 408-13
34. Le Vine, op. cit., p. 30
35. Mveng, op. cit., p. 344
36. Le Vine, op. cit., p. 29; Mveng, pp. 309–10
37. Rudin, op. cit., p. 116
38. Ibid., p. 283
39. Le Vine, op. cit., p. 36

40. Ibid., p. 37
41. See E. Ardener, 'The Kamerun Idea' in *West Africa*, 1958, pp. 533 ff. and 559
42. See G. Smith, 'The British Government and the Disposition of the German Colonies in Africa, 1914–1918' in Gifford and Louis (eds.), op. cit., pp. 275–300; Le Vine, op. cit., pp. 32–5; Mveng, op. cit., pp. 361–3

3. FROM TUTELAGE TO AUTONOMY UNDER THE FRENCH

1. On the mandate system in general, see Quincy Wright, *Mandates under the League of Nations*, and R. F. Logan, *The African Mandates in World Politics*
2. For this section and others relating to the UN's role in relation to Cameroun, I have drawn heavily on the material in Prof. David Gardinier's study, *Cameroon: United Nations Challenge to French Policy*
3. Art. 76
4. Op. cit., pp. 4–7
5. See Le Vine, *The Cameroons from Mandate to Independence*, pp. 89–90, for a synopsis of the policy of association as expanded by Albert Sarraut, the French Minister of Colonies, in 1923. Gardinier, op. cit., pp. 10–13, compares the policies. On their history, see Roberts, *History of French Colonial Policy 1870–1925*; Buell, *The Native Problem in Africa*, Vol. II p. 86 ff.; Betts, *Assimilation and Association in French Colonial Theory, 1890–1914*
6. E. Mveng, *Histoire du Cameroun*, p, 376
7. Le Vine, op. cit., p. 94
8. 'It goes without saying that considering the inorganic state of indigenous society, there would be no question of any form, however vague and distant it might appear, of a representative *régime*': letter from Commissioner Marchand to the *chef de circonscription* at Ngaoundéré on the establishment of a *Conseil de Notables*, quoted by Le Vine, pp. 92–3
9. Ibid., p. 96
10. Ibid., pp. 101–3
11. p. 101.
12. By the *Loi Laminé Gueye* of May 7, 1946
13. Gardinier, op. cit., p. 19, points out that the word 'self-government' in the Brazzaville test was given in English to emphasise the foreign nature of the notion and its incompatibility with 'the work of French civilisation accomplished by France in the colonies'.
14 Gardinier, op, cit., pp. 8–9

15. Ibid., pp. 18–19
16. Le Vine, op. cit., p. 137; Gardinier, op. cit., p. 21
17. Le Vine, op. cit., p. 136
18. Gardinier, op. cit., p. 50
19. Decree No. 57–501, April 16, 1957
20. Le Vine, op. cit., p. 120, gives the total number of properties expropriated in this way as 362; 147 went to the French authorities, 132 to Frenchmen or French firms, 29 to Camerounians and 40 to Englishmen or English firms
21. Ibid., p. 118
22. The total number in secondary schools only exceeded 150 for the first time after the end of World War II. See Le Vine, op. cit., Table 9, pp. 78-9.
23. Mveng, op. cit., p. 393. There were 150 medical centres and 50 doctors in Cameroun in 1939. For a moving tribute to Dr Jamot and his work on sleeping sickness see Ketchoua, *Contribution à l'Histoire du Cameroun*, pp. 132–9
24. The tax was levied on men, women and children over the age of 12. Women had never been taxed by the Germans, and the new tax led to widespread protests, and even a riot in Douala in 1932. Le Vine, op. cit., p. 105 and p. 247, n. 47
25. On forced labour under the mandate see Buell, op. cit., Vol. II, pp. 320 ff; Hailey, *An African Survey*, 1938, pp. 608 ff.
26. Le Vine, op. cit., Table 9, pp. 78-9
27. Ibid., Table 10, p. 83
28. Gardinier, op. cit., pp. 29,30
29. Le Vine, op. cit., p. 57, citing Chaffard, 'Cameroun à la veille d'Indépendance', in *Europe France-Outre-Mer*, No. 355, June 1959, p. 65
30. Le Vine, op. cit., p. 53, Table 5; and p. 55, Table 6
31. Ibid., p. 64
32. See Welch, *Dream of Unity*, p. 181
33. For a description of the movement led by Ganty on behalf of the Douala, see Le Vine, op. cit., pp. 114–17
34. Op. cit., p. 41
35. It was allied to the *Rassemblement Démocratique Africain* (RDA), a political grouping established in 1946 throughout francophone sub-Saharan Africa, which, in turn, was allied to the French Communist Party
36. Gardinier, op. cit., p. 44; J-M. Zang-Atangana, 'Les Partis Politiques Camérounais', in *Recueil Penant*, December 1960, p. 683. Le Vine, op. cit. p. 144, incorrectly suggests that it 'disintegrated after only several months of existence'

37. Le Vine, op. cit., pp. 147–8, gives a detailed description of the party apparatus, which consisted of local cells, headed by a central *Comité-Directeur*, elected by a Congress, and comprising a Political Bureau, a Secretariat and a Treasury. It resembled the kind of structure established elsewhere in Africa by RDA parties
38. Le Vine, op. cit., p. 147
39. Gardinier, op. cit., p. 47
40. Le Vine's phrase, op. cit., p. 144. Esocam attended the KUNC congress in December 1951 and opposed the resolutions on independence and unity; Welch, op. cit., p. 179.
41. Ajoulat had apparently become too liberal for the French voters in Cameroun and sought a seat on the predominantly African roll. The number of seats for the French National Assembly had been increased from 2 to 3; it is suggested that this was done to provide Ajoulat with a base. Gardinier, op. cit., p. 49
42. Le Vine, op. cit., pp. 239–43, lists more than 40 such ethnic or 'pseudo-ethnic' bodies
43. Gardinier, op. cit., p. 65
44. Gardinier, op. cit., p. 68 attributes Ajoulat's campaign to personal resentment at the fact that the UPC had supported Soppo Priso in the ATCAM presidency election at which Ajoulat was ousted. This seems too narrow a view, given Ajoulat's earlier moves. The UPC's influence in such matters could not have been very great. The fact that Ahidjo was elected Vice-President of ATCAM at the same time is probably a better indication of the changes taking place in ATCAM members' attitudes; it heralded the coming north-south alliance which was to dominate Cameroun politics thereafter
45. Le Vine, op. cit., p. 154
46. Gardinier, op. cit., p. 70
47. See Le Vine, p. 160, for a detailed description of some of these acts on the two days, December 18–19, in the Bassa region
48. Ibid., p. 161. There was also a low percentage poll in the north, though this was almost certainly the result of a lower turnout by women and a weaker tradition of political participation
49. Le Vine, Table, p. 249; there were also three independents

4. INTEGRATION AND DEVOLUTION IN BRITISH NIGERIA

1. Gardinier, 'The British in the Cameroons, 1919–1939' in Gifford and Louis (eds.), *Germany and Britain in Africa*, p. 526
2. Mandate, Article 9.
3. A practice which led to the pointed, but not altogether just, description of the Southern Cameroons later as a 'colony of a

region of a colony': Johnson, *The Cameroon Federation*, p. 94. See below for examples of the lack of development in administrative fields and social services generally.

4. See, in general, N. U. Akpan, *Epitaph to Indirect Rule*, passim

5. The British Cameroons Ordinance No. 3, of 1924, extended the Nigerian legal system to the territories, replacing German law; Ordinance No. 3 of 1925 required Nigerian legislation to specify that it was to obtain in the Cameroons

6. Gardinier, op. cit., p. 542

7. On the traditional political system in the grassfields, see Kaberry, 'Retainers and Royal Households in the Cameroons Grassfields' in *Cahiers d'études Africaines*, 3, 1962, and 'Traditional Politics in Nsaw' in *Africa*, Vol. 29, 1959; Chilver and Kaberry, 'From Tribute to Tax in a Tikar Chiefdom' in *Africa*, Vol. 30, 1960, and 'An Outline of the Traditional Political System of Bali-Nyonga, Southern Cameroons' in *Africa*, Vol. 31, 1961; as well as McCulloch et al, *Peoples of the Central Cameroons*, and Dugast, *Inventaire Ethnique du Sud Cameroun*. On other parts of the territory, see E. Ardener, *Coastal Bantu of the Cameroons*, and Meek, *Land, Law and Custom in Nigeria and The Cameroons*

8. See, in general, Akpan op. cit., and R. E. Wraith, *Local Government in West Africa*

9. P. M. Kale, *Political Evolution in the Cameroons*, 1967, pp. 21–2. The proposals were made by the Cameroons Welfare Union, and three names were put forward. None was accepted

10. Kale, op. cit., p. 34

11. Ezera, *Constitutional Developments in Nigeria*, pp. 68–9

12. See J. S. Coleman, *Nigeria—Background to Nationalism*, Ch. 12

13. Ezera, op. cit., p. 195; Kale, op. cit., p. 43

14. *Report of the Conference held on the Nigerian Constitution, held in London in July and August*, 1953, Cmnd. 8934, pp. 22–3

15. Ezera, op. cit., p. 324; Le Vine, *The Cameroons From Mandate to Independence*, p. 207

16. Le Vine, op. cit., p. 121; Bederman, *The Cameroons Development Corporation, Partner in National Growth*, p. 15, points out that the Germans got their former properties back at very favourable prices

17. By 1936, the proportion of plantation property owned by Germans was even greater. Gardinier, op. cit., p. 549, says that in that year they held 293,678 acres, while British-owned acreage only amounted to 19,053

18. Between 1931 and 1938, German imports actually grew from 70·7 to 81·88 per cent of the total. Cameroons' imports from Germany decreased from 58·55 to 52·4 per cent of the total over the same

period. British exports declined from 22·55 to 13·18 per cent, though imports rose from 4·08 to 7·1 per cent. Source: Gardinier, op. cit., pp. 549–50. Welch, *Dream of Unity*, p. 155, gives figures which confirm this general picture for the year 1937, though British imports were slightly more at 11·9 per cent.

19. Ex-Enemy Lands (Cameroons) Ordinance No. 30, of 1946; Cameroons Development Corporation Ordinance No. 39, of 1946; Bederman, op. cit., p. 19

20. Bederman, op. cit., p. 21; Johnson, op. cit., p. 98

21. £38,028 in 1957, £25,188 in 1960; no profit was realised at all in 1955 and 1959; Johnson, p. 102

22. Johnson, op. cit., pp. 102–3

23. See the pamphlet prepared by E. T. Egbe and J. Epale of the Kamerun Society in 1957, entitled 'Economic and Financial Problems of the Cameroons' quoted by Welch, op. cit., p. 193

24. *Report on the Financial, Economic and Administrative Consequences of Separation from Nigeria;* Johnson, op. cit., p. 106

25. Because of the tendency to base this nationalism on the territorial unity which existed in the period before the mandates, the term often preferred in this context is the German 'Kamerun', which was used by nationalists in both trust territories and accordingly adopted in their writings by authorities such as Ardener, Johnson and Welch. The expression 'The Kamerun Idea' is used by all three (though coined by the first) to epitomise nationalist feeling on the subject. In this work, the German spelling is only used where it appears as part of a proper name or in a quotation; the French form seems to have more meaning in the light of the union which ultimately emerged

26. Kale, op. cit., p. 51; Welch, op. cit., p. 160. Kale gives the date of the formation of the CYL as March 27, 1940, Welch and Le Vine some time in 1939; but there is other evidence in Kale's booklet to suggest that the CYL was already in existence in 1940, although he refers to it as the Victoria branch of the CWU (p. 22). Kale, who continued to play a part in Cameroun politics over the next twenty-five years, was a school-teacher; he later became Speaker of the West Cameroun House of Assembly

27. Kale, op. cit., pp. 51-5 sets out the memorandum in full

28. Ibid., p. 27

29. Ibid., p. 34

30. See, in general, Warmington, *A West African Trade Union*, pp. 22–52

31. Welch, op. cit., pp. 164–6

32. Ibid., p. 163, citing UN Petition No. 4/16-5/7 of December 9, 1949

33. Ibid., pp. 173–4
34. *West Africa*, August 6, 1960; Welch, op. cit., p. 177; Johnson, op. cit., p. 121
35. Coleman, op. cit., p. 401, and Welch, op. cit., pp. 184 ff.
36. Statement of Azikiwe on August 25, 1963, quoted by Kale, op. cit., p. 39
37. Welch, op. cit., p. 187
38. E. Ardener, 'The Political History of Cameroon' in *The World Today*, August 1962, p. 348; Welch, op. cit., p. 191
39. Johnson, op. cit., pp. 129–30
40. Kale, op. cit., pp. 43–4
41. Le Vine, op. cit., pp. 207

5. FROM SELF-GOVERNMENT TO INDEPENDENCE AND FEDERATION

1. Both Le Vine, *The Cameroons From Mandate to Independence*, p. 163, and Gardinier, *Cameroon: United Nations Challenge to French Policy*, p. 82, also attribute Mbida's unpopularity to his authoritarian personality, his inability to get along with colleagues and the fact that he antagonised French officials in the administration
2. Resolution of October 24, 1958
3. Gardinier, op. cit., p. 88. This matter was to prove of some importance during the later UN debates, when an attempt was made to press Ahidjo into calling a further general election before independence
4. The *Démocrates* were reduced to 8 members (out of their original 20) by the time Mbida went into exile in January 1959; Le Vine, op. cit., p. 168
5. His appointment as Prime Minister had been confirmed by 45 votes to none, with 16 abstentions; ibid., p. 167
6. Mveng, *Histoire du Cameroun*, p. 439
7. These included an alleged imperviousness to bullets; see Le Vine, op. cit., p. 171
8. Appeal made in July 1957; ibid., p. 164
9. Le Vine, op. cit., p. 165 suggests that the Bamiléké and Moungo areas were raided from bases in the British Cameroons.
10. Some 10,000–15,000 people were thus moved and about 150 arrests had been made by the end of 1957; Le Vine, ibid.
11. Report of the UN Visiting Mission on the Cameroons under French Administration (UN Document T./1427, January 1959), p. 51. 75 civilians were reported killed, 90 wounded and 90 abducted, and about 200 houses set on fire
12. Mveng, op. cit., p. 439

13. Effigies of Um Nyobe were carried through the streets at the time of independence; Mveng, loc. cit.
14. Even Mveng (ibid.) is prepared to consider it possible that Um Nyobe was opposed to violence! and suggests that, although he was communist, he probably favoured a 'more liberal' communism.
15. Le Vine, op. cit., p. 170; Gardinier, op. cit., p. 87, gives the total number of defectors as 2,500
16. In the Fourth Committee, the African bloc was only able to obtain a maximum of 28 votes for its proposals. The first was defeated by 46 to 28 with 7 abstentions, the second by 42 to 28 and 11 abstaining. The entire resolution was approved by 56–9, with 16 abstentions. On the debate, see Le Vine, op. cit., pp. 172–80; Keesings Contemporary Archives, pp. 16821–3; and Gardinier, op. cit., pp. 89–90
17. This resolution was carried by 56–0, with 23 abstentions
18. Johnson, *The Cameroon Federation*, estimates a total of 7,500. An indication of the scale of the violence is to be obtained from Mveng, op. cit., p. 440, who tends to emphasise anti-church activities. He gives the following examples:
   Night of July 25–6, 1959 attack on the mission at Nyombe, with Paoli injured; *August 27*: attack on Bandjoung, Fr Moroni injured; *August 30*: Fr Musslin killed in the parish of Bonaberi; *September 6*: Mr Ralph Nitcheu, catechist of Bafang, is killed; *Night of November 29–30*; attack on Bafang, Fr Giles Heberlé and Brother Saron killed, the Camerounian sister Marie-Noëlle injured; *January 31, 1960*: the mission at Kamoko pillaged; *May 2*: the monitor, Benoît Boufon, of Makenene, decapitated; *August 15*: Fr John Courtecuisse killed in the village of Botko; there were four other Camerounian priests who were kidnapped: Abbés M. Kamgang, J. Kejuipia, G. Siyam and Th. Fondjo. Two pastors were killed: a Camerounian, David Nenkam, and a Swiss (pastor Kopp). (Author's translation)
19. Gardinier, op. cit., p. 93, says that they obtained 'modern weapons and supplies' from the Soviet Bloc via Guinea, but does not indicate in what quantity. Johnson, op. cit., p. 357, claims that a guerrilla leader in Yabassi only received a total of 8 Czech pistols and that 'the very few 12-gauge shot-guns in their possession they either stole in Douala or got through customs officials'
20. Johnson, op. cit., pp. 356–7
21. Gardinier, op. cit., p. 94
22. Le Vine, op. cit., p. 182
23. The debates were exceedingly acrimonious, with deputies shouting,

stamping their feet and hammering their desks. They are described by Le Vine, op. cit., pp. 184–8
24. Constitution, Art 20
25. Le Vine, Table p. 249; Gardinier, op. cit., pp. 107–8
26. It is claimed by Gardinier, op. cit., p. 107, that the delimitation of the seat was so arranged as to ensure that Bell would win
27. Mveng, op. cit., p. 441, gives his name as William Betchel, and attributes the information to the report of an official enquiry conducted by the Swiss federal police
28. Report on the Trust Territory of the Cameroons under British Administration, UN Document T./1426 (January 1959), p. 82
29. Resolution No. 1350 of March 13, 1959
30. Le Vine, op. cit., p. 209
31. Ibid., p. 210; Johnson, op. cit., p. 147
32. The term is Welch's. Examples of KNDP scare stories, which claimed that a vote for Nigeria would mean 'calling 2,000,000 Ibos into the Cameroons; seizure of Cameroon land by Ibos . . . seizure of all important jobs, Government and private, by Nigerians', are taken by him from Le Vine, 'P. Day in the Cameroons' in *West Africa*, March 1961, p. 236. See also, Johnson, op. cit., pp. 146–52 and E. Ardener, 'Crisis of Confidence in the Cameroons' in *West Africa*, August 1961, pp. 878 ff., on the campaign as a whole. Welch, *Dream of Unity*, p. 232, cites equivalent examples of CPNC propaganda, involving the prospect of bloodshed and terrorism as a result of a decision to enter Cameroun
33. The value of this is to be doubted. Already in March 1960, the KNDP's fragile majority was destroyed when one of its members crossed the floor because he disagreed with Foncha's policy on reunification, thus leaving government and opposition equally balanced. The government nearly fell shortly afterwards, when another member also changed sides (allegedly in response to a bribe of £2,000), but reverted to the KNDP later; Welch, op. cit., pp. 211–12

6. The Character of Camerounian Federalism

1. Le Vine, *The Cameroons From Mandate to Independence*, p. 211
2. Johnson, *The Cameroons Federation*, p. 170; Gardinier, *Cameroon*, p. 118
3. Record of the All-Party Conference on the Constitutional future of the Southern Cameroons held at the Community Hall, Bamenda, from June 26–8, 1961; and Johnson, op. cit., Ch. 8, passim
4. Johnson, op. cit., pp. 176–86; Ardener, 'The Nature of the

Reunification of Cameroon' in *African Integration and Disintegration*, (ed.) Hazlewood, pp. 306–7

5. Constitution of West Cameroun, Section 5

6. The danger of possible *coups d'état* in East Cameroun was thus diminished. See Ardener, 'The Nature of the Reunification of Cameroon', op. cit., p. 310

7. See Johnson, loc. cit., for a description of the differences between the delegations at Bamenda

8. Johnson, op. cit., p. 184

9. Constitution of the Federal Republic, Article 1 (1), which established the new designations of the federated states

10. Federal Constitution, Arts. 6 and 38

11. Enonchong, *Cameroon Constitutional Law*, p. 109, n. 16; Ardener 'The Nature of the Reunification of Cameroon', gives only the former reason.

12. The suffrage and the ballot are among the few rights conferred on the individual citizen by the Constitution: See Arts 2 (2) and 16. An interim arrangement enabled the members of the National Assembly to be elected by the respective state legislatures

13. Federal Constitution, Art. 3 (1)

14. See Chapter 7, below

15. Le Vine, op. cit., p. 228; Enonchong, op. cit., p. 112

16. The quotation is taken from the official translation, which is the same as that which appears in the constitution published separately in Buea in 1963 and in the 1968 *Annuaire National* (Yaoundé, 1969), the official yearbook. The emphasis is added. Enonchong gives a correct précis of the clause, but his interpretation does not stress the discretionary character of the President's power

17. Federal Constitution, Art. 47 (2), (4)

18. Ibid., Art. 47 (2) proviso

19. Ibid., Art. 47 (3)

20. Ibid., Art. 47 (1)

21. Ibid., Arts. 6 (2) and (3)

22. Ibid., Arts. 5 and 6

23. Ibid., Art. 24

24. Op. cit., p. 123

25. P. F. Gonidec, *La République Fédérale du Cameroun*, p. 40, (author's translation). He does not, however, appear to be correct in stating that the National Assembly is confined to the matters specified in Art. 24

26. Le Vine, 'The Cameroun Federal Republic' in *Five African States*, (ed.) G. Carter, p. 310

27. Op. cit., p. 129, though there is less evidence for his view that

the presidency was the 'offspring' of the American one and only 'remotely a direct descendant' of the French

28. Federal Constitution, Art. 9. The only other qualification for office, apart from being in possession of 'civic and political rights' is a minimum age of 35
29. Gonidec, op. cit., p. 40
30. Federal Constitution, Arts. 9 (3) and 52
31. Enonchong, op. cit., pp. 120 and 140–4
32. Federal Constitution, Art. 6
33. Ibid., Art. 12 (12) proviso
34. Federal Constitution, Art. 39
35. Ibid., Art. 44 (2)
36. Gonidec, op. cit., p. 37
37. Federal Constitution, Art. 12
38. As defined in the Federal Constitution, Arts. 5 and 6
39. Federal Constitution, Art. 24
40. Enonchong, op. cit., p. 146
41. Jurgensmeyer, 'African Presidentialism. . . .', in *Journal of African Law*, Vol. 8., No. 3, 1964, p. 171
42. Gonidec., op. cit., p. 39
43. Federal Constitution, Art. 36
44. Ibid., Art. 11
45. Ibid., Art. 11 (2)
46. Enonchong, op. cit., p. 132; Johnson, *The Cameroon Federation*, p. 311
47. Johnson, op. cit., p. 314
48. Ibid., p. 315
49. Enonchong, op. cit., p. 141
50. Federal Constitution, Art. 33 (2)
51. J. A. C. Smith, R. Gilg and J. A. O'B. Quinn, 'The Federal Republic of Cameroon' in *Judicial and Legal Systems in Africa*, (ed.) A. N. Allott, p. 109
52. Federal Constitution, Arts. 14 and 29
53. Enonchong, op. cit., p. 226
54. Federal Law 65-LF-29 (November 19, 1965); see Smith et. al., op. cit., pp. 109–10; Enonchong, op. cit., pp. 235–6
55. Federal Constitution, Art. 33, and Federal Ordinance No. 61-05-6 of October 4, 1961
56. Smith et. al., op. cit., p. 110
57. Law No. 66-LF-1 of June 10, 1966
58. Federal Penal Code, Book 1, Sec. 101
59. Enonchong, op. cit., pp. 169–70
60. Johnson, *The Cameroon Federation*, p. 209

61. In 1969, there were 30 *préfets* and 61 *sous-préfets* in East Cameroun, and 9 *préfets* in West Cameroun.
62. Decree No. 15, October 20, 1961
63. Johnson, op. cit., p. 209
64. The information on the court systems is derived from Smith et. al., op. cit. See also, Enonchong, op. cit., Ch. 8
65. Both the substantive law and the rules of procedure differ greatly for each state in nearly every field, except the unified federal Penal Code, which was introduced in 1967, and the federal Labour Code. Criminal procedure has still not been unified. In general, East Cameroun's law derives from French law as applied first in French West Africa and then in French Equatorial Africa, together with statutes passed locally durng the mandate period and the period of trusteeship, and by the Republic of Cameroun and the East Cameroun state legislature. West Cameroun's law derives from the common law, doctrines of equity and English statutes of general application in force in 1900 and received at that date in Nigeria; legislation passed in Nigeria and made applicable to the Southern Cameroons under the mandate and trusteeship regimes, and enacted by the West Cameroun legislature since federation. Customary law applies in both states
66. There used to be an appeal in matters concerning land to the Prime Minister of West Cameroun, but this was abolished in 1968
67. Johnson, op. cit., p. 188
68. See L. Rubin and P. Murray, *The Constitution and Government of Ghana*, 2nd. edn., 1964, p. 222
69. See the judgement of the Ghana Court of Appeal in *Re Akoto*, 1961
70. Enonchong, op. cit., pp. 182 ff. His argument is only made in relation to the West Cameroun constitution. But it seems reasonable to suppose that it applies equally to the East Cameroun situation as well. The question is, however, complicated in that case by the fact that the Republic of Cameroun actually adopted the Federal Constitution in 1961 to replace its own constitution of 1960, whereas the Southern Cameroons legislature never did so: its constitution simply lapsed on its incorporation into the Federal Republic as the federated state of West Cameroun

7. THE REALITIES OF REUNIFICATION

1. Speech during an official visit to the Nyong and Sanaga region, January 1964. Author's translation
2. See his press conference of November 11, 1961, and his address to the uc congress at Ebolowa, 1962

3. Speech to the National Council of the UNC, November 1967
4. Press Conference, November 1961
5. In April 1962, the UC had 77 deputies, the *Démocrates* 8, the UPC 7, and there were 8 independents; Gardinier, *Cameroon*, p. 122
6. See Le Vine, 'The Cameroun Federal Republic' in Carter (ed.) op. cit., pp. 320–4, and Johnson, op. cit., pp. 247–53
7. Ibid.
8. Le Vine, *The Cameroons*, p. 222, is incorrect in saying that there was only one party by mid-1962
9. Johnson, op. cit., pp. 254–6
10. Johnson, in Lewis, (ed.), *French-speaking Africa*, p. 214
11. This was first disclosed in *L'Effort Camérounaise*, a Catholic weekly, which was promptly seized by the government, and its editor deported. A subsequent issue was also banned when it reported the deportation. The news of the prisoners' deaths was, however, reported in *Le Monde* and in *West Africa*. A judicial enquiry was held into the incident
12. Le Vine, 'Cameroun (1955–1962)', p. 255
13. Ibid; Johnson, *The Cameroon Federation*, pp. 352–3
14. S. Daoudou (Minister in charge of the Armed Forces), 'L'Evolution de l'Armée Camérounaise' in *Cameroun 1966: Bilan de Cinq Années d'Indépendance*, Yaoundé 1966, pp. 48–50. The armed forces accounted for approximately 30 per cent of the federal budget in 1965–6
15. Le Vine, 'Cameroun (1955–1962)', p. 262
16. The CPNC candidates (on a single list) lost their deposits, polling just less than 25 per cent of the votes
17. The course of the contest is described in detail by Johnson, *The Cameroon Federation*, pp. 269–76
18. Ardener, 'The Nature of Reunification in Cameroon', op. cit., says that there was an atmosphere of 'intellectual ferment' at the time, involving a 'generational revolt', but the issues raised in this connection do not seem to have figured overtly in the dispute
19. Johnson, *The Cameroon Federation*, p. 324: 'The party served the function of aggregating the élites rather than the mass'
20. Ibid., p. 361
21. R. N. Nordau, 'Cameroon-Cameroun', *Africa Report*, January 1970, p. 4
22. *Le Monde*, August 22, 1970
23. Communication to the Federal National Assembly, May 23, 1967. Author's translation
24. Ahidjo, General Policy Report to the First National Congress of the

243

UNC, Garoua, March 10, 1969, (English version, Ministry of Information, Yaoundé), p. 101

25. Johnson, *The Cameroon Federation*, gives examples of some of the problems encountered, which included currency hoarding and black-marketeering in the west

26. Ardener, op. cit., p. 321

27. See Nordau, op. cit., pp. 5–6

28. Op. cit., pp. 325–7

29. See J. A. C. Smith, 'The Cameroun Penal Code: Practical Comparative Law' in *International and Comparative Law Quarterly*, Vol. 12, Pt. 3, July 1968

30. See his articles 'A case for early bilingualism' in the bilingual Cameroun journal *Abbia*, Nos. 4 and 5, 1963 and 1964. He also advocated the policy strongly in his capacity as member of the National Education Council

31. *The Cameroon Federation*, p. 300

32. *Cameroun, 10 ans d'indépendance*, special number, Agence Camérounaise de Presse, January 1970, pp. 36–7

33. According to Ardener, op. cit., this was largely the result of substantial aid provided by US AID, including the use of Peace Corps volunteers as teachers. Nevertheless, primary education in West Cameroun has grown at a rate of 12 per cent p.a., giving it a per capita rate which is second only to the most developed parts of East Cameroun

34. *Annuaire National*, p. 59

35. Also a major beneficiary of US AID; Ardener, loc. cit.

36. Teachers in both Law and English are provided by Britain, as part of the aid programme to the university

37. Of approximately 100 members of the teaching staff in 1967, 28 were Camerounians

8. UNIFICATION AND ECONOMIC DEVELOPMENT

1. Speech to the Council on Foreign Relations, New York, October 1967. See, *The Political Philosophy of Ahmadou Ahidjo*, Yaoundé, 1968, p. 93

2. For a critical appraisal of the successes and failures of the First Plan 1960–65, see Ph. Hugon, *Analyse du Sous-développement en Afrique Noire*, Paris, 1968, pp. 249–51

3. Ibid., p. 241

4. Gaboux and Rathery, *Etude sur le niveau de vie dans la zone cacoayère*, 1965, p. 14

5. Hugon, loc. cit.

6. Press Conference, February 17, 1968
7. Johnson, *The Cameroon Federation*, p. 329, n. 29
8. Annual production figures 1967/8: *Cameroun, 10 ans d'indépendance*, Yaoundé, January 1970, Agence Camérounaise de Presse, p. 24.
9. Hugon, op. cit., p. 121
10. Ibid., p. 104
11. See *Africa Research Bulletin* (Economic, Financial and Technical Series), 1970, p. 1667; and Hugon, op. cit., p. 114
12. *Africa Research Bulletin*, 1970, p. 1712
13. Hugon, op. cit., p. 108. This means that the unemployed are only 50,000 fewer than the total number in receipt of wages
14. P. Billard, *Le Cameroun Fédéral*, Vol. II, *Essai de Géographie Humaine et Economique*, Paris, 1968, p. 320; and Hugon, op. cit., p. 237
15. Hugon, op. cit., p. 236. The figures are for 1965, but little increase is likely to have occurred since wages were unchanged until 1969, when a 4 per cent increase was granted
16. Ibid., pp. 231, 238 and 303; 15 per cent of the population received 60 per cent of the total national income in 1966
17. R. N. Nordau, *Africa Report*, January 1970, p. 3; allowances paid by embassies and foreign companies to expatriate personnel are alleged to be higher than in all but three or four countries in the world
18. Confidential information, based on an economic survey by a visiting economist from an international agency
19. See Johnson, op. cit., pp. 335–6, for the effect of this in favouring small businessmen in West Cameroun. Billard, op. cit., p. 266, gives the number of licences granted in 1965 as 182 in East Cameroun and 236 in West Cameroun, but says that by 1967 the numbers had been reduced to 39 and 106 respectively
20. *Africa Research Bulletin*, 1970, p. 1671
21. Hugon, op. cit., pp. 169 ff.
22. Ardener, 'The Nature of the Reunification of Cameroon', op. cit., p. 317; Hugon, op. cit., p. 195, gives the total figure for subventions to both federated states as 2·6 billion francs CFA. By the time of the 1970–71 budget the two subventions together were estimated at 3·7 billion francs CFA: *Africa Research Bulletin*, p. 1765
23. Hugon, op. cit., p. 303
24. *Africa Research Bulletin*, 1970, p. 1677
25. Hugon, op. cit., p. 231, drawing on a table compiled in Yaoundé by Rathery and Ghuyssen
26. Op. cit., p. 200. Author's translation
27. *Cameroun 10 ans d'indépendance*, p. 33

28. Hugon, op. cit., p. 171
29. UN Economic and Social Council: *Prospects for Industrial Development in Cameroun*, 1965, p. 6
30. Ibid., p. 14
31. See note 18 above
32. Ibid., and 'Total Export/Import Figures Covering 41 African Countries', 1967/8, *Africa Research Bulletin*, 1970, p. 1634 (based on figures from the Economic Commission for Africa's quarterly statistical bulletin for Africa)
33. Source as in note 18
34. Johnson, *The Cameroon Federation*, p. 331
35. See Ardener, op. cit., p. 317
36. Ardener, loc. cit., gives figures which indicate that in 1962 it was nearly half that of 1958, though how much of this decline took place after unification, or as a consequence of it, is not known
37. Johnson, op. cit., points out that West Cameroun firms were able to gain from the new system of import licensing, which favoured smaller firms, pp. 333–6, and see note 19 above
38. Gonidec, *La République Fédérale du Cameroun*, p. 13
39. Speech at Douala, December 9, 1963. Quoted in *Ahmadou Ahidjo par lui-même*, p. 52. Author's translation

9. CAMEROUN, AFRICA AND THE WORLD

1. See, inter alia, M. Roberts, 'Political Prospects for the Cameroun' in *The World Today*, Vol. 16, July 1960, pp. 305 ff.; H. Kitchen, 'Cameroun faces troubled Future' in *Africa Special Report*, January 1960, p. 14; *West Africa*, 1960–61, passim
2. As late as 1965, the *Union Nationale des Etudiants Kamérounais* maintained an active branch in Paris, and the Committee of African Organisations in London grouped exiled students there and published UPC material
3. See 'Cameroun Vignettes of Power Rivalries', *The Times*, January 7, 1960, p. 7
4. Le Vine, 'The Cameroun Federal Republic' in Carter, (ed.), *Five African States*, p. 354
5. Ibid.
6. See *Case Concerning the Northern Cameroons*, Reports of Judgements and Advisory Opinions of the International Court of Justice, Judgement of December 2, 1963, The Hague. The decision was taken on a preliminary objection by the UK, based on the fact that the UN had decided in 1961 to terminate the trust status of the territory, and that the Court had no power to deal with the matter

7. See Africa Research Bulletin, 1969, p. 1437
8. See Legum, *Pan-Africanism: a short political guide*, pp. 50 ff.
9. In March 1969, 340 Ibos were arrested on charges involving rioting in Bamenda; some 40 were ultimately charged, and 4 were convicted. The interest aroused by the case in West Cameroun was considerable, though by no means uniformly sympathetic to the accused, whose presence had long been a source of resentment
10. The majority are of Nigerian origin and work on cocoa plantations. Camerounians are said to number about 1,000. See Bolaji Akinyemi, 'Nigeria and Fernando Po' in *African Affairs*, Vol. 69, No. 276, July 1970, p. 241
11. Ibid., pp. 247–8
12. At the first Congress of the UNC at Garoua in 1969, he singled out this subject for mention in relation to the alleged 'humanitarian' considerations which motivated 'some countries' in supporting the rebel Biafra. Niether the irony nor the vagueness hid the fact that it was France that was being criticised.
13. See Fonlon, 'Will we Make or Mar?', *Abbia*, No. 5, March 1964
14. See, in general, Welch, *Dream of Unity*
15. Johnson, *The Cameroon Federation*, p. 289
16. Speech at Ntui, 1964
17. p. 290
18. Ibid., p. 289, n. 2
19. Speech to the UC Congress at Bafoussam, November 1965. Author's translation

Select Bibliography

Ahidjo, A., *Contribution à la construction nationale*, Présence Africaine, Paris 1964; *The Political Thought of Ahmadou Ahidjo*, Monaco 1968; *Ahmadou Ahidjo par lui-même*, République Fédérale du Cameroun, Yaoundé 1968

Akpan, N. U., *Epitaph to Indirect Rule*, Cassell, London 1956; Barnes and Noble, New York 1956

Ardener, E., *Coastal Bantu of The Cameroons*, International African Institute, London 1956; 'The Kamerun Idea' in *West Africa*, Nos. 2147, 2148, 1958; 'The Political History of Cameroon' in *The World Today*, Vol. 18, London 1962; 'The Nature of the Reunification of Cameroon' in A. Hazlewood (ed.), *African Integration and Disintegration*, Oxford University Press, London 1967

——, Ardener, S., and Warmington, W. A., *Plantation and Village in The Cameroons*, London 1960

Ardener, S., *Eye-Witness to the Annexation of Cameroon, 1883–1887*, Government Printer, Buea 1968

Bederman, S. H., *The Cameroons Development Corporation: Partner in National Growth*, CDC, Bota 1968

Billard, P., *Le Cameroun Fédéral*, 2 Vols. Imprimerie des Beaux Arts, Lyons, 1968

Buell, R. L., *The Native Problem in Africa*, Vol. 2, Bureau of International Research, Harvard University and Radcliffe College, New York, 1928

Chaffard, G., 'Cameroun à la veille de l'indépendance' in *Europe France-Outre-Mer*, No. 355, Paris 1959

Chilver, E. M., 'Native Administration in the West Central Cameroons, *1902–1954*' in K. Robinson and F. Madden (eds.), *Essays in Imperial Government presented to Margery Perham*, Oxford University Press, Oxford 1963

——, and Kaberry, P., *Traditional Bamenda: Precolonial History and Ethnography of the Bamenda Grassfields*, Government Printer, Buea 1967; *Zintgraff's Explorations in Bamenda, 1889–1892*, Buea 1966

Coleman, J. S., *Nigeria: Background to Nationalism*, University of California Press, Los Angeles 1958

Crowder, M., *The Story of Nigeria*, rev. ed., Faber, London 1966; Praeger, New York 1966

Dugast, I., *Inventaire Ethnique du Sud-Cameroun*, IFAN, Yaoundé 1949

Enonchong, H. N. A., *Cameroon Constitutional Law: Federalism in a Mixed Common Law and Civil Law System*, Yaoundé 1967

Ezera, K., *Constitutional Developments in Nigeria*, Cambridge University Press, London 1960

Fonlon, B., 'The Case for Early Bilingualism' in *Abbia*, Yaoundé 1964; 'Will We Make or Mar?', in *Abbia*, Yaoundé 1964; *The Task of Today*, Cameroon Printing and Publishing Co., Victoria 1966

Froelich, J., *Cameroun-Togo*, Editions Berger-Levrault, Paris 1956

Gardinier, D., *Cameroon: United Nations Challenge to French Policy*, Institute of Race Relations, Oxford University Press, London 1963; 'The British in The Cameroons, 1919–1939' in P. Gifford and W. R. Louis (eds.), *Britain and Germany in Africa. Imperial Rivalry and Colonial Rule*, Yale University Press, New Haven 1957

Gonidec, P., *La République Fédérale du Cameroun*, Paris, 1969

Green, R. H., 'The Heirs of Le Clerc' in *The New African*, London 1965

Hailey, Lord, *An African Survey*, rev. ed. Oxford University Press, London 1956

Hodgkin, T., *Nationalism in Colonial Africa*, Muller, London 1956; New York University Press, New York 1957

Hugon, P., *Analyse du Sous-Développement en Afrique Noire: l'example de l'économie du Cameroun*, Presses Universitaires de France, Paris 1968

Johnson, W. R., *The Cameroon Federation. Political Integration in a Fragmentary Society*, Princeton University Press, Princeton 1970; 'The Cameroon Federation: Political Union between English and French-speaking Africa' in W. H. Lewis (ed.) *French-Speaking Africa*, Walker, New York 1965

Kaberry, P., *Women of The Grassfields*, HMSO, London 1952; 'Traditional Politics in Nsaw' in *Africa*, Vol. 29, London 1959

Kanga, V., *Le Droit Coutumier Bamiléké au contact des droits Européens*, Government Printer, Yaoundé 1959

Ketchoua, T., *Contribution à l'histoire du Cameroun de 450 avant Jésus-Christus à nos jours*, Yaoundé 1962

Kirk-Greene, A. H. M., *Adamawa, Past and Present*, Oxford University Press, London 1958

Le Vine, V. T., *The Cameroons from Mandate to Independence*, University of California Press, Los Angeles 1964; 'The Cameroon Federal Republic' in G. Carter (ed.), *Five African States*, Cornell University Press, Ithaca 1963; 'Cameroon Political Parties' in J. S. Coleman and C. Rosberg, *Political Parties and National Integration in Tropical Africa*, University of California Press, Berkeley 1964

Logan, R. F., *The Operation of the Mandate System in Africa, 1919–*

1927, Washington, D.C. 1942; *The African Mandates in World Politics*, Public Affairs Press, Washington, D.C. 1948

Lugard, F. D., *The Dual Mandate in British Tropical Africa*, Blackwood, London 1923

McCullough, M., Littlewood, M., and Dugast, I., *Peoples of the Central Cameroons*, International African Institute, London 1954

Meek, C. K., *Land Tenure and Land Administration in Nigeria and The Cameroons*, HMSO, London 1957

Moumié, F-R., *Rape of The Cameroons*, London 1959

Moumié, F-R., (Mrs), *Dr Félix-Roland Moumié, My Memories of his life*, Conakry 1960

Mveng, E., *Histoire du Cameroun*, Présence Africaine, Paris 1963

Perham, M., *Native Administration in Nigeria*, London 1937; *Lugard*, 2 Vols. Collins, London 1956

Ritzenhaler, R. and P., *Cameroons Village. An Ethnography of the Bafut*, Milwaukee 1962

Roberts, Margaret, 'Political Prospects for The Cameroun' in *The World Today*, Vol. 16, London 1960

Roberts, S. H., *History of French Colonial Policy*, Shoestring Press, London 1929

Robinson, R., Gallagher, J., and Denny A., *Africa and The Victorians*, Macmillan, London 1961; Doubleday, New York 1968

Rudin, H., *Germans in The Cameroons, 1884–1919*, Yale University Press, New Haven 1938

Tardits, C., *Les Bamiléké de l'Ouest Cameroun*, Berger-Levrault, Paris 1960

Um Nyobe, R., 'Cameroun, Naissance du Mouvement National' in *Cahiers Internationaux*, Vol. 6, No. 52, Paris 1954; 'Cameroun, Objectifs immédiats du Mouvement National' in *Cahiers Internationaux*, Vol. 6, No. 53, Paris 1954; 'Cameroun, Où en est le nationalisme camérounais?' in *Cahiers Internationaux*, Vol. 6, No. 54, Paris 1955

Union des Populations du Cameroun, *La révolution kamérounaise, ses objectifs, sa signification et ses répercussions dans le continent africain*, Cairo 1960; *Unification immédiate du Cameroun*, 1952

Warmington, W. A., *A West African Trade Union*, Oxford University Press, London 1960

Welch, C. E., *Dream of Unity: Pan-Africanism and Political Unification in West Africa*, Cornell University Press, Ithaca 1966

Wright, Q., *Mandates Under the League of Nations*, University of Chicago Press, Chicago 1930

Zang-Atangana, J. M., 'Les Partis Politiques Camérounais' in *Recueil Penant*, No. 684, Paris 1960

Index